People-Centered Social Innovation

T0382674

Social Innovation is emerging as an alternate interdisciplinary development pathway of knowledge and practice that aims to understand and address contemporary complexities and multidimensional social realities. However, though Social Innovation is a widely-used term; its conceptual understanding and the specific relation to social change remains under explored.

People-Centered Social Innovation: Global Perspectives on an Emerging Paradigm attempts to revisit and extend the existing understanding of Social Innovation in practice by focusing on the lived realities of marginalized groups and communities. The emerging field of people-centered development is placed in dialogue with theory and concepts from the more established field of social innovation to create a new approach; one that adopts a global perspective, engaging with very different experiences of marginality across the global north and south. Theoretically, *People-Centered Social Innovation: Global Perspectives on an Emerging Paradigm* draws on "Northern" understandings of change and improvement as well as 'Southern' theory concerns for epistemological diversity and meaning-making. The result is an experiment aimed at reimagining research and practice that seriously needs to center the actor in processes of social transformation.

Swati Banerjee, PhD, is Professor and Chairperson at the Centre for Livelihoods and Social Innovation, School of Social Work, Tata Institute of Social Sciences (TISS), Mumbai, India, and Coordinator of the Right Livelihood College (RLC)–TISS.

Stephen Carney, PhD, is Associate Professor in Comparative Education Policy at Roskilde University in Denmark.

Lars Hulgård, PhD, is Professor of social entrepreneurship, Roskilde University, Denmark, and visiting professor at Tata Institute of Social Sciences, Mumbai, India.

Routledge Studies in Social Enterprise & Social Innovation
Series Editors: Jacques Defourny, Lars Hulgård, and Rocío Nogales

Social enterprises seek to combine an entrepreneurial spirit and behaviour with a primacy of social or societal aims. To various extents, their production of goods or services generates market income which they usually combine with other types of resources. A social innovation consists of the implementation of a new idea or initiative to change society in a fairer and more sustainable direction.

Routledge Studies in Social Enterprise & Social Innovation seeks to examine and promote these increasingly important research themes. It particularly looks at participatory governance and social innovation dynamics in social enterprises and more widely in partnerships involving third sector and civil society organizations, conventional businesses and public authorities. In such perspective, this series aims at publishing both breakthrough contributions exploring the new frontiers of the field as well as books defining the state of the art and paving the way to advance the field.

Social Enterprise in Latin America
Theory, Models and Practice
Edited by Luiz Inácio Gaiger, Marthe Nyssens and Fernanda Wanderley

Social Entrepreneurship and Innovation in Rural Europe
Edited by Ralph Richter, Matthias Fink, Richard Lang & Daniela Maresch

People-Centered Social Innovation
Global Perspectives on An Emerging Paradigm
Edited by Swati Banerjee, Stephen Carney and Lars Hulgard

For more information about this series, please visit: https://www.routledge.com/Routledge-Studies-in-Social-Enterprise--Social-Innovation/book-series/RSESI

People-Centered Social Innovation

Global Perspectives on an Emerging Paradigm

**Edited by Swati Banerjee,
Stephen Carney and Lars Hulgard**

Routledge
Taylor & Francis Group

LONDON AND NEW YORK

First published 2020 by Routledge

2 Park Square, Milton Park, Abingdon, Oxon, OX14 4RN
605 Third Avenue, New York, NY 10017

Routledge is an imprint of the Taylor & Francis Group, an informa business

First issued in paperback 2020

Library of Congress Cataloging-in-Publication Data
Names: Banerjee, Swati, editor. | Carney, Stephen, editor. |
    Hulgêard, Lars, editor.
Title: People centered social innovation : global perspectives on
    an emerging paradigm / edited by Swati Banerjee,
    Stephen Carney and Lars Hulgard.
Description: New York, NY : Routledge, 2020. |
    Series: Routledge studies in social enterprise &
    social innovation | Includes index.
Identifiers: LCCN 2019017050 | ISBN 9780815392170
    (hardback) | ISBN 9781351121026 (ebook)
Subjects: LCSH: Social entrepreneurship. | Technological
    innovations—Social aspects. | Social change.
Classification: LCC HD60 .P379 2020 | DDC 658.4/08—dc23
LC record available at https://lccn.loc.gov/2019017050

ISBN: 978-0-8153-9217-0 (hbk)
ISBN: 978-0-367-78532-1 (pbk)

Typeset in Sabon
by Apex CoVantage, LLC

In memory of Professor, Dr. Chandrakant Puri, friend, scholar and activist

Contents

1 People-Centered Social Innovation: An Emerging
  Paradigm with Global Potential   1
  SWATI BANERJEE, STEPHEN CARNEY AND LARS HULGÅRD

2 Social Innovation Learning From Critical Social
  Entrepreneurship Studies: How Are They Critical,
  and Why Do We Need Them?   17
  LUISE LI LANGERGAARD

3 Arenas for Gendering Social Innovation and
  Marginalized Women's Collectives   42
  LINDA LUNDGAARD ANDERSEN AND SWATI BANERJEE

4 Genealogy and Institutionalization of People-Centered
  Social Innovation in Kudumbashree, Kerala, India   69
  P. K. SHAJAHAN AND LARS HULGÅRD

5 Ethos of Social Innovation: In Search of a Decolonizing
  Analysis   89
  ADRIANE VIEIRA FERRARINI

6 Informal Entrepreneurship as Adaptive Innovation:
  Strategies Among Migrant Workers in Indian Cities   110
  SUNIL D. SANTHA AND DEVISHA SASIDEVAN

7 Buen Vivir as an Innovative Development Model   128
  ANDRES MORALES, ROGER SPEAR, MICHAEL NGOASONG
  AND SILVIA SACCHETTI

8 Indian Diasporic Communities: Exploring Belonging,
  Marginality and Transnationalism   156
  RASHMI SINGLA, P. K. SHAJAHAN AND SUJATA SRIRAM

 9 Innovations in Multistakeholder Partnerships for
    Sustainable Development: Fostering State–University–
    Community Nexus   179
    ABDUL SHABAN AND PRASHANT B. NARNAWARE

10 Social Innovation in Africa: An Empirical
    and Conceptual Analysis   195
    JEREMY MILLARD, MOHAMED WAGEIH AND BEV MELDRUM

11 Social Innovations as Heretical Practices   225
    SILLA MARIE MØRCH SIEVERS

    Notes on the Authors   239
    Index   245

1 People-Centered Social Innovation: An Emerging Paradigm with Global Potential

Swati Banerjee, Stephen Carney and Lars Hulgård

Introduction

On the dusty plains of Andhra Pradesh, Madhavayya found his father's limp body in the small hut where he would rest from the midday sun. Scorched by debt and despair and at the mercy of both harsh weather and fickle markets, Mallappa took his own life rather than continue what seemed like an endless struggle for moderate prosperity on his own land. His story—one shared by hundreds of thousands of struggling farmers across India—only made global headlines because Mallappa had planned his funeral in advance. After purchasing the white cloth that would cover his body, as well as garlands, incense and a laminated photo for his grave, he left a final note to his family that explained that he had made these preparations in order to ease their burden during the hard days ahead. A good farmer who had planned the use of his land with care, Mallappa had no control of the price of his crops, access to markets or the conditions for financing short-term hardships. Indeed, these factors appeared to work actively against him. Madhavayya has now left his father's land, joining a growing exodus of young people to India's mega-cities in search of a different future but equally dependent on circumstance and the small favors of global capitalism.

In another case, this time closer to our own work in rural India, a group of poor and marginalized women explained their desire to create a small-scale livestock farming project. Like Mallappa, their aim was to create a livelihood that might provide a degree of autonomy, security and social justice. Their ultimate goal, however, was something else: to enable their children to obtain a level of education that would free them from the struggles of rural existence and open the way for a different type of future in the metropolis. For one farmer, the aim may be to live securely in the familiar surrounds of home. For another, it is the prospect of transcending that: to leave and never return. While examples from the global South seem somehow extreme or more urgent, the experience of hardship, despair, desire and human initiative is global. Such experiences frame capitalism wherever it takes form. How, then, can we understand

and act with respect for such perspectives while holding firmly to our commitments to change unjust structures at their roots, help others in egalitarian ways and make a fairer world?

The contested concept of "development" is about change and some understanding of progress or improvement, but the distinctive contribution of the approach we outline in this book—a people-entered approach to Social Innovation—suggests that such change must take as its starting point the ontological, social and political perspectives of those it aims to support. Following the work of Boaventura de Sousa Santos (2016), our starting point is an acknowledgment that "the understanding of the world by far exceeds the Western understanding of the world". Additionally, there can be "no global social justice without global cognitive justice' and that 'emancipatory transformations in the world" might well "follow grammars and scripts other than those developed by Western-centric critical theory" (p. viii). This radical perspective requires an equally radical and courageous reassessment of the role and potential of academic work at what many acknowledge to be a turning or *tipping* point in the history of humanity. For change to be meaningful, something meaningful has to change in the way we approach the world.

Making a Difference in an Age of Ideas

Our time is definitely complex and increasingly marked by the clash and conflict of interests and policies. Growing social and economic inequality and the concentration of wealth marks our time as dangerous and unstable. Some claim that the unfolding 21st century may be the *most* unequal period ever faced by humanity (Piketty, 2013). In spite of their active engagement in developing and maintaining societal inequality, individuals of extreme wealth and the foundations that carry their names and message have successfully created a headline-grabbing policy agenda. Here, we see a small fraction of the profits of such work used to set the agenda for social innovation globally. With marvelous *linguistic* innovation, we are offered the promise of "catalytic philanthropy", "corporate social innovation", "social impact investment" and, for example, "scaling for impact". Such word craft rarely stands alone from the heroic individuals it celebrates. Ashoka, a leading body promoting social entrepreneurship gives British business tycoon Richard Branson its seal of approval. With a long history of for-profit entrepreneurship packaged as socially aware and alternative, Branson's metamorphous from businessman to determined social innovator was complete after his cameo appearance in Al Gore's groundbreaking documentary *An Inconvenient Truth*. Responding to Gore's home visit where he was given a personal PowerPoint presentation, Branson remarked that it was "one of the best presentations I have ever seen in my life . . . As I sat there and listened to Gore, I saw that we are looking at Armageddon" (Klein, 2014: 231).

On the spot, Branson gave a pledge to turn his Virgin Group into Gaia Capitalism, a notion he invented that would redefine and celebrate the earth as a single living organism. Following this pledge, he publicly announced a commitment to spend US$3 billion to develop biofuels as an alternative to oil and gas. Thus spoke the social entrepreneur, innovator, savior and collective conscience of the planet. One man, one voice, one vision, all based on a privileged right to speak and act.

On the surface, such passion and vision seem a service to the majority of the population but avoids another "inconvenient truth" that collective challenges are best met by political consensus and the establishment of common resource pools through systems of taxation and the shared sense of ownership and obligation they engender. While the charismatic change agent offers a new perspective and can possibly break an impasse in public policy making, other perspectives are closed down or obscured. Some social activists have noted that while committed wealthy individuals have a role to play, they and their corporate connections are able to extend their wealth as the spotlight of change shifts from the state, its democratic institutions and the people who, ultimately, have most at stake. What happened to Richard Branson's pledge? According to Naomi Klein, the investment in biofuel was well under $300 million in 2014 only two years before the $3 billion target was to be reached in 2016. By 2018, some environmental lobby groups had claimed that less than 3% of the original commitment had been honored.[1] Klein ends her analysis of Branson as a change maker for the common good by indicating that the skeptics may be right. "Branson's various climate adventures may indeed prove to have all been a spectacle, a Virgin production, with everyone's favorite bearded billionaire playing the part of planetary savior to build his brand, land on late night TV, fend off regulators, and feel good about doing bad" (Klein, 2014: 251).

Rather than solely a critique of certain strategically motivated individuals, we may be seeing the beginning of a new phase in the political process where media, charismatic leadership and our collective desperation to find solutions make us especially vulnerable to the image, slogan and unsubstantiated promise. Clearly, it appears that powerful business tycoons such as Richard Branson and, for that matter, policy makers, do not need to implement their ideas in order to be celebrated as successful and passionate change makers. In the airline industry, Branson needed planes in the air to achieve his success as a tycoon. In social innovation, he only needed to outline his vision in the broadest of strokes. When business leaders enter the field of social innovation, they often do so with exaggerated goals that are a large part of a strategy for recognition. Pamela Hartigan of the Skoll and Schwab Foundations, one of the most influential discourse makers in the world of social innovation, once noted "that a social entrepreneur is what you get when you cross Richard Branson with Mother Teresa" (World Economic Forum, 2003). Just by *entering* the field with ideas and visions, the global social innovator reaches the goal of having an impact. He *becomes* a change maker for the common good.

Following the legacy of Joseph Schumpeter, it was assumed that innovation and social innovation had to be *implemented* in order to be successful. This capacity for implementation distinguished an inventor from an innovator. Here, the practical development of new products or procedures had to take place: while the ability to envision something entirely new was a precondition, actual change had to be achieved. This need not necessarily take the form of a new service or product but could also emerge as changed societal power relations driven by social movements. However, in contemporary times, it seems that business leaders, in particular, can become successful social innovators by simply launching an idea aimed at seducing people and policy makers to open their hearts, minds and funds. Top-down, energetic, authoritative, connected but, nonetheless, distant from any lived understanding of the challenges faced by marginalized groups. Supported by a short-term media cycle and an emerging political culture where message outruns action, our genuine and collective impulse for socially oriented change is in danger of being transformed into understandings of the world and strategies for engaging with it that will only intensify the damaging pathologies of the previous century.

Using rhetoric to ride the wave of interest in social innovation may serve the ends of those select superrich and their network of corporate partners but stops the vast majority of human beings from contributing to immense societal challenges that range from demographic and climate change, rising inequality, xenophobia and a contemporary political disorder marked by a populism. In some countries, typically in the global North, these changes appear to have a lesser impact but, even here, we see a kind of permanent crises of consciousness, particularly amongst the young who face precarious futures and a failing political system. As such, to advocate for social innovation is to also advocate for a people-centered perspective: one where strategies of change are first envisaged in dialogue with those who stand most to lose but, by the same token, have most to offer.

Approaching People-Centered Social Innovation

A people-centered approach to social innovation rests on a number of important assumptions. First, social innovation was never a question of how to use the capitalist firm or the conventional market model as a blueprint for serving the needs of people. The dominance of a market-centered approach to social innovation is, in fact, quite recent. Neither innovation or, for that matter, *social* innovation can be thought of as originating from the market economy (Moulaert et al., 2017; Godin, 2015). Indeed, the origins of the concept of innovation precede those of social innovation by many centuries (Moulaert et al., 2017) and are grounded in two characteristics: "the quest for freedom" and a prioritizing of practice over "contemplation" (Godin, 2015: 6). In its earliest iterations, innovation can be located in Western religious texts in the 15th century (Moulaert et al., 2017) but has more ancient roots in 5th-century-BCE Greece. Here, innovation stems from the word *kainos* (new). Initially, *kainotomia* had nothing to do with our current or dominant meaning of innovation as commercialized technical invention. Instead, *innovation* meant "cutting fresh into" and was used in the context of concrete thinking ("opening new mines") as well as abstract thought ("making new"): "In the hands of ancient philosophers and writers on political constitutions, innovation is introducing change into the established order" (Godin, 2015: 19). Benoit highlights an additional feature of innovation that is crucial for the people-centered approach articulated here. Innovation was initially envisaged as "subversive" and inherently political, "it is regulated by Kings, forbidden by law and punished. Books of manners and sermons urge people not to meddle with innovation" (Godin, 2015: 22). Innovation was also understood as reflecting diverse struggles for freedom. As such, we can say that *social* innovation has been concerned historically with issues of emancipation and self-determination: an inherently political concept today dramatically emptied of its original meaning and potential. Since the quest for freedom and emancipation lies the core of any activity labelled as innovation, one may wonder if there is even a need to develop theory about social innovation, especially for any understanding that positions people at the center of the change process.

Second, the people-centered approach to social innovation adopted in this volume takes an important point of departure in Karl Polanyi's understanding of economic activity which, he warned, could never be reduced to the virtues of markets:

> Let us make our meaning more precise. No society could, naturally, live for any length of time unless it possessed an economy of some sort; but previously to our time no economy has ever existed that, even in principle, was controlled by markets. In spite of the chorus of academic incantations so persistent in the nineteenth century, gain and profit made on exchange never before played an important part in human economy. Though the institution of the market was fairly common since the later Stone Age, its role was no more than incidental to economic life.
>
> (Polanyi, 1957: 43)

Polanyi made a distinction between a formal and a substantive view of the economy. Economy, in the formal sense, is about economizing scarce resources, whereas

> the latter centers on how human beings organize and allocate the pursuit of the things needed to sustain human life, humans are social

animals; they define and realize themselves in relation to others. It is collectively through social arrangements that human beings work out how they will secure their livelihood.

(Block and Somers, 2014: 30)

Economic activity is as much about actions shaped by changing configurations of redistributive and reciprocal actions as of the actions of a market. To Polanyi, "robust human freedom depends on a coalition of state and civil society that has the power to protect society against the destructive forces of marketization" (Block and Somers, 2014: 4). This perspective lives on in the claims of influential economists such as Nobel Prize recipient Joseph Stiglitz who has reiterated the need for social innovations that can address the inequalities produced by conventional market economies. To Stiglitz (2011), "[t]he problem is that the growth that has been achieved may not be sustainable and the benefits of the growth that has occurred are accruing to but a fraction of the population". As such, "social innovations are as important as technological innovations" and the lessons from recent economic crises are moral as well as a structural.

This moral dimension is emphasized when he argues that the same people who brought the global community to the abyss due to their greed were, in the wake of the economic crisis, allowed to walk away with much more than they deserved by successfully managing to externalize the full costs of their actions. In structural terms, he adds that the growth produced by the conventional market economy is neither sustainable nor able to benefit the majority of society (Stiglitz, 2011). Inequality is on the rise everywhere, also in countries that used to be pioneers in reducing inequality and income differentials. No one doubts that we are blessed with talented social innovators and policy makers but if we are to build and reinforce policy conditions and ecosystems of social innovation that fundamentally challenge the view of the market as a driver of social innovation, people have to find their way to the center of change processes.

The third foundation for a people-centered approach to social innovation lies in a commitment to promoting what Boaventura de Sousa Santos calls "ecologies of knowledge" (Santos, 2016) to challenge the monocentric approach that has led us to the precipice of irreversible inequality and environmental devastation. An approach that identifies ecologies of knowledge would recognize material differences and injustices and make visible alternative worldviews, values and epistemologies. In research terms, it requires that we go beyond classical paradigms of Western and Northern thought in order to engage with other equally valid knowledge(s). This commitment is fundamental to a people-centered approach to social innovation as it creates not only new spaces for discussing the meaning of progress and innovation but also for inviting otherwise silenced voices into conversations about our common future.

Some "Southern knowledge" perspectives view modernity itself as a European phenomenon constituted dialectically "with a non-European alterity that is its ultimate content" (Dussel, 1993: 65–66). Here, the global South is defined not on its own terms but by its difference from the supposed norms and ideals of the global North. For de Sousa Santos, "Northern" thinking is "abyssal" because it operates in a space that relies upon "non-existence, invisibility, nondialetical absence" (Santos, 2016: 118). As such, a "Northern" perspective erases "nonmetropolitian experience" even though such experiences are vital to establishing what *can* be said:

> Modern knowledge and modern law represent the most accomplished manifestations of abyssal thinking. They account for the two major global lines of modern times, which, though being different and operating differently, are mutually interdependent. Each creates a subsystem of visible and invisible distinctions in such a way that the invisible ones become the foundation of the visible ones. In the field of knowledge, abyssal thinking consists in granting to modern science the monopoly of the universal distinction between true and false, to the detriment of two alternative bodies of knowledge: philosophy and theology . . . that cannot be fitted into any of these ways of knowing. On the other side of the line, there is no real knowledge; there are beliefs, opinions, intuitions, and subjective understandings, which, at the most, may become objects or raw materials for scientific inquiry
>
> (Santos, 2016, p. 119)

By exploring the empty spaces created by abyssal thinking—what de Sousa Santos fashions as a "sociology of absences"—we find the *subject* of social innovation waiting patiently for a time when voices of singularity, difference and experience become the foundation of programs of social justice as well as of research-based knowledge.

None of this is to suggest that the major structural problems of today can be solved without linking top-down actions by the state with the bottom-up actions of civil society, the third sector and the social and solidarity economy (Somers, 2008). This is probably the most important challenge confronting public policy makers wishing to harness the potential of social innovation. In a seminal report for the European Union (EU) written by a team of scholars led by Frank Moulaert, 30 EU-funded research projects totaling 91 million euros in funding were examined to explore how public policies underpin the bottom-up initiatives of social change makers (Moulaert et al., 2017). Two observations stand out. First, the term *innovation* is far from new and originates in the sphere of religion rather than the spheres of technology or economy. It has a moral and ethical dimension that insists we place the citizenry and the commons above the parochial interests of the private sector: innovations must be social in both their "ends and means" (BEPA, 2011). Second, while initiatives should be grounded in local understandings of need, they must relate to the public sphere and to political leaders who are charged with ensuring their sustainable implementation.

Interrogating People-Centeredness: Some Conceptual Issues

While *social innovation* is a widely used term, its conceptual understanding and specific relation to social change remain underexplored. This book aims to revisit earlier conceptual developments and to extend them by focusing on the lived realities of peoples and communities as they seek change. The emerging field of people-centered development is placed in dialogue with theory and concepts from the more established field of social innovation to create a new approach, one that adopts a global perspective, engaging with very different experiences of advocacy, participation, marginality and precariousness across the global North *and* South. Theoretically, we draw on "Northern" understandings of change and improvement as well as "Southern" theory concerns for epistemological diversity and situated meaning-making. The result is an experiment aimed at reimagining research and practice for social transformation.

A number of perspectives are worth clarifying before we elaborate our own approach to people-centered social innovation. To begin, we acknowledge that the category of 'people' is not viewed as homogenous but, rather, located within an understanding of complexity, heterogeneity and the complexity of relations of power. A focus on experience thus becomes essential to unfolding subjectivity and actorhood, where politics, power, ideology and struggle frame the daily lives of people and their life worlds. A focus on agency helps us to understand the ways in which material conditions and discursive frameworks intersect to present certain choices for individuals and groups. Ultimately, this orientation recognizes the affective desire to reach the types of outcomes that have become enshrined in global frameworks (e.g., Women Development Report, World Bank, 2012). Building on Amartya Sen (1999: 4), we are also conscious of the powerful trope of freedom as a perspective that "enhances the ability of people to help themselves, and to influence the world". This does not imply a continuation of earlier welfare approaches. Like Dreze and Sen (1989: 373), we recognize the capacity of the people to actively participate in developmental processes where the public is not merely constructed as "the patient" whose well-being commands attention but also as the "agent" whose actions can be transformative. Agency is an important factor for social value creation and therefore social innovation.

Beyond such clarifying work, it is also necessary to acknowledge the ways in which the landscape of social innovation takes shape across disciplinary borders that make interconnected perspectives possible. These include epistemologies that extend beyond Northern ways of knowing (Santos, 2008), diverse theories of social change (Jessop et al., 2013) and orientations that transcend the "institutionalized field(s)" of public or private action (Moulaert et al., 2013). This last perspective is critical: social innovation comes to the fore when traditional, dominant approaches to change are unable to address the problems of "poverty, exclusion, segregation and deprivation or opportunities for improving living conditions" (Moulaert et al., 2013: 2).

This leads us to people centered development as a way of positioning (and theorizing) actors and agency in processes of social innovation. Originating in alternative ideas about development, including postdevelopment, postcolonialism and poststructuralism, a people-centered approach to development attempts to question mainstream strategies to change. By deconstructing established notions of representation, it challenges universalist frameworks for action and by elevating the importance of engagement it positions purpose and intention at the center of theory, policy and practice.

The Politics of Practice in People-Centered Social Innovation

A people-centered orientation to social innovation is thus one powerful way to address the multidimensional challenges that confront policy makers, activists and marginalized groups worldwide. Such an orientation must theorize societal context in ways that enable us to work with the situational or contextual dimensions of the social, cultural, economic and political spaces at various levels: macro, meso and micro. The aim here is to better identify challenges and problems from the perspective of actors themselves. Developing a politics of practice also invites for the articulation of "innovation solutions" that can provide insights into the proposed new idea as well as the new knowledge and learning that can inform it. The identification of key societal problems includes things that are immediately pressing at the local level as well as larger societal challenges that combine both economic and social concerns as well as deeply entrenched societal and systemic inequities and strategic needs.

The development of an innovation strategy helps us to understand the entire pathway of innovation from idea to implementation, diffusion and scaling. It also helps locate the barriers and drivers along that pathway. As we shall see in the chapters presented here, the varied nuances and complexities of societal context, innovation strategy, innovation solution and actors/ actorhood come together through the optique of people-centered social innovation.

Between Imaginary and Reality: Centering People in Practice

Any discussion of the "local" and the "community" must grasp that it is diverse, compromising multiple and hierarchical power relations and affective dispositions. Avoiding essentialist or romanticized appeals to the "other", participation in social innovations occurs in complex, interconnected networks and spaces. Guijit and Shah (2006) remind us that "community" is often viewed naively or, in practice, dealt with as a harmonious and internally equitable container. Indeed, it is only possible to talk of an "ideal" community by neglecting the discontinuities and irresolvable differences that lie *within* any social hierarchy. This has serious implications for practice as any innovation or intervention is in danger of re-creating the very power imbalances and hierarchies it seeks to address. Andrea Cornwall (2002: 8) elaborates by suggesting that "power relations pervade (all) spaces for participation" where spaces established by the powerful may be "discursively bounded to permit only limited citizen influence, colonizing interaction and stifling dissent". Here, the well-rooted structural inequities of caste, class, gender and race gain new legitimacy and purchase and obscure the deeper forces that social innovation strategies attempt to expose and counter.

The outside gaze of the policy maker, researcher or institutionally located activist can impede our understanding of grassroots realities and processes of engagement. Following Chambers (2008: 31), it is important to identify biases in both research and practice that can reinforce misperceptions about people and their contexts. These include spatial, project, person (elite/male, etc.), seasonal, diplomatic and professional issues. Without an understanding of such biases, participation can only remain at the level of rhetoric. Crawley (2006: 24) notes that "the application of participatory approaches has raised increasingly critical questions about their impact". A simple example comes from our own participatory fieldwork in rural communities in India. Exploring "context" one morning, we realized that women were not part of our mapping exercise. Were they unimportant? Uninterested? Unable? Being aware of the rhythms and flows of particular places, we soon realized that they had moved on to household chores and therefore could *not* be present. Sometimes, "voice" becomes a simple commitment to ensuring that all are heard, not assuming that those who have an interest—or are interesting to researchers and activists—will *make* themselves heard. In this sense, and above all else, a people centered approach to social innovation is about a willingness to share expertise, to co-produce understanding and to work toward social value creation that serves the interests of all.

The Contributions

The themes and perspectives opened up here suggest numerous ways to approach this emerging field. With its genesis in a research and development collaboration between Tata Institute of Social Sciences, Mumbai, India, and Roskilde University, Roskilde, Denmark, the book reflects diverse perspectives on people-centered social innovation from leading researchers and practitioners from across the world. In the process, it embodies the very diversity and difference of the people-centered approach itself.

We start with a chapter that explores the theoretical richness and potential of social innovation as a research lens with which to conceptualize change processes. **Luise Li Langergaard** provides a conceptual opening by considering the related area of social entrepreneurship. Often presented as a panacea for solving social problems, this influential way of approaching social change remains a contested concept. Despite its clear normative and political implications, critical studies of social entrepreneurship are limited. She presents and analyses the types of critique employed in the literature and discusses the implications of these for understandings of social change and emancipation. One important insight to emerge here is that these critical studies, as they exist, tend to emphasize discourse and resistance, as well as an empirical methodology, rather than questioning the inherent normativity and ideology of the field. The limitations on the framing of critique place, in turn, limitations on how we might conceptualize the social itself. Drawing on early critical theory, she develops a more coherent and thorough conceptual outline of the literature and thus provides us with a greater understanding of the normative and political dimensions of social innovation and social entrepreneurship as well as their potential.

In their chapter on gendering social innovation, **Linda Lundgaard Andersen and Swati Banerjee** explore marginalized women's collectives, positioning them in the largely "uncharted" realm of gendered social innovation which they unfold through an intersectional research awareness. Building on Gibson-Graham's work they argue that "a much wider range of social relations bear on economic practices" than hitherto captured by much of the policy and research literature. These include "trust, care, sharing, reciprocity, cooperation, future orientation, collective agreement, coercion, bonding, guilt, love, community pressure, equity, self-exploitation, solidarity, distributive justice, stewardship, spiritual connection, environmental and social justice" (Gibson-Graham, 2014: 151). Through rigorous casework, grounded in this broader awareness, they conclude that temporality is an "important feature" in people-centered social innovation: empowering marginalized women takes time and focus beyond that usually provided by external bodies and funding agencies.

In the second of three TISS/Roskilde collaborative chapters, **P. K. Shajahan and Lars Hulgård** provide a genealogical analysis of the institutionalization of people-centered social innovation in Kerala, India. The Kerala State Poverty Eradication Mission, better known as Kudumbashree, was initiated by the government of Kerala to de-root absolute poverty from the state. Treating women not as isolated individuals and entrepreneurs, but in the "totalities" of their communities and everyday life, Kudumbashree combines microcredit, entrepreneurship and empowerment (social, economic and political) initiatives to strengthen the solidarity economy of the community. Their work is heavily indebted to de Sousa Santos's "ecologies of knowledge" perspective, one taken up further by **Adriane Vieira Ferrarini** in her decolonizing analysis of the ethos of social innovation. Here, the concept of *ethos* is used as an analytical device for epistemological and methodological considerations of economic rationality (where the "the social" is given primacy over "the economic") and where the ethical-political intentions of actors can be understood in relation to the quality of participation. She concludes that if the critical epistemological debate proves necessary in the North, it is indispensable in practices aimed at overcoming poverty in the South. In effect, social innovation cannot be restricted to solving societal problems alone: it also creates, legitimates and therefore consolidates constellations of knowledge and power.

Notwithstanding the potential of decolonial analyses to uncover embedded marginalities, this orientation also enables us to reimagine existing processes of social innovation. **Sunil D. Santha and Devisha Sasidevan** argue that adaptive innovations are social innovations that are context specific, developmental and always committed to the values of social justice and environmental sustainability. They involve processes by which social innovators understand the political economy of the larger social system and apply their knowledge, networks and skills to shape or modify these social systems to adapt to diverse risks and uncertainties. Their chapter describes how informal entrepreneurship could be developed and strengthened as adaptive social innovation in order to counter livelihood insecurity. By using a social innovation "lens" they illustrate the livelihood adaptation strategies of migrant informal workers, highlighting their capacities as active subjects. The outcome is an ambitious framework that blends agency-based adaptation with a socio-ecological system perspective on innovation.

Such cutting-edge concept work continues in the chapter by **Andres Morales, Roger Spear, Michael Ngoasong, and Silvia Sacchetti**. Drawing on indigenous community organizations (ICOs) in Colombia, they examine "Northern" understandings of development with Buen Vivir, a community-centric, ecologically balanced and culturally sensitive development model which challenges the "dominant" market-based model of capitalism adopted by Latin American countries in the wake of colonialism. Drawing on the thought of postcolonial theorists such as Homi Bhabha, Gayatri Spivak and Edward Said, they examine the transformation of indigenous peoples' organized groups into ICOs within the social and solidarity economy, showing processes of hybridization that provide not only institutional protection but also the threat of incorporation into dominant Western forms of organization. Their research points to the ever-present abyssal power of hegemonic frames of thought that always threaten the possibilities for alternative forms of action.

A final trio of chapters extends our gaze much further outward. In the chapter on Indian diasporic communities, **Rashmi Singla, P. K. Shajahan and Sujata Sriram** explore the intersections of belonging, marginality and transnationalism, applying a people-centered approach grounded in what they call "first-person voices and interests". This perspective enables them to identify spaces such as places of worship as addressing the (often) unmet demands of people who fall through the cracks of formal 'state integration' efforts. By retaining an openness to those (non)state institutions that play a central role in actual lives, we are able to see the potential role that deeply established local organizations can play in social innovation. In this way, integration becomes the collective responsibility of state *and* community partners rather than something driven only by the obligations, interests and field of vision of government and its private-sector partners.

Another institution of central importance in the creation of social value—one often overlooked or reduced to the realm of the formal economy—is the university. **Abdul Shaban and Prashant B. Narnaware** ask, "How can we look at development alternatives or alternatives to development in an increasingly neoliberal world with its deepening marginalities?" Their case study of state–university–community partnerships takes a different turn from the long tradition of such collaborations by starting from the perspective of the local. With the example of the Tuljapur Campus of the Tata Institute of Social Sciences—an initiative designed primarily to serve local stakeholders—we see the potential of the university for bringing together the agenda of the state (here, the district administration), civil society groups and educational providers. The result is an experiment in transformative and sustainable change that could inspire higher education systems globally.

The global potential of people-centered social innovation is captured in the mapping research of **Jeremy Millard and Mohamed Wageih and Bev Meldrum**, who draw on worldwide experiences of social innovation and sustainable development initiatives to reflect on achievements across much of the African continent. Their analysis suggests that the 'crisis of development' in Africa can be addressed in part by policies that promote social innovation and entrepreneurship at the local level *alongside* top-down regulatory frameworks. The growth of the cooperative movement resonates with a long tradition of similar approaches to social value creation in Europe and suggests an alternative pathway to change in Africa that can mediate the effect of uncertain governmental and funding regimes and that centers people (and grassroots democratization) in change processes. Often overlooked in global studies of social change and development, the African experience of rapidly declining inequalities, youth-driven entrepreneurship and growing links between civil society and the public and private sectors, as well as international donors and investors, suggest a dynamic set of practices that may come to inform if not lead our understanding of social innovation into its next phase.

Finally, in an especially provoking piece, **Silla Marie Mørch Sievers** explores the origins of the concept of social innovation from the reformation to the 19th century when it was regarded as unwelcome and where innovators were often looked at as heretics who disturbed an accepted order. She argues that the disturbance of order can be viewed as a central feature of social innovation, something that is also key to Schumpeter's idea of innovation as "creative destruction". However, in the social innovation literature we see an imbalance favoring "creativity" and other positive aspects where its full(er) potential is lost in favor of less dangerous forms of change. Viewing social innovation as a heretical practice may be one way of reimagining it as a tool for deeper structural action.

An Invitation and Opening

The chapters presented here make clear that there can never be one approach to people-centered social innovation. To think so would be to misunderstand the very *idea* of a social innovation generated by and for people. We hope that the contributions in this book—some theoretical, others methodological and practical—do some degree of justice to the rich, context-specific nature of an emerging approach to working together toward our common humanity. We invite you to join this journey!

Note

1. http://theoilpalm.org/branson-weighs-in-on-palmand-fails/.

References

Amartya, Sen. (1999). *Development as Freedom*. Oxford: Oxford University Press.
BEPA. (2011). *Empowering People, Driving Change: Social Innovation in the European Union*. Luxembourg: Publications Office of the European Union.
Block, F. and Somers, M. R. (2014). *The Power of Market Fundamentalism: Karl Polanyi's Critique*. Cambridge: Harvard University Press.
Chambers, Robert. (2008). *Revolutions in Development Inquiry*. London: Earthscan.

Cleaver, F. (2005). "The Inequality of Social Capital and the Reproduction of Chronic Poverty," *World Development*, 33(6), pp. 893–906.

Cornwall, Andrea. (2000). *Making a Difference: Gender and Participatory Development*. IDS Discussion Paper 378. www.participatorymethods.org/sites/participatorymethods.org/files/Dp378.pdf.

Cornwall, Andrea. (2002). *Making Spaces, Changing Places: Situating Participation in Development*. IDS Discussion Paper 170. www.accountabilityindia.in/sites/default/files/document-library/52_1236482684.pdf.

Crawley, Heaven. (2006). "Living Up to the Empowerment Claim? The Potential of PRA," in Guijit Irene and Shah Meera (eds.), *The Myth of Community: Gender Issues in Participatory Development*. London: Intermediate Technology Publications Ltd, p. 24.

Dhingra, P. (2007). *Managing Multicultural Lives: Asian American Professionals and the Challenge of Multiple Identities*. Stanford: Stanford University Press.

Dreze, J and Sen, A. (1989). *Hunger and Public Action. WIDER Studies in Development Economics*. Oxford: Clarendon Press, pp. Xviii, 373.

Dussel, E. (1993). "Eurocentrism and Modernity (Introduction to the Frankfurt Lectures)," *Boundary 2*, 20(3), pp. 65–76.

Gibson-Graham, J. K. (2014). "Rethinking the Economy with Thick Description and Weak Theory," *Current Anthropology*, 55(S9), pp. S147–S153. https://doi.org/10.1086/676646.

Godin, B. (2015). *Innovation Contested. The Idea of Innovation Over the Centuries*. New York: Routledge.

Guijit, Irene and Shah, Meera. (2006). "Waking Up to Power, Conflict and Process," in Guijit Irene and Shah Meera (eds.), *The Myth of Community: Gender Issues in Participatory Development*. London: Intermediate Technology Publications Ltd.

Jessop, B., Moulaert, F., Hulgård, L. and Hamdouch, A. (2013). "Social Innovation Research: A New Stage in Innovation Analysis?" in F. Moulaert, D. MacCallum, A. Mehmood and A. Hamdouch (eds.), *The International Handbook on Social Innovation. Collective Action, Social Learning and Transdisciplinary Research*. Cheltenham: Edward Elgar.

Klein, N. (2014). *This Changes Everything: Capitalism vs. Climate*. New York: Simon & Schuster.

Moulaert, F., MacCallum, D., Mehmood, A. and Hamdouch, A. (eds.). (2013). *The International Handbook on Social Innovation. Collective Action, Social Learning and Transdisciplinary Research*. Cheltenham: Edward Elgar.

Moulaert, F., Mehmood, A., MacCallum, D. and Leubolt, B. (eds.). (2017). *Social Innovation as a Trigger for Transformations. The Role of Research*. Luxembourg: Publications Office of the European Union.

Piketty, T. (2013). *Capital in the Twenty-First Century*. Cambridge: Harvard University Press.

Polanyi, K. (1957). *The Great Transformation*. Boston: Beacon Press.

Santos, B. S. (ed.). (2008). *Another Knowledge Is Possible: Beyond Northern Epistemology*. London: Verso.

Santos, B. S. (2016). *Epistemologies of the South: Justice Against Epistemicide*. London: Routledge.

Somers, M. R. (2008). *Genealogies of Citizenship: Markets, Statelessness, and the Right to Have Rights.* Cambridge: Cambridge University Press.

Stiglitz, J. (2011). "Introduction," in J. Schumpeter (ed.), *Capitalism, Socialism and Democracy.* Oxon: Routledge Classics. eBook version: Taylor & Francis e-Library.

World Bank. (2012). *Women Development Report.*

World Economic Forum. (2003). *Social entrepreneurship: What it is and why should you care? A conversation with Pamela Hartigan, Managing Director, Scwhab Foundation.* Copyright 2003: World Economic Forum. Available at http://web.worldbank.org/archive/website00818/WEB/OTHER/SOCIAL_E.HTM. Accessed 13.05.2019.

2 Social Innovation Learning From Critical Social Entrepreneurship Studies

How Are They Critical, and Why Do We Need Them?

Luise Li Langergaard

Introduction

Social entrepreneurship is often represented as a panacea for solving social problems, such as exclusion, marginalization, poverty and inequality, in Western societies, as well as in developing countries (see Dacin et al., 2011; Dey and Teasdale, 2013). Social entrepreneurship is defined as new ways of serving unmet social needs in society (Gawell, 2013) or as entrepreneurial activities undertaken with the aim of producing social (rather than commercial) value (Dees and Centennial, 1998; Dart, 2004). In the global South, it has gained a prominent role in the provision of public goods and in attempts to find local solutions to poverty and social deprivation (Nicholls, 2009) and as a means for women's empowerment (Haugh and Talwar, 2016). The potential invested in the idea of social entrepreneurship is high.

In that sense, social entrepreneurship is a concept that implies progressive social change and societal transformation also in a broader sense. The question is, What kind of change and what kind of societal transformation? The question arises because social entrepreneurship is also an ambiguous and contested concept that is often portrayed as theoretically underdeveloped (Hulgård and Andersen, 2012) and as an ill-defined concept (Hervieux et al., 2010) in which the social dimension is largely unexplored (Barinaga, 2012). Others again criticize the entire field for inconsistencies and contradictions (Schofield, 2005). A reason for this may be that the concept is stretched between approaches emphasizing community-oriented collective logics, on one hand, and individual, market-based dynamics, on the other (Hulgård and Andersen, 2012; Hervieux et al., 2010). Consequently, the political implications and underpinnings of both the phenomenon and the concept of social entrepreneurship are ambiguous and unclear. Swedberg (2006) emphasizes that social entrepreneurship, in contrast to the "traditional" Schumpeterian concept of entrepreneurship, is not related to a broader theory of entrepreneurship and is often used more like an inspiring phrase or a slogan (Swedberg, 2006). In combination with the very positive connotations associated with the term, the risk is that it becomes deployed to give legitimacy to policies and initiatives in ways that suspend a critical examination of the concept, including the types of change and societal transformation that social entrepreneurship actually contributes to and how we can normatively evaluate these. When we conceive of social entrepreneurship as a means toward social change, it necessarily has political and ethical consequences (Steyaert and Dey, 2010: 233). In this sense, any potential for the concept to more precisely define, conceptualize or guide progressive social change seems to be threatened by its ambiguity and widely different uses. This calls for a concise and precise discussion of the conceptual, as well as normative, vagueness currently associated with social entrepreneurship. The chapter addresses this challenge by applying and discussing the concept of 'critique' in an analysis of a number of critical studies in the research field of social entrepreneurship. Such critical studies address precisely this ambiguity of social entrepreneurship and denaturalize certain understandings, thereby opening up for discussion alternative ways of conceptualizing or understanding social entrepreneurship. Furthermore, critique as a research strategy in social theory has traditionally been associated with an emancipatory aim of research and explicit reflections about the role of research in societal transformation (Delanty, 2011; Horkheimer, 1970; Habermas, 2005). Seeing social entrepreneurship as a concept of social change, such explicit reflections will aid the clarification of the potentials and limitations of current understandings of social entrepreneurship and current ways of conducting research about it.

In the context of this book about people-centered social innovation, the aim of the chapter is to shed light on issues that are relevant not only to social entrepreneurship research but also to social innovation research more generally. Social entrepreneurship can be considered as a particular field in the broader range of social innovation research, and the concept represents some of the same ambitions and addresses the same challenges as social innovation. *Social innovation* is also a term that is used in many ways, and its ambiguous meaning is thus something that researchers continually work on clarifying and overcoming (Moulaert et al., 2013). People-centered social innovation focuses on the empowerment and sociopolitical mobilization of people and a desire to address issues of social injustice (Hulgård and Shajahan, 2013). From a normative perspective, one could say that our challenge as researchers is to identify understandings and commitments that allow us to do research and theory on social injustice and social entrepreneurship as a way of addressing injustice, without adding further layers of difference and distance. This chapter addresses this challenge by elucidating different dimensions of critique in research and theory on social entrepreneurship in a discussion of what it means to have a critical position in the area of social entrepreneurship and social innovation research.

The Aim and Approach of the Chapter

The chapter started by suggesting that there is a need for critical approaches to social entrepreneurship. However, it is not evident what *critique* more specifically could mean in this context and what different critical strategies would imply for empirical and conceptual studies in the field. Consequently, the question is, Which types of critique could be significant contributions to the field of social entrepreneurship studies? The chapter focuses on three dimensions of critique in particular, namely, the implications for social entrepreneurship as a concept of social change, methodological considerations about the position of the researcher and the role of normativity. The choice of these particular dimensions has to do with, first of all, the argument that social entrepreneurship is a concept of change and, second, because it is along these dimensions especially that we see variations among critical contributions in the field. It has not been possible to identify a particular current of the field concerned with critical studies, and the contributions vary in the way that they understand and employ a critical methodology or strategy.

The chapter analyzes and discusses critique as a research strategy in social entrepreneurship studies by in-depth analysis of 10 contributions that conduct some form of critique. The 10 contributions (articles and conference papers) have been selected (three nonnormative critical discourse analyses, three normatively informed critiques, and four conceptual contributions) because they all provide examples of critique, enabling a discussion of what critique could mean as a strategy for social entrepreneurship research. Some researchers use the term *critique* explicitly, while others do not, albeit still conducting their research in a way that can be recognized as critical in the sense that they draw systematically on established positions in critical social theory. The ambition is not to make a comprehensive overview including all critical approaches or types of critique but, rather, to identify a selection of critical approaches that provide a good basis for discussion of the implications of different notions of critique for social entrepreneurship research. Some of the contributions use the term *social enterprise*, while others use the term *social entrepreneurship*. As the two terms, policies and academic literature, are closely related and, to a large extent, seem to refer to the same phenomenon, both are included here.

Structure of the Chapter

The chapter contains three analysis sections and a conclusion. The first section visits the arguments found in the research field for why we need critical social entrepreneurship studies and presents an overview of the main critiques and what they have in common. A common denominator of existing studies is the object of critique, namely, the influence of neoliberal logics of managerialism, individualism and marketization in nonprofit and civil society organizations. The way critique is understood and conducted, however, varies, and this is what the subsequent two analysis sections look into. The second analysis section presents a number of critical approaches that all put counterdiscourse and resistance at the center of their critical analysis and discuss the implications and limitations of these approaches. Despite their common focus, they vary with regard to the role of normativity and the role of theory and thereby also by ascribing different roles to the researcher in practicing critical research. Another common trait of these studies is that critique plays a role and has implications for ways of conducting empirical research but has limited reflections and consequences for the conceptualization of social entrepreneurship. Thus, the third section presents and discusses a number of conceptual takes on social entrepreneurship. They all present suggestions for concepts or definitions of social entrepreneurship; however, none of them actually explicitly address the question of what it means to conceptualize. Conceptualization as a critical strategy thereby remains largely unexplained and unarticulated across all critical social entrepreneurship studies. This means that the current conceptual approaches have limitations because the discussion of *criteria* for conceptualization is not systematically addressed. Finally, the conclusion discusses the implications and limitations of the existing critiques and suggests a way forward.

What Is *Critique* in Social Entrepreneurship Studies?

Before getting into the substance of the critical approaches, a few remarks should be made about how to understand *critique* in the first place. As indicated earlier, critical contributions to social entrepreneurship studies do not constitute a coherent strand of research. Rather, we can note a variety of approaches, each using the term *critique* in different ways, or exercising something that may be characterized as a critique for differing purposes. So, before we can identify existing critical approaches in social entrepreneurship research, we must determine what constitutes a critical approach in the first place. Are they only the approaches that use the term *critique* or *critical*, and if so, can all these contributions be considered critical? Or do we also find approaches that can be designated *critical* without, however, using the term explicitly?

Among research contributions that call their approach *critical*, some are clearer and more explicit in their use of the term than others. Even those that use the word *critique* do not always articulate what is meant by it. Nor do they all represent well-known critical social theoretical positions. In some of these contributions it can be difficult to see what *critique* means and what role it is playing in theory, in policy, or in organizational or societal development. In these cases, the term *critique* is often employed in a more everyday sense of the word rather than as a distinctive research strategy. We can also see a number of approaches in which, even if they do not explicitly use the word *critique* to describe what they do, nevertheless researchers conduct their research in ways that could be called critical. For example, their studies may aim at denaturalizing certain dominant understandings of social entrepreneurship (e.g., Barinaga, 2012) and can thus be considered to be critical in the sense that they reveal the historical and contingent meanings attached to the concept, thereby opening up for discussion the underlying assumptions of its contemporary use. Or they express concerns about a dominant managerial ideology taking precedence over the social dimension of social enterprise (e.g., Hulgård and Andersen, 2012; Pestoff and Hulgård, 2016). Last, a group of contributions use the term *critique* to characterize what they do and follow certain critical strategies explicitly drawn from social theory. They thereby conduct a certain systematic and explicit type of critique, for example, critical discourse analysis (e.g., Dey and Teasdale, 2013).

That critical approaches are relatively rare is confirmed by Dey and Steyaert (2012) and Steyaert and Dey (2010), who have contributed to some of the few systematic presentations of critical research on social entrepreneurship. These articles constitute an important starting point for the chapter and are significant contributions to critical social entrepreneurship studies because they explicitly develop potential critical strategies. For example, in their 2010 article, Steyaert and Dey outline a number of critical research strategies found in existing social entrepreneurship research and reimagine current research approaches to the field. A central point of the article is that social entrepreneurship research creates certain images of social entrepreneurship and thereby contributes to constituting it rather than just studying something that is essentially there prior to the act of research (Steyaert and Dey, 2010: 232). This chapter follows up on this endeavor but works with some other distinctions, for example, between empirical and conceptual studies, in order to open new debates about the implications of certain critical strategies deployed in the field.

The Content of and Arguments for Critique in Social Entrepreneurship Studies

When it comes to the content of critique, all critical approaches seem to have the same object of critique. Concerns about the influence of neoliberal logics of managerialism, business principles, individualism and marketization in nonprofit organizations, in nongovernmental organizations, in community organizing, in public services or more generally that activities with social aims are somehow being subjected to managerial logics dominate these critical perspectives (see also Hervieux et al., 2010). Most arguments for the need of critical studies start with a call for an alternative to the neoliberal discourse or business-oriented view apparently dominating the field (Bull, 2008). We see a number of contributions that emphasize the cooperative, collective and participatory dimensions of social enterprise and suggest an alternative frame of reference for understanding it. The trend described here is that the third sector, which historically was built on ideals of community and trust, is being challenged by the introduction into it of the well-known dynamics of managerialism and business-like practices. An argument is that the amalgamation of the social and enterprise legitimizes a narrative where there seems to be no contradiction between economic and social aim, and where social enterprise is represented as a way of doing business where success in the market will allow social aims to more or less to take care of themselves (Bull, 2008). Examples abound of critical approaches analyzing the impact of neoliberalism on the shaping of social entrepreneurship and indicating the ways in which social entrepreneurship is deployed politically to introduce market-based logics and funding mechanisms, as well as business methods, into third-sector organizations (Dey and Teasdale, 2013; Dey, 2010).

As indicated, however, the critiques take different forms. Some contributions are explicitly normative while others are not. Some contributions stress the participatory governance dimensions and cooperative ways of working on the basis of a historical and empirical sensitivity to social enterprise and the roots these organizations have, especially in a European context (Pestoff, 2014; Pestoff and Hulgård, 2016). It is relevant to mention that the perspective represented by Pestoff and Hulgård (2016) is developed and shared by a larger network of European researchers in the EMES (L'EMergence de l'Entreprise Sociale en Europe) network, in particular, and thus does not represent a niche position. Others take a more explicitly normative position when they suggest that we should understand social entrepreneurship and social enterprise in terms of, for example, ethical capital (Bull et al., 2010), recognition and social justice (Froggett and Chamberlayne, 2004), equality, emancipation and democracy (Curtis, 2008) or participatory and deliberative democracy and citizen identities (Eikenberry, 2009) rather than in business and market-based terms. In this light, it is fair to doubt the unanimous dominance of a taken-for-granted and mainstream understanding of social entrepreneurship associated with neoliberalism, marketization and the privatization of welfare, as a number of the critical contributions take as their starting point for why we need critique. It seems that there are already a number of alternative perspectives available in the field, actually to such an extent that we can hardly call the alternative position marginalized. The question is thus what can be gained from taking on a more explicitly critical research approach, beyond ascertaining a dominant neoliberal discourse and suggesting a community-based alternative.

Despite the ambiguity about the concept, and thus also about the normative dimensions of social entrepreneurship, and the use of the concept in political agendas for the development of Western welfare systems and for empowerment in the global South, social entrepreneurship is often represented as something unquestionably positive and associated with great optimism (Bull, 2008; Dacin et al., 2011; Mason, 2012). In that sense, it is a powerful concept, with a political significance, which calls for a critical reflection on the political and practical implications of methodological and conceptual choices made in the research field. Critique can thus be a strategy for self-reflection of the research field itself, not merely something directed toward practitioners and policies. This is something that critical studies should be able to offer, and this is an important argument for why we need them. Without such reflection, the concept can easily be used ideologically to support and legitimize certain political agendas, and research may provide further support for that, unwittingly perhaps but nevertheless effectively. Critical studies, therefore, can potentially contribute to denaturalizing the concept, thus opening up for discussion what social entrepreneurship is and could be, also from a more political perspective. But they can also provide suggestions for ways of understanding it, including as a driver for social transformation. In that sense, critical research may contribute to shaping and not only studying social entrepreneurship and thereby play a role in social transformation itself. In the following, we take a look at ways of using critique to question a certain neoliberal interpretation of social entrepreneurship.

Empirical Studies of Resistance and Counterdiscourse

In the field of social entrepreneurship research, a number of studies conduct critical discourse analyses as a research strategy. Common to these is their focus on practitioners' resistance, which can be traced in different types of counter discourse to what is portrayed as a hegemonic business-oriented social entrepreneurship discourse. It is thus at the micro level that alternatives to the mainstream are detected and through the small discontinuities and contestations that cracks can appear. The studies vary in their understanding of discourse, as well as in their methodological approach, especially in the sense that some researchers take a nonnormative stance while others build on explicitly normative theories and concepts in their analysis. In the following we first take a look at some nonnormative analyses and thereafter at some normatively informed critiques.

By deploying the Foucauldian concept of *dispositif*, Dey (2010) analyzes how linguistic constructions of social entrepreneurship stipulate the correct conduct of community affairs, thereby playing a role in identity-forming processes of practitioners in the field. But according to Dey, something escapes this metadiscourse. Ambivalences in the linguistic self-representations of social entrepreneurs suggest that the metadiscourse fails in the sense that the individual social entrepreneur never fully accedes to the symbolic placement offered by the matrix of the *dispositif*. Dey suggests that, rather than pointing to a monolithic dominant discourse and spelling out one particular alternative or strategy of resistance, we should embrace the discursive ambivalences, ideological dilemmas and processes of transgressive self-formation. Such a critical strategy makes it possible to

> approach the sign 'social entrepreneurship' not in terms of its ontology (i.e. what it really means), but based on meticulous analyses of the . . . structures and practices that constitute the conditions of possibility of social entrepreneurship and of which social entrepreneurship is an effect.
>
> (Dey, 2010: 16–17)

It offers a distance from taken-for-granted assumptions and invites reflection on the political reality into which social entrepreneurship is transformed. According to Dey, such reflective detachment provides a means of repoliticizing social entrepreneurship by seeing it as primarily belonging to society and not only to the economy. It thus becomes possible to embrace different, and at times antagonistic, semantic possibilities and leave space for more variegated images of social entrepreneurship, thereby taking a step toward a multiplication of the meaning of social entrepreneurship. He argues that the little narratives of practitioners lay out a promising path toward justice, not "because the truth lies in the local but because any recognition of difference depends on the 'ruthless discipline of context' " (Dey, 2010: 32).

A similar strategy is taken up by Dey and Teasdale (2013), who also deploy a discourse analysis to point out oppositional and antagonistic identity politics in the field of social enterprise. They explore the identity work of third sector practitioners by relating dis/identification with social enterprise discourse to issues of agency. They show that resistance, dis-identification and counter-identification of actors in the field take a variety of forms and thereby demonstrate that social enterprise does not work deterministically as a *muscular discourse* in the third sector, shaping practitioners' identities in an all-embracing manner (p. 263). In this article, the focus on agency is articulated even more strongly than in Dey (2010), as the authors explicitly distance themselves from types of more deterministic discourse analysis. They stress that they see the actors not as docile bodies who blindly endorse the policy context of which they are part but rather as revealing notable levels of agency, in particular in the ways they oppose the discourse of social enterprise. As is argued in the following, this is relevant to the understanding of critique as a research strategy.

A third example to be mentioned here is Mason's (2012) critical analysis of social entrepreneurship discourse in the United Kingdom. He points to the importance of counterposing the heroic narratives that are often used to describe social entrepreneurship with critical analyses of its role in society. Mason interrogates the notion that social entrepreneurship has become a *governable terrain* through the struggle for hegemony. Through a quantitative and qualitative analysis of key words and word frequencies in UK government documents and speeches that define social entrepreneurship in the period from 2002 to 2008, he finds that policy language contributes to creating an artificial business-like identity. Like Dey (2010) and Dey and Teadale (2013), Mason focuses on counterdiscourse and resistance from actors by holding onto a *minorizing* social enterprise identity and to an oppositional grassroots identity (Mason, 2012). He argues that resistance and counterdiscourses are important to understanding how hegemony is challenged and that "discursive contestation ensues where ideology, values and legitimacy clash, representing the struggle by nonhegemonic participants against domination" (Mason, 2012: 126).

We can detect a difference in the understanding of discourse, as well as counterdiscourse, between Dey (2010) and Dey and Teasdale (2013), on one hand, and Mason, on the other. For Dey (2010) and Dey and Teasdale (2013), discourse, as well as counterdiscourse, is portrayed as something constituted by possible fragmentation, disharmony, discontinuity and ambivalence; for Mason (2012), however, the mainstream discourse is represented as an overarching hegemony to be countered by its opposite, namely, a grassroots discourse. This is relevant because the discourse concepts and the concept of symbolic violence or domination revealed by the authors indicate how they understand power, as well as emancipation or resistance to power. The contrast here could be presented as between minorizing the dominant discourse by giving space to one specific counterdiscourse of grassroots identity versus opening the possibility of multiple counterdiscourses pointing in different directions and thereby also suspending the dominance of certain business-oriented narratives and stories of hero entrepreneurs. Such strategies of *deconstructing hegemony* by pointing to a plurality of already-existing alternatives or possibilities are also present in recent critical approaches to capitalism (Gibson-Graham, 2006a, 2006b; Laville, 2010) and to a monoculture of the universal and global associated with neoliberal globalization (Santos, 2009). Dey and Teasdale express an explicit concern for upholding a symmetry between researchers and actors and for avoiding any normative judgments. In this sense, the relationship between critique and social transformation is closely linked with the critical disputes and acts of resistance of the actors (Dey and Teasdale, 2013: 250). Both these studies locate the potential for a different social entrepreneurship discourse/ agenda in the resistance of actors in the field. To the researcher, critical engagement seems to be restricted to methodological choices, to pointing out the potential and need for alternative arenas for negotiation and identity shaping of social entrepreneurship. From a perspective of critical social theory, these contributions represent a certain modesty with regard to a more explicit normative engagement of the researcher. The emphasis on the agency and the competence of practitioners in the field bears some similarity to the sociology of critical practice of Boltanski and Thévenot in the sense that the empirical object of study is critical practices carried out by the actors in the field (Boltanski, 2013; Boltanski and Thévenot, 1999, 2006). In that respect, the researchers do not provide specific normative suggestions about what an alternative social entrepreneurship discourse could entail, except for opening up to seeing the phenomenon as something connected to society and not merely to the market. In this way, the researcher can contribute to social change by unmasking and challenging existing agendas of social entrepreneurship and by identifying resistance but is not the driver of change per se and does not provide any substantial content or normative input to the change to guide it in a certain direction. The following section focuses on studies that take a more normative approach.

Normatively Informed Critiques

A number of normatively informed critiques also focus on counterdiscourse as a critical strategy. The difference is that the normatively informed approaches to critical discourse analysis explicate certain normative counterpositions or counterconcepts to the mainstream neoliberal social entrepreneurship discourse. So even if the normatively informed approaches share similarities with the critical discourse approaches mentioned earlier, there are also significant differences in terms of the critical strategies employed.

Curtis (2008), for instance, conducts a critical analysis in which he distances himself from what he presents as mainstream social enterprise research. He critically comments on the depoliticization of social services and the managerial decision-making governed by financial constraints and market economics rather than ethics, inclusivity and democracy. He describes his approach in the following terms: "the goal of research is not the interpretation of the world, but the organization of transformation" (Conti, 2001, as cited in Curtis, 2008: 277). He sees the role of critical theory as identifying and challenging assumptions, recognizing the influence of culture and social position, exploring alternatives and disrupting routines and established orders. Thereby social transformation becomes an explicit aim of social research. He also stresses the resistance of actors in the field and argues that the counterposition to the mainstream discourse of social entrepreneurship implies that new voices are heard, such as the voices of the beneficiaries of social services. Curtis

(2008: 276) advocates that critique is about "finding the grit" that makes a pearl, that is, the obstruction that prevents the neoliberal system from running smoothly: the resistance, recalcitrance and obstruction. He is thus explicit about how he defines critique and about that of which he is critical, or from which he distances his research, namely, mainstream social enterprise literature with its focus on managerialism. If we take Curtis's view of critique as something that challenges assumptions and points out alternatives by mentioning equality, emancipation and democracy as more appropriate foundational principles for social enterprise (Curtis, 2008), one could argue that his critique is normatively informed. Even though he does not unpack what he means by these concepts, he nevertheless suggests some concepts that provide a normative alternative to neoliberal discourse.

Froggett and Chamberlayne (2004) develop a critique of neoliberalism and positivist approaches to policy evaluation inspired by Honneth's concept of recognition (Froggett and Chamberlayne, 2004: 72–73). They further suggest empirical methods, which could support critical studies of social entrepreneurship, such as biographical methods that contribute to stimulating powerful critiques of neoliberal and rational choice thinking. Biographical methods reveal contradictions and make it possible to challenge certain one-sided discourses of performative activism and active citizenship underpinning representations of social entrepreneurship and community activism (Froggett and Chamberlayne, 2004). By furthermore suggesting an alternative conceptual framework of recognition, suffering and caring, social entrepreneurship can be conceptualized in political terms and with a focus on social solidarity and justice. The implication of such a critical strategy is that it provides alternative categories with which to associate social entrepreneurship than the ones emerging from a neoliberal discourse of individualism, consumerism and managerialism (Froggett and Chamberlayne, 2004: 72–73). Again, we see a strong focus on the actors and their resistance—on this occasion, however, accompanied by a normative conceptualization and theorization. The difference here is that the normative theoretical framework makes explicit what the authors see as threatened by the neoliberal version of social entrepreneurship (i.e., recognition, active citizenship, community activism), and thus, it becomes possible to discuss this from a normative perspective of justice and injustice.

Eikenberry (2009), too, conducts a critical analysis of democratic discourse for voluntary and nonprofit organizations, including social enterprises. Eikenberry explicitly situates her research within critical and normative theorizing in the nonprofit sector, with the aim of challenging taken-for-granted assumptions underpinning the prevailing market discourse. Eikenberry sketches a development in which the nonprofit sector is driven to conform to a neoliberal ideology, entailing an increased focus on entrepreneurial behavior, market-based solutions to social problems and a greater reliance on income-generating activities. Social entrepreneurship is presented as an important part of this ideology. Marketization has become a threat to the democratic contribution of third-sector organizations and she suggests an alternative discourse of participatory and deliberative democracy and citizen identities to replace the emphasis on consumer identities. She argues that, by the pursuit of market-based rather than community-based activities, social enterprises attempt to find the most entrepreneurial way to address a social problem but thereby risk losing sight of the root causes of the social problems that they aim to address. This weakens the role of nonprofit and voluntary organizations in social transformation, and in order to resist this, she argues, we must imagine and promote democratic movements "that reject the dominant market discourse 'and pursue more just, more humane, and more social cooperative' futures" (Eikenberry, 2009: 583). Eikenberry portrays the market discourse as a "pervasive 'ideology that views all aspects of human society as a kind of a market'" (Zimmerman and Dart, 1998: 16 as cited in Eikenberry, 2009: 582). Her intention in proposing alternative democratic counterdiscourses is not to create another hegemonic discourse but, rather, to encourage a diversity of perspectives and discourses in studies of the nonprofit sector (Eikenberry, 2009: 593).

Implications of the Critical Discourse Analyses

Despite the variations in method and critical strategy, the approaches presented point more or less unanimously toward managerialism, marketization or neoliberalism in an amorphous sense (Dey and Teasdale, 2013; Dey, 2010; Dey and Steyaert, 2010; Bull, 2008; Curtis, 2008; Eikenberry and Kluver, 2004; Eikenberry, 2009; Bull et al., 2010). Through discourse analyses they all highlight resistance and counterdiscourses of the actors in the field as important for creating the cracks in the mainstream discourse that can lead the way for the emergence of alternative interpretations of social entrepreneurship, and thereby for new practices. However, they also display differences, for example, in their understanding of power and resistance. Dey (2010) and Dey and Teasdale (2013) portray social entrepreneurship discourse (and resistance to it) as fragmented, discontinuous and ambiguous rather than as one coherent, hegemonic discourse to be resisted through a certain counterdiscourse. The normatively informed critical approaches, on the other hand, develop alternative normative conceptual frameworks by the use of concepts of such as recognition, cooperation, justice, democracy or emancipation—but without seemingly offering any specification of what these may actually entail practically in terms of organization, management or conduct. Normatively informed critiques thereby suggest a certain direction of change by leaning on more or less elaborated normative ideals. Such differences have implications for the role of the researcher, in particular in relation to the actors under study, and furthermore for critique as a driver of social change—whether driven by the resistance of practitioners or by a critical strategy of the researcher.

Typical arguments against normatively informed critiques include that they risk becoming paternalist. They are said to claim a detached, privileged position of the researcher that allows him or her to unmask ideologies and power relations that work behind the backs of the agents and that they may not even be aware of. A position that is more sensitive toward the actors and gains a deeper understanding of them requires a hermeneutically more sensitive researcher who insists on the primacy of practice, of the agent's perspective and self-understanding over the standpoint of science or theory that claims the privilege of detachment (Celikates, 2006). The flipside of this, if taken to its extreme, is a position deprived of the possibility of raising any critique of what practitioners are doing and what is done to them beyond what is already available to them (Celikates, 2006). In other words, the risk is to end up in an affirmative, rather than a critical, position, and one that is cementing rather than challenging the phenomena and social orders that it is concerned with studying. Furthermore, some argue that even the negativist version of critical theory has a utopian component, that it implicitly relies on an idea of the good society—or, at least, of a society in which the conditions that are criticized are not present. For Cooke (2009), for example, critical theory of society is unthinkable without a more or less specific idea of the good society (or at least of a better society). One could argue that, as a consequence, such research should be conscious and transparent about the ideals that it implicitly or explicitly works from. The normatively informed critiques presented here also have a strong focus on the worldview and resistance expressed by the practitioners in the field and, in this sense, do not attempt to unmask something that takes place behind the backs of the practitioners. Furthermore, in these studies the normative concepts of democracy, participation and cooperation do not seem to contradict the self-understanding of the practitioners in the third sector and their grassroots identity.

But the position of the researcher in relation to the critical practices of the agents in the field also has implications for how change can be viewed. As mentioned, social entrepreneurship can be considered a concept and practice of social transformation, but the question is how to view this in light of these critical studies. As mentioned, Curtis saw "the goal of research is not the interpretation of the world, but the organization of transformation" (2008: 277). Such an ambition has been part of critical research since Marx and with the Frankfurt school (Habermas, 2005). The question is whether and how these critical strategies in themselves relate to social change.

In these studies, counterdiscourses and the resistance of actors seem to be seen as potential drivers of change. As for the role of the researcher in critical work, identifying critique empirically and making it visible through research becomes the central task. This could be seen as a way of avoiding being accused of paternalism and insensitivity toward the actors in the field, while at the same time conducting critical research that denaturalizes certain understandings of social entrepreneurship and points to alternatives. Critique then becomes part of the empirical field under study rather than something the researcher does or employs in relation to pointing out alternatives or arguing for the implications of certain social entrepreneurship discourses. By making critique part of the empirical object under study, these contributions represent a view of critique that is similar to the French sociology of critical practices of Boltanski and Thévenot, as described earlier. In addition to this, normatively informed critiques apply theories to empirical studies, theories with normative content, which means that the researcher gets a role, too, in the formulation of alternatives to neoliberalism and managerialism. A limitation of this could be, as mentioned earlier, that studies that focus solely on the resistance of the actors in the field remain at a micro level of analysis, thus becoming blind to the broader structural, political and societal dimensions of change, and may not be able to account for how these acts of micro-resistance play into and initiate a broader movement of transformation. Furthermore, the relationships among theory and practice, the researcher and the actors in social transformation, and not least the role of social entrepreneurship, as practice, phenomenon and concept, are not considered explicitly, even in normative approaches.

Social entrepreneurship is, as mentioned, about social change and development of society. Socially entrepreneurial initiatives have, given that they lead to changes in society, political and ethical implications. This calls for considerations and arguments about the normative dimensions of the changes carried out in the name of social entrepreneurship. Theorizing about social entrepreneurship means more than merely describing a phenomenon. It is also part of constituting the phenomenon and the activities carried out in its name. What is interesting is that critical studies rarely address the issue of social change and social entrepreneurship as a concept of change explicitly. Instead, the focus is on the distinction between the social (which is associated with democracy, community, and other positive things) and the economic (which is associated with neoliberalism, marketization; see also Barinaga, 2012). Relevant questions that could be addressed more explicitly are What are the main driving forces of social change, and how can we understand the relation between micro and macro levels, between researchers and actors, and between theory and practice? What is social entrepreneurship from this perspective, theoretically speaking? and How can we distinguish between normatively desirable change and undesirable change that social entrepreneurship has a role in? Even if it may seem like there are implicit assumptions about the drivers of social change related to social entrepreneurship, these are not explicated and thus not developed in a way that allows for critical scrutiny or conceptual discussion of them.

The role of the normative concepts in that sense seems to be to substantiate the "social" side of social entrepreneurship, but the question is whether this really leads to theoretical development in the field and if it helps us to overcome conceptual ambiguity. My answer to these questions would be yes, it does lead to theoretical development, or, at least, theoretical anchoring, of the field of social entrepreneurship in the sense that it provides a conceptual, theoretical framework that clarifies the broader societal context of social enterprises as well as the organizing principles and logics in play. These studies do not, however, directly address and attempt to clarify the concept of social entrepreneurship itself. These discourse analytical approaches seem more engaged with empirical studies than with conceptual work. The normatively informed critiques suggest different theoretical frameworks, which stress democracy, community and emancipation that are applied in empirical studies, rather than discussed in conceptual terms. They focus on the phenomenon of social entrepreneurship and social enterprise rather than on the concept, except for the concept being part of the empirical object of study and the discourses that the concept organizes in certain ways. Social entrepreneurship becomes a practice, a discourse or a *sign* (Dey, 2010) to be studied empirically. In that sense, the concept seems to be reduced to an empirical phenomenon, which can be studied, and critically discussed in light of its political and practical implications but without the researcher subsequently engaging in conceptualization as an academic practice, as I indicated earlier. The question of how such critical methods and empirical strategies should have consequences for the conceptualization of social entrepreneurship is not addressed. But should critical research also throw itself into the conceptual battle? And if so, how? Or should we accept that social entrepreneurship is so imbued with neoliberal thinking that it is better to give it up and use different terms and practices? In the following, we take a look at some of the attempts to critically reflect on the very concept of social entrepreneurship and explore how we can find answers to such questions.

Conceptual Debates in Social Entrepreneurship Studies

As mentioned at the beginning of the chapter, the field is claimed to be immature and undertheorized with only very few critical contributions. Other researchers resist these representations of the field and see the field as mature enough for us to identify certain different substrands and distinctions in it (Defourny et al., 2014). In any case, the question is not merely about empirical studies, or about which theories to apply, but also about conceptualization. A question that is not answered by empirical studies, whether normative or nonnormative, is, If social entrepreneurship is already implicated in so-called neoliberal agendas and practices, what can we then do with it, presuming that we find this agenda potentially problematic? Should we discard the concept and accept that it is too sullied by managerialism and neoliberalism, or should we redefine the concept? The critical empirical studies may suggest alternative arenas from which new meanings of social entrepreneurship can emerge (Dey, 2010) or alternative theoretical frameworks for understanding social entrepreneurship (such as Eikenberry, 2009; Froggett and Chamberlayne, 2004), but they do not engage directly in conceptual development. In the following, we take a look at research contributions that work with conceptualizing social entrepreneurship.

One contribution that engages in conceptualizing is Peredo and McLean (2006), who set themselves the task of undertaking an analytical, critical and synthetic examination of the concept of social entrepreneurship. They argue that the concept needs to be clarified and that we need to understand what social entrepreneurship actually is and what constitutes social entrepreneurship. Their method for pursuing the question is to look into scholarly definitions of social entrepreneurship, by first considering definitions of *entrepreneurship* and then attempting to identify the *social* in social entrepreneurship. Their reflections about what a concept is, what it means to conceptualize or what is appropriate or good conceptualization in the specific case are mainly about whether a definition should include normative characteristics. They state that there are good reasons to resist this temptation. They argue that a satisfactory definition of the entrepreneurship component of social entrepreneurship should avoid building on the notions of success and worthiness and allow for social entrepreneurs who may be unsuccessful, inconsistent or otherwise less than exemplary (Peredo and Mclean, 2006: 59). In their review and discussion of the social dimension of social entrepreneurship, they draw on different definitions with varying takes on, in particular, the nonprofit dimension and the relation between social mission and the pursuit of profit. They also deploy a number of cases and examples of social entrepreneurship in order to investigate whether profitability is consistent with social entrepreneurship (Peredo and Mclean, 2006). As a result, they end up with a rather broad definition in which social entrepreneurship is distinguished from other types of entrepreneurship by the commitment to provide social value. They see social entrepreneurship as an untidy concept and explain that this is a reflection of the untidiness of the world. If we look, for a moment, beyond the content of the concept that they suggest and instead take a look at what they actually do in their conceptualization exercise, we may also learn something about what they understand by a *concept*, which is interesting for understanding the research field.

Looking at it from a methodological point of view we can trace a double movement in the way Peredo and McLean work with the concept.

On one hand, they indicate that mirroring reality, namely, what social entrepreneurship actually is, is one criterion for a concept while also contending that the concept is not tidy due to the untidiness of reality. And, as mentioned, they also argue that we should avoid the temptation to include normative dimensions in the concept. On the face of it, this appears to equate with a value-free descriptive attitude which is primarily interested in creating theories and concepts on the basis of some kind of ordering of empirical facts. On the other hand, they also have a more practical, or pragmatic, interest related to managing social entrepreneurship. One reason given for why we need a concept of social entrepreneurship in the first place is that we must be able to distinguish it from entrepreneurship per se, because the type of managerial competencies appropriate to successfully pursuing social goals may differ in significant ways from what is relevant to entrepreneurship without such a social component. In that sense, one could argue that this discussion about the concept of social entrepreneurship basically rests on a positivist and technical scientific approach to conceptualization. Approaching the concept in this way does not create any clear link between social entrepreneurship and broader societal change, and certainly not in any politically normative sense, as social transformation. Neither does this conceptual exercise take into consideration that the concept of social entrepreneurship is also used to legitimate certain political agendas or initiatives over others, and this can have political implications. Nevertheless, the contribution is relevant to include, first, because it is symptomatic of many of the conceptual attempts that operate without explicit criteria for conceptualization and, second, because it becomes difficult to see by what criteria a certain concept or definition of social enterprise is judged better than other definitions.

A different way of entering the conceptual debate is seen with Pestoff and Hulgård (2016). They are representatives of the approach to social entrepreneurship developed in the research network EMES, which emphasizes the roots in civil society and the cooperative tradition. They explicitly incorporate an additional dimension to the understanding and conceptualization of social enterprise besides the distinction between social and economic purposes, namely the dimension of participatory versus nonparticipatory decision-making, governance structures and processes (Pestoff, 2014). Pestoff and Hulgård (2016) argue that much of the conceptual confusion could be dispersed with a more concise and focused definition of social enterprise that is contextually specific rather than vaguely universal. They discuss what should be included in a definition of social entrepreneurship and social enterprise and distance themselves from both very broad and very narrow definitions by also discussing how such definitions serve to support certain policy agendas or pursuits of legitimization of large corporations. A definition encompassing the social, economic and participatory dimensions of social enterprise, they argue, allows us to more accurately denote and delimit the space for the development of social enterprise in Europe. They specify that social entrepreneurship aims to create social change by addressing unmet needs, demands or market failures (Pestoff and Hulgård, 2016). However, I argue that it is not entirely clear if the relationship between social entrepreneurship and social change refers to the *efforts* to create social change in the practice field or on the determination that social change *has occurred* from a research perspective, irrespective of the aims and ambitions of the practitioners. Besides, it is not clear whether and how we should understand social entrepreneurship as a driver of progressive social transformation or of social change more generally (whether good or bad), even though there does seem to be some normative underpinnings to this approach with its emphasis on social economy and democracy. However, it is not made explicit how we should understand the normative dimension of these. Rather than as a normative dimension, the emphasis could also be read as sensitivity to the history and empirical knowledge of social enterprises, especially in a European context, where, to a great extent, they have grown out of the tradition of cooperatives, mutuals and associations (Pestoff and Hulgård, 2016). In that sense, Pestoff and Hulgård do not explicitly position themselves as normative or engage in any normative justification. Defourny and Nyssens (2010) also present the EMES definition of social enterprise by pointing out a number of criteria that an organization should meet in order to be classified as a social enterprise. They refer to the definition as a Weberian ideal type. By that they mean "an abstract construction that enables researchers to position themselves within the 'galaxy' of social enterprises" (Defourny and Nyssens, 2010: 43). The criteria for social enterprises are not meant as prescriptive criteria but, rather, as constituting a tool that will make it possible for researchers to locate the position of an organization in the social enterprise field and eventually to identify subsets of social enterprises.

A final conceptual approach to be included here is one by Bull et al. (2010), whose declared aim is to conceptualize social enterprise as holding the potential for higher moral and ethical ground in business. They argue that this higher ground claim is one of the defining characteristics of social enterprise. In that sense, it is a conceptual approach, not one that focuses strictly on the question of a definition but, rather, one that aims to develop a normative, theoretical framework for analyzing social enterprises. They explore the implications involved in merging a social mission with the culture of market ideology, and the trade-offs involved in that balancing act. Their reason for emphasizing ethical capital is also to contribute to the development of the sector and to understand the value of social entrepreneurs and transformations of capital in driving social change. They present this as an attempt to break away from the usual ways of looking at social entrepreneurship and as an alternative to both the enterprise-oriented view (with a basis in mainstream economics) and the social capital lens. This conceptualization of social enterprise opens a way of understanding the ethical dimension of social enterprise and seeing it as a vehicle for moral management (Bull et al., 2010). In that sense, they aim to contribute to development of the field by elaborating the normative dimension of social enterprise by distinguishing, for example, between conventional morality (moral norms shared by society, in general) and critical morality (the critical reflection on the normative value of these norms; Bull et al., 2010). This contribution is clearly normative and has the aim of contributing to change through an increased understanding of ethical management; it also points to an alternative to the neoclassical economic view of understanding management and organization.

Discussion of the Conceptual Contributions

The contributions above engage in conceptual debate, but questions about what a concept is, what it means to conceptualize and what we wish to do with the concept are rarely explicitly addressed, except as an ideal type that enables researchers to position themselves within the "galaxy of social enterprise". The impression is that, despite the numerous attempts to define and conceptualize, the field would benefit greatly from a more systematic metareflection on the enterprise of conceptualizing. I argue that such metareflective considerations—the criteria for the concept and what is required of a good or appropriate concept of social entrepreneurship—are highly relevant to the field. For example, should a concept mirror or order empirical reality as accurately as possible, should it work as a tool for management or should it be a driver for emancipation and social transformation? What it means to conceptualize and what the criteria for a good concept are, in this context, could thereby become explicit and the epistemological, pragmatic and normative dimensions of the concept could be separated out. The *epistemological* dimension regards questions about what type of knowledge is reflected in the concept. This also involves reflections about the relationship between the concept and the phenomenon. for example, if the concept is meant to mirror an empirical phenomenon (as indicated by Peredo and McLean, 2006). Is it concerned with what it is that is out there, and if so, how should the ambiguous empirical reality relate to the concept? Or is conceptualization aimed at understanding in a more hermeneutic sense? We can also accept that a concept can structure and affect the phenomenon, knowingly or unknowingly, in a way where it is realized that the concept also does something to the phenomenon. Likewise, conceptualization can be driven by certain knowledge constitutive interests (see Habermas, 2005), such as an interest in technical control or in emancipation. We can see the *pragmatic* dimension as regarding what the concept is thought to or supposed to do—for example, to make the management of social enterprise possible or to distinguish between different organizational forms in order to develop new and better legal frameworks. The *normative* dimension refers to the political and ethical dimensions of the concept, meaning the political and ethical implications of conceptualizing social entrepreneurship in certain ways—for example, that a strict focus on the social-economic distinction can risk losing sight of the political dimensions of the concept and thereby perhaps unintentionally risks contributing to a depoliticization of social entrepreneurship. These three dimensions refer to different but interrelated questions about what is meant by a concept more specifically. The latter two dimensions, especially, relate closely to how the concept could be understood in relation to social change or transformation. Applying these dimensions to the concept could also lead to answering the question about whether social entrepreneurship should be understood mainly as a concept for describing and understanding social change that can be observed empirically or if it should be understood mainly as a concept-leading and -defining progressive social transformation and perhaps be connected to an emancipatory ideal. The implications for research and clarification of the concept would be very different, depending on which of the two understandings of the concept one chooses to pursue. One way to enter the conceptual debate in a less confusing manner would be to become clearer about these dimensions, thereby enabling a debate that reflects metatheoretically on the enterprise of doing research, whether critical or not. In early critical theory with, for example, Horkheimer (1970) and Habermas (2005), distinctions between ways of theorizing and conceptualizing are explicated. Applying some of the distinctions found in this critical tradition could be a starting point for meta-reflection on the concept of social entrepreneurship. This would also make it possible to see conceptualization as a critical, research enterprise, and move beyond seeing the concept as merely a part of the empirical phenomenon to study and critically analyze in terms of its discursive effects. Not that this is not also a potentially important element of critical studies, as the effects and normative implications of certain conceptualizations thereby become questionable and open for redefinition and debate, but it is not first and foremost a conceptual one.

Conclusion

Finally, I shall return to the question I raised at the outset of this chapter: Why do we need critical studies in social entrepreneurship? The chapter started by arguing that there is a need for critical approaches to overcome the ambiguities of the concept, something that was essential not only because of its normative connotations and influence on policy and practice but also because the field is generally considered undertheorized and conceptually underdeveloped. However, it was not evident what critique more specifically could mean in this context and what different critical strategies would imply for empirical and conceptual studies in the field.

The chapter has analyzed and discussed critique as a research strategy in social entrepreneurship studies by in-depth analysis of 10 contributions that conduct some form of critique. After attempting to paint a broader picture of how critique appears in social entrepreneurship studies and what these critiques point toward—namely, managerialism and neoliberalism—the chapter analyzed two approaches in particular: first, an empirical one that focuses on discourse and resistance and then a conceptual one engaging with concepts of social entrepreneurship.

The studies focusing on discourse and resistance were divided into a normative and a nonnormative strand. Both entail empirical studies of how practitioners in the social entrepreneurship field create counter-discourses and resistance to certain managerialist or neoliberal social entrepreneurship discourses. Consequently, critique becomes part of the empirical object under study. The explicitly normative approaches supplement this with normative theories or categories (such as community, recognition or emancipation) as alternatives to market-oriented understandings from which to understand social entrepreneurship. This appears to be one way of seeing critique as a driver for social change, namely, the resistance of the actors in the field as leading the way for new understandings and practices of social entrepreneurship. The way research can play a role in this change is mainly by shedding light on alternatives and thereby denaturalizing certain market-oriented or neo-liberally imbued understandings and ideals of social entrepreneurship. Such critical studies can therefore contribute to opening up for discussion what social entrepreneurship is and could be and what the political implications of it are. Without these, the concept of social entrepreneurship may remain *scientific ideology*, a loose and tentative term that, due to its fuzziness, can function as a boundary concept that is able to reorganize debates among different disciplines, discourses or fields. Part of this involves *reification*, where an abstract and tentative term becomes represented as a presumably given, self-evident and tangible entity (Miettinen, 2002). A number of critical studies in the field manage to counter exactly such a process by denaturalizing certain conceptions of social entrepreneurship, and sometimes also by suggesting alternative ways of seeing it. Some also explicitly recognize that such a reification process can take place (e.g., Dey, 2010). However, a more systematic discussion of the concept of social entrepreneurship is not present in these empirical studies.

By looking into conceptual studies of social entrepreneurship, contours of certain criteria for conceptualization become visible, thereby opening up for reflection the enterprise of conceptualizing in itself. Basic questions about the relationship between the concept and the phenomenon and the epistemological dimensions of the concept tend to be overlooked or mixed up with pragmatic and normative criteria for conceptualization rather than separated out and treated systematically and coherently. This makes it difficult to distinguish between different dimensions or intentions with the concept. For example, when is the concept of social entrepreneurship understood as a way of descriptively comprehending and subsuming specific empirical phenomena, such as specific organizational forms or certain types of social change that we have experienced empirically? When is the concept supposed to work as a tool in attempting to control and alter the social world, for example, through certain management techniques, in a more pragmatic sense? And when is social entrepreneurship understood as a normative, political and ethical concept of emancipatory social transformation related to societies and the human condition in a broader sense? From a critical perspective, a one-sided focus on the descriptive side runs the risk of becoming affirmative and ideological. A focus on the pragmatic dimension without a corresponding consideration of the broader political and societal aspects runs the risk of becoming managerialist. We need critical conceptual studies that are aware of and explicit about these three dimensions of the concept if social entrepreneurship is supposed to be a concept of societal change or transformation. So even if both the empirical and conceptual critical contributions are important and necessary, there is still some work to do for future research to include such criteria and methodological considerations in relation to conceptualization as a critical enterprise. Furthermore, there is a need for a clearer distinction between the concept and phenomenon of social entrepreneurship and corresponding reflections upon what critique means in empirical and conceptual studies respectively.

The questions and the critical strategies addressed in the chapter concern issues that are relevant not only to social entrepreneurship but also to the broader field of social innovation, as well as to people-centered social innovation. Questions about the role of normativity in social research, the ideological dimensions of knowledge and the relation between the researcher and the actors in the field are all relevant themes in the research of people-centered social innovation. People-centered social innovation places empowerment as an intrinsic part of the social change process, focuses and collaboration and the creation of a "people's democracy" in a desire to address issues of social injustice and human dignity (Hulgård and Shajahan, 2013: 93). In people-centered social innovation, we also find critiques of science being at the service of certain forms of hegemonic globalization (Santos, 2009) that bear similarities with critiques of neoliberalism that are represented in critical social entrepreneurship studies. People-centered social innovation research, with its interest in the transformative potential of social practices and its emphasis on epistemological alternatives to "coloniality of knowledge and power" in the context of marginalized communities (Hulgård and

Shajahan, 2013: 96), in itself represents a normatively informed critical approach in the broader field of social innovation—a field which shares a number of similarities with the field of social entrepreneurship, in the sense that it, too, is characterized by "terminological confusion" (Moulaert et al., 2013: 13) in a tension field between the social versus the economic and between neoliberalism, managerial and market thinking versus a broader concern for satisfying human needs and setting agendas for a better future (Moulaert et al., 2013: 16). Hopefully, the systematic discussion of what critique could mean in the field of social entrepreneurship can also provide analytical tools to navigate the field of social innovation. It might provide a basis for discussing potential research positions and roles of research when balancing between giving voice to (previously absent) singularities, differences and experiences (as mentioned in the introduction to this book; Santos, 2009) and taking on a clear and explicit role as researchers when conceptualizing as well as empirically studying social innovation.

References

Barinaga, E. (2012). "Overcoming Inertia: The Social Question in Social Entrepreneurship," in D. Hjort (ed.), *Handbook on Organizational Entrepreneurship*. Cheltenham: Edward Elgar, pp. 242–256.

Boltanski, L. (2013). "A Journal Through French-Style Critique," in P. du Gay and G. Morgan (eds.), *New Spirits of Capitalism—Crises, Justifications, and Dynamics*. Oxford: Oxford University Press, pp. 43–59.

Boltanski, L. and Thévenot, L. (1999). "The Sociology of Critical Capacity," *European Journal of Social Theory*, 2(3), pp. 359–377.

Boltanski, L. and Thévenot, L. (2006). *On Justification*. Princeton and Oxford: Princeton University Press.

Bull, M. (2008). "Challenging Tensions: Critical, Theoretical and Empirical Perspectives on Social Enterprise," *International Journal of Entrepreneurial Behaviour & Research*, 14(5), pp. 268–275.

Bull, M., Ridley-Duff, R., Foster, D. and Seanor, P. (2010). "Conceptualising Ethical Capital in Social Enterprise," *Social Enterprise Journal*, 6(3), pp. 250–264.

Celikates, R. (2006). "From Critical Social Theory to a Social Theory of Critique: On the Critique of Ideology After the Pragmatic Turn," *Constellations*, 13(1), pp. 21–40.

Cooke, M. (2009). "Zur Rationalität der Gesellschaftskritik," in R. Jaeggi and T. Wesche (eds.), *Was ist Kritik?* Frankfurt am Main: Suhrkamp Verlag, pp. 117–133.

Curtis, T. (2008). "Finding the Grit Makes a Pearl. A Critical Re-Reading of Research into Social Enterprise," *International Journal of Entrepreneurial Behaviour & Research*, 14(5), pp. 276–290.

Dacin, M. T., Dacin, P. A. and Tracey, P. (2011). "Social Entrepreneurship: A Critique and Future Directions," *Organization Science*, 22(5), pp. 1203–1213.

Dart, R. (2004). "The Legitimacy of Social Enterprise," *Nonprofit Management and Leadership*, 14(4), pp. 411–424.

Dees, J. G. and Haas Centennial, M. P. (1998). *The Meaning of Social Entrepreneurship, Kaufmann Center for Social Entrepreneurship.* https://csistg.gsb.stanford.edu/sites/csi.gsb.stanford.edu/files/TheMeaningofsocialEntrepreneurship.pdf.

Defourny, J., Hulgård, L. and Pestoff, V. (2014). "Introduction to the 'SE Field'," in J. Defourny, L. Hulgård and V. Pestoff (eds.), *Social Enterprise and the Third Sector—Changing European Landscapes in a Comparative Perspective.* Oxon and New York: Routledge, pp. 1–14.

Defourny, J. and Nyssens, M. (2010). "Conceptions of Social Enterprise and Social Entrepreneurship in Europe and the United States: Convergences and Divergences," *Journal of Social Entrepreneurship*, 1(1), pp. 32–53.

Delanty, G. (2011). "Varieties of Critique in Sociological Theory and Their Methodological Implications for Social Research," *Irish Journal of Sociology*, 19(1), pp. 58–92.

Dey, P. (2010, June 22–25). "The Symbolic Violence of 'Social Entrepreneurship': Language, Power and the Question of the Social (Subject)," *The Third Research Colloquium on Social Entrepreneurship—Säid Business School of Oxford.* www.alexandria.unisg.ch/64861/1/SE%20Colloquium_PDey_full%20paper.pdf.

Dey, P. and Steyaert, C. (2010). "The Politics of Narrating Social Entrepreneurship," *Journal of Enterprising Communities: People, and Places in the Global Economy*, 4(1), pp. 85–108.

Dey, P. and Steyaert, C. (2012). "Social Entrepreneurship: Critique and the Radical Enactment of the Social," *Social Enterprise Journal*, 8(2), pp. 90–107.

Dey, P. and Teasdale, S. (2013). "Social Enterprise and Dis/identification—The Politics of Identity Work in the English Third Sector," *Administrative Theory and Praxis*, 35(2), pp. 248–270.

Eikenberry, A. M. (2009). "Refusing the Market: A Democratic Discourse for Voluntary and Nonprofit Organizations," *Nonprofit and Voluntary Sector Quarterly*, 38(4), pp. 582–596.

Eikenberry, A. M. and Kluver, J. D. (2004). "The Marketization of the Nonprofit Sector: Civil Society at Risk?" *Public Administration Review*, 64(2), pp. 132–140.

Froggett, L. and Chamberlayne, P. (2004). "Narratives of Social Enterprise: From Biography to Practive and Policy Critique," *Qualitative Social Work*, 3(1), pp. 61–77.

Gawell, M. (2013). "Social Entrepreneurship: Action Grounded in Needs, Opportunities and/or Perceived Necessities?" *Voluntas: International Journal of Voluntary and Nonprofit Organizations*, 24(4), pp. 1071–1090.

Gibson-Graham, J. K. (2006a). *The End of Capitalism (As We Knew It)—A Feminist Critique of Political Economy.* Minneapolis and London: University of Minnesota Press.

Gibson-Graham, J. K. (2006b). *A Postcapitalist Politics.* Minneapolis and London: University of Minnesota Press.

Habermas, J. (2005). "Erkendelse og interesse," in J. Habermas (ed.), *Teknik og videnskab som ideologi.* Frederiksberg: Det Lille Forlag, pp. 119–136.

Haugh, H. and Talwar, A. (2016). "Linking Social Entrepreneurship and Social Change: The Mediating Role of Empowerment," *Journal of Business Ethics*, 133(4), pp. 643–658.

Hervieux, C., Gedajlovic, E. and Turcotte, M-F. B. (2010). "The Legimization of Social Entrepreneurship," *Journal of Enterprising Communities, People and Places in the Global Economy*, 4(1), pp. 37–67.

Horkheimer, M. (1970). "Tradisjonell og kritisk teori," in Ragnvall Kalleberg (ed.), *Kritisk Teori*. Oslo: Gyldendal, pp. 1–44.

Hulgård, L. and Andersen, L. L. (2012). "Socialt Entreprenørskab: velfærdsafvikling eller arenaer for solidaritet?" *Dansk Sociologi*, 4(23), pp. 11–28.

Hulgård, L. and Shajahan, P. K. (2013). "Social Innovation for People-Centred Development," in F. Moulaert, D. MacCallum, A. Mehmood and A. Hamdouch (eds.), *The International Handbook on Social Innovation: Collective Action, Social Learning and Transdisciplinary Research*. Cheltenham and Northhampton, MA: Edward Elgar, pp. 93–104.

Laville, J-L. (2010). "Plural Economy," in K. Hart, J-L. Laville and D. Cattani (eds.), *The Human Economy*. Cambridge: Polity Press, pp. 77–83.

Mason, C. (2012). "Up for Graps: A Critical Discourse Analysis of Social Entrepreneurship Discourse in the United Kingdom," *Social Enterprise Journal*, 8(2), pp. 123–140.

Miettinen, R. (2002). *National Innovation System—Scientific Concept or Political Rhetoric*. Helsinki: Edita.

Moulaert, F., MacCallum, D. and Hillier, J. (2013). "Social Innovation: Intuition, Precept, Concept, Theory and Practice," in F. Moulaert, D. MacCallum, A. Mehmood and A. Hamdouch (eds.), *The International Handbook on Social Innovation: Collective Action, Social Learning and Transdisciplinary Research*. Cheltenham and Northhampton, MA: Edward Elgar, pp. 13–24.

Nicholls, A. (2009). "We Do Good Things, Don't We? 'Blended Value Accounting' in Social Entrepreneurship," *Accounting, Organizations and Society*, 34(6–7), pp. 755–769.

Peredo, A. M. and McLean, M. (2006). "Social Entrepreneurship: A Critical Review of the Concept," *Journal of World Business*, 41(1), pp. 56–65.

Pestoff, V. (2014). "The Role of Participatory Governance in the EMES Approach to Social Enterprise," *Journal of Entrepreneurial and Organizational Diversity*, 2(2), pp. 48–60.

Pestoff, V. and Hulgård, L. (2016). "Participatory Governance in Social Enterprise," *Voluntas*, 27(4), pp. 1742–1759.

Santos, B. D. S. (2009). "The World Social Forum: Toward a Counter-Hegemonic Globalisation (Part 1)," in J. Sen and P. Waterman (eds.), *World Social Forum—Challenging Empires*. Montreal: Black Rose Books, pp. 191–204.

Schofield, S. (2005). "The Case Against Social Enterprise," *Journal of Co-Operative Studies*, 38(3), pp. 34–39.

Steyaert, C. and Dey, P. (2010). "Nine Verbs to Keep the Social Entrepreneurship Agenda 'Dangerous'," *Journal of Social Entrepreneurship*, 1(2), pp. 231–254.

Swedberg, R. (2006). "Social Entrepreneurship: The View of the Young Schumpeter," in C. Steyaert and D. Hjort (eds.), *Entrepreneurship as Social Change: A Third New Movements in Entrepreneurship Book*. Cheltenham and Northampton, MA: Edward Elgar, pp. 21–34.

Zimmerman, B. and Dart, R. (1998). *Charities Doing Commercial Ventures: Societal and Organizational Implications*. Toronto, ON: Trillium Foundation.

3 Arenas for Gendering Social Innovation and Marginalized Women's Collectives

*Linda Lundgaard Andersen
and Swati Banerjee*

Introduction and Conceptual Framing

In this chapter, we bring together two cases from different corners of the world: Neighborhood Mothers in Denmark and Design and Dignity in India. In so doing, we provide a starting point for a discussion of the ways and formats of people-centered social innovation that sustain women's agency, empowerment and intersecting identities, based on old and new cultures, livelihoods and peer learning. Neighborhood Mothers engages and fosters resources with migrant women using knowledge and everyday actions aimed at the family network, local community and close neighbors. Design and Dignity is a craft and marketing social enterprise aimed at social and economic empowerment of marginalized women by selling an ethnic range of products. Our focus, therefore, is on marginalized women. By presenting in-depth cases, we follow Gibson-Graham's 2014 work on "rethinking the economy with thick description and weak theory". Gibson-Graham advocate "a move away from 'strong theory,' with its 'embracing reach' and 'reduced, clarified field of meaning' . . . toward 'weak theory,' which, through 'little more than description' . . ., powerfully attends to nuance, diversity and overdetermined interaction" (Gibson-Graham, 2014: S149). Gibson-Graham argue that

> a much wider range of social relations bear on economic practices, including . . . trust, care, sharing, reciprocity, cooperation, divestiture, future orientation, collective agreement, coercion, bondage, thrift, guilt, love, community pressure, equity, self-exploitation, solidarity, distributive justice, stewardship, spiritual connection, and environmental and social justice.
>
> (Gibson-Graham, 2014: S151)

It is in the apprehension of these multiple determinations that ethnographically thick description comes into its own and leads the way toward rethinking the economy (Cameron et al., 2014; Gibson-Graham, 2014). Thus, exploring cases on marginality and gendered social innovation adds to rethinking social innovation, economy and social justice.

Gendered social innovation is still an uncharted phenomenon, and in general, the innovation system is understood as gender-neutral (Ljunggren et al., 2010). The gender gap in entrepreneurship is still very big (Pines et al., 2012), and women are described as more influenced by *push* than *pull* factors—that is, when women are forced by economic conditions, they can be much more entrepreneurial (Weiler and Bernasek, 2001). Research also suggests that a sense of mission and commitment to service as opposed to profit also characterize women and, compared to traditional commercial entrepreneurial activity, that women are relatively more prevalent in social entrepreneurial activity than men—pointing to a smaller gender gap than in conventional entrepreneurship (Huysentruyt, 2014: 6). However, a gendered analysis of women as social entrepreneurs is sparse, in spite of the many single-case success stories about women as social entrepreneurs and innovations where women are participants in the same, including social entrepreneurship initiatives. Thus, as mentioned by Banerjee, in the South Asian region,

> one of the success stories in social innovation . . . over the past 30 years has been the development of micro-finance institutions (MFIs) and the formation of self-help groups (SHGs) as institutional forms of poor that facilitate financial inclusion and social empowerment of women [including] SEWA in India and Grameen Bank in Bangladesh.
>
> (2018: 159)

However, the discourses around such innovations are largely approached from a "women and development" perspective wherein the targeted participation of women is seen as contributing to addressing macro concerns like poverty and do not necessarily unpack patriarchy and entrenched gendered relations, despite women being active participants in such innovations. We therefore find that research on social entrepreneurs remains largely dependent on the assumption that there is a common set of characteristics inherent to social entrepreneurs—leading to a kind of universal definition of the social entrepreneur—and to social innovation. This is problematic in the context of female social entrepreneurs since it relies on individual characteristics and might ignore the collective nature of entrepreneurship, failing to address the real diversity of social entrepreneurs (Humbert, 2012: 11). Therefore, we endeavor to provide an in-depth study and analysis of gendered people-centered social innovation.

The chapter is organized as follows. Since our cases pinpoint hybridity, social innovation, collectivity and livelihood promotion in different parts of the world, we first outline these concepts, adding a discussion from a gendered and global/local perspective. Second, we display and analyze our two cases applying a thematic grid that identifies the needs and drivers in a people, societal and community context, their institutional and organizational structures, their innovation and implementation strategies and their potentials and challenges. Third, we return to our key questions summing up similarities and differences in our cases and furthering our conceptual profiling and findings of how people-centered social innovation can sustain women's agency, empowerment and intersecting identities based on old and new cultures and livelihood.

Hybridity

Our conceptual framing combines hybridity as a significant feature of social entrepreneurship and civic and local community organizations—linking this to intersectional learning as learning arenas. *Hybridity* is a concept that refers to corporate and organizational forms that intersect and combine different formats like those of private, public and civil society. Hybrid organizations incorporate profit and nonprofit components and display not only competitive advantages and challenges but also difficulties that could affect their mission, business and organizational ideology and value orientation (Andersen, 2015c; Mair and Noboa, 2003). Hybrid organizations in human service and health care are part of an increasing development in welfare systems in many countries seeking to strengthen an alternative economy, new forms of solidarity, of business and organizational models, of empowerment and democracy, of co-production between professionals and citizens. They usually engage several stakeholders, have larger and differentiated goals and mix resources combining governmental subsidy, market income and charity. Some perceive this as an organizational asset and an advantage (Billis, 2010; Brandsen et al., 2005; Mair et al., 2015), while others point to the potential weakness because of its volatile nature, which threatens to affect or change organizational structure and mission over time (Buckingham, 2011; Evers, 2005; Pestoff, 2014).

Currently, many social entrepreneurial organizations find themselves in hybrid processes of transformation, in which market pressure, demands for resource mix, participatory governance and efficiency are significant features (Andersen, 2018: 27). But simultaneously, social entrepreneurial organizations take on the shape of "both drivers and arenas of change" (Wijkström and Zimmer, 2011: 10). In general, we see "a transformation in the division of labor" between the different institutional sectors and spheres, leading to "a changing portfolio of activities"(Wijkström and Zimmer, 2011: 12) for civil society organization and public- and private-sector organizations (Wijkström, 2011). This transformation of a typical hybrid character of civil society in the 20th century could be described as *half movement* and *half government*, the relationship today has transformed its character into *half charity* and *half business*, which is more activities of entrepreneurship and business activity (Wijkström, 2011). Hybridity, then, could be understood as both sector-centered and mechanism-centered and the latter should be paid more attention. Sector-centered hybridity refers to the well-known definition in which hybrid organizations intersect private, public and civil features, whereas mechanism-centered refers to latent hybridity that enables us to detect agency, dynamic organizational change, mutuality and reciprocity in a broader range of phenomena. Seibel argues for a middle-ground approach combining both dimensions since this provides a more dynamic and nuanced understanding (Seibel, 2015: 708). Both our cases share features of manifest and latent hybridity, not only being hybrid organizations in origin but also seeking agency, reciprocity and mutuality.

In addition, as mentioned earlier, our cases focus on social innovation, processes of collectivization, collective agency and livelihoods promotion in two different parts of the world. Here, social innovation serves as a process of change, which aims to address and transform marginalities. Simultaneously, processes of collectivization and collective agency are seen as a strategy for the social change process within an understanding of hybrid institutions. Further empowerment and livelihood promotion can be seen as a progressive impact and outcome of the social change process. We therefore briefly outline these concepts from a gendered perspective.

Gender and Social Innovation

Social innovation is increasingly seen as an alternative development pathway for trying to address contemporary societal challenges with newer strategies. The term has been variously defined but the core of most of these definitions attempts to understand the relationship of social innovation with social change and social transformation. The SI-Drive definition of social innovation as mentioned by Howaldt and Hochgerner (2018: 19) elaborates that social innovation is a new combination of social practices in certain areas of action or social contexts. The idea of the *social* is also explained by BEPA, a European commission report that defines social innovation as "innovations that are social in both their ends and means" (BEPA, 2011). Furthermore, Banerjee (2018: 158) emphasizes the understanding and relevance of the potential of social innovation as a process of social change, especially within the context of poverty, marginalization and multiple forms of deprivation. Moulaert and Van den Broeck (2018: 28) highlight the importance of the interaction between new socially innovative initiatives, on one hand (housing experiments, people-centered learning, solidarity-based workspaces, alter networks, and action research, etc.), and governance and institutionalization processes, on the other hand. Evers, Ewert and Brandsen add further dimensions emphasizing how social innovations are "in a significant way, new and disruptive toward the routines and structures prevailing in a given (welfare) system or local setting. Whether or not they can be seen as "better" (more effective/social/democratic) is a question of its own that can only be answered in retrospective [*sic*]" (Evers et al., 2016: 11). Consequently, it is quite difficult to decide beforehand if a social innovation applies to the criteria. Mulgan and co-authors further add a people-change dimension to our understanding of social innovation when, in a theory of difference, they clarify that three dimensions are important: first, developing new combinations or hybrids of existing elements to be realized; second, developing radical innovations across organizational, sectoral and disciplinary boundaries; and, third, developing compelling new social relationships between previously separate individuals and groups, fueling a cumulative dynamic in which each innovation can lead to further innovations, thereby developing capacity to exercise power (Mulgan et al., 2008: 34–35). This definition departs from Schumpeter's concepts on incremental and radical innovation, but as Andersen (2016b) underlines, Mulgan and colleagues revisit the original Schumpeterian concepts of innovation by adding empowerment and a change-driven and people-centered approach (Andersen, 2016b; Casebourne, 2014). In doing so, they further push social innovation, highlighting how we need to include people change and people development as a significant conceptual aspect. However ambitious this take on social innovation might be, this very much applies to our two cases. They are both each in their own way preoccupied with the same objectives. Finally, von Hippel's open innovation situating a democratic innovation that positions citizens as end users and co-producers of services or products, providing social synergy, open distribution and bottom-up innovation also add a cutting edge to our social innovation perception (von Hippel, 2005). As we will demonstrate, this is very much at the heart of our two cases, but simultaneously this also provides a huge challenge for marginalized women and their co-workers.

As for gendering social innovation, this is still a case to be further developed. As mentioned, social innovation discourse, in general, is largely gender- and intersectionality-neutral and does not necessarily take into account the underlying power relations emerging from the same—or the societal context and its impact. In addition,

> innovation and women's empowerment are rarely discussed within the same context but each has essential value for human progress. There is significant evidence that progress on poverty reduction and human development are related to advancements in both innovative capacities and gender equality.
>
> (Malhotra, 2009: 3)

Based on an Indian case, Haugh and Talwar (2016) frame emancipatory social entrepreneurship as processes that empower women and contribute to changing the social order in which women are embedded.

Departing from this, Haugh and Talwar conclude that innovative models enabling women to generate income, acquire new skills and expand their networks in ways that comply with existing norms are thus likely to have empowerment potential (Haugh and Talwar, 2016: 5). Thus, social innovation offers an important pathway for gender equity and transformation of gender relations.

Marginalities, Processes of Collectivization and Collective Agency

Marginality is generally used to describe and analyze sociocultural, political and economic spheres, where disadvantaged people struggle to gain access to resources and full participation in social life (Andersen and Larsen, 1998). Within the context of exclusion of marginalized communities, the marginalization and exclusion of women belonging to marginalized communities are layered and multiplied—this is visible in the situational contexts of the women in our case studies. Furthermore, gendered marginalities, which are often located within various intersections including caste, ethnicity, class and generation, not only multiply but also become invisible to popular discourses and policy frameworks (Banerjee, 2015). Therefore, there is a renewed need to understand relevant strategies to address the issue of gendered marginalities. This chapter explores social innovations as pathways to address such marginalities through innovation strategies of collective social enterprises, civil society organizations and collectivization of marginalized women. Processes of collectivization are intrinsically linked to an expansion of creative agency, which further helps in dealing with inequitable social structures and multiple marginalities. "Agency is about more than observable action; it also encompasses the meaning, motivation and purpose which individuals bring to their activity, their sense of agency, or the power within" (Kabeer, 1999: 438). Agency can therefore be both individual and collective. When we are specifically talking of marginalized women's collectives, the focus is on women's collective agency, which helps them to deal with various marginalities that arise from both intersectionalities of gender and other axes of marginality. The discourse on intersectionality from a feminist understanding further suggests that gender relations intersect with other oppressive relations such as those based on class, race, ethnicity and so forth (Wieringa, 1994).

The construct of agency further implies that

> [t]he transpositions of schemas and remobilizations of resources that constitute agency are always acts of communication with others. Agency entails an ability to coordinate one's actions with others and against others, to form collective projects, to persuade, to coerce,

and to monitor the simultaneous effects of one's own and others' activities. Moreover, the extent of the agency exercised by individual persons depends profoundly on their positions in collective organizations.

(Sewell, 1992: 21)

Processes of collectivization are therefore significant in reworking and reintegrating the agency of marginalized groups, leading to a collective understanding of power and *power-with* that has implications for the transformation of both the individual and the marginalized group as a whole. In addition, the notion of hybridity in collective organizations or collective social enterprises, as mentioned earlier, helps in the expansion of this collective agency, leading to processes of empowerment in addressing various marginalities including livelihood insecurities.

Gendered Livelihoods

Chambers (1995) defined *livelihood* as the "means of gaining a living, including tangible assets (resources and stores), intangible assets (claims and access), and livelihood capabilities", including coping abilities, opportunities and diverse freedoms. This definition tries to have a holistic and sustainable understanding of livelihoods. The construct of sustainable livelihoods incorporates the key ideas of capability, equity and sustainability, where *capability* refers to an ability to make full use of livelihood opportunities and a capacity to deal with adverse scenarios, stress and shock. *Equity* refers to not just income equity but also equitable access to assets, capabilities and opportunities. *Sustainability* refers to both environmental (global concerns of pollution, deforestation, etc.) as well as social dimensions of maintaining livelihoods along with preserving the asset bases on which livelihoods depend (Chambers and Conway, 1992). However, the hierarchical societal structures of inequity, including gender, determine the access and control over assets. Thus, often the access to livelihoods of poor and marginalized communities gets impacted, especially women within these communities. This gendered understanding of livelihoods is further explored by Krishna (2007), where she points out the gendered inequities not only with respect to local communities but also with respect to development initiatives of the state, which she says further reinforces the gendered and local power structures. Thus, livelihood promotion activities should not only aim to reduce livelihood insecurities by enhancing livelihood assets but should also work toward the expansion of agency and equitable access to livelihood resources. This is also seen in the case study from India where dignity and capability development are seen as key factors toward livelihood promotion through the collective enterprise Dignity and Design.

Intersectional Learning and Collective Enterprises of Marginalized Women: Case Narratives from Denmark and India

While our case arenas display a rich variety of activities, learning and agency that contribute to substantial results and outcome, we label these *intersectional learning* as developed by Andersen (2012, 2015a). Intersectional learning is, as it says, learning in intersections. The term *intersectional learning* departs from the concept of intersectionality by Crenshaw and McCall as a methodology of studying "the relationships among multiple dimensions and modalities of social relationships and subject formations" (McCall, 2005: 1771). In a further development, Andersen suggests that *intersectional learning* involves studying the multiple dimensions and modalities of learning, social relationships and subject formations—and inquiring if and how this leads to equality and inequality as well as empowerment, competencies and life skills. This approach then accentuates how hybrid organizations aiming at human growth, empowerment and social values through the production of welfare services or products via market dynamics offer blended and intersectional learning in multiple learning arenas. In these arenas, marginalized citizens work and learn alongside different professionals in shared positions and actions, through co-creation and co-production. In our two cases, we identify that they apply peer-to-peer learning, social learning, vocational training, role-modeling, school-based learning, action learning and practicing democracy and governance. In our case narratives, we demonstrate that these take place either in different, parallel or displaced arenas, all located in the same organization. We further argue that these learning trajectories mutually affect and intersect each other and cannot be understood as separate entities since they are intertwined—for better or for worse—but, in the long run, often lead to transformative learning, agency and competence development (Andersen, 2012, 2015a). Moreover, the result and outcome that our two case narratives have accomplished over the years are closely related to their learning and empowering approach. Hybrid organizations are rich in learning and competence development, and in brief, they often apply combinations of experiential and collaborative learning, social learning, situated or action learning and more concepts that are critical, such as sociological imagination and critical pedagogy. Learning, however, can not only be ambiguous and ambivalent due to its capacity to transform human lives, social structures and organizations but can also function as an effective tool for political, societal and professional needs and performances (Andersen, 2015b). Therefore, as we show in our case narratives, we see that learning trajectories are not linear but often take detours, go in circles or even include a setback.

We now turn to show the two cases by identifying the needs and drivers in a people, societal and community context, their institutional and organizational structures, their innovation and implementation strategies and their potentials and challenges. The two-case analysis, then, provides a starting point for a final discussion of the ways in which a people-centered social innovation approach can be informed by our theoretical framework addressing the development of women's agency, empowerment and intersecting identities based on old and new cultures, livelihood and peer learning.

Neighborhood Mothers in Denmark

Introduction and Overview

Neighborhood Mothers (NM) is an award-winning civil society organization in Denmark based on the power of migrant women that works through a combination of volunteering, learning and enlightenment, skills training, local participation, empowerment and networking. The objectives of NM is to develop and foster resources like knowledge and everyday actions aimed at the family network and the local community and neighbors. The key actor in these objectives is the individual women—labeled *neighborhood mothers*—acting out the thought that, provided with the information and support they require, women in need will be able to control and influence their own lives and make decisions they believe are right for themselves, their family and their children (Neighborhood Mothers, 2013). NM focuses its efforts on engaging women living in isolation, who do not know much about the society they live in, who are challenged by the Danish language and many of whom are distrustful of the municipal and public system (CFBU, 2010). In numbers, NM nationally and via local outreach covers more than 600 active neighborhood mothers; almost 40 NM units are distributed throughout Denmark in local group networks. Neighborhood mothers speak 54 different languages and represent 41 different nationalities; an NM group receives an average of three calls per month and uses a total of 137,000 volunteer hours yearly (Neighborhood Mothers, web: https://bydelsmor.dk/english). The majority of neighborhood mothers (48%) have had a long-lasting affiliation to Denmark of more than 15 years; about 40% have been living in Denmark for 5 to 15 years, while only 6% have arrived in Denmark within the last five years (Thomsen and Ravn-Mortensen, 2012: 11). The variety of topics and activities covered includes Danish and intercultural children's upbringing (in discussions with a family therapist), youth, alcohol and drugs, health, food and exercising by a local health visitor, visiting the local employment center and local day-care institutions, how to engage in local outreach work, the nature of relations and responsibilities among authorities, neighborhood mothers and isolated local women by a local social worker, tools and ideas for outreach work by a local integration consultant (CFBU, 2010).

This case is drawn from a number of inquiries, evaluation reports and dissemination activities performed by a variety of researchers and consultants based on different methods and data. This includes university researchers and MA students (Delica and Nielsson, 2012; Krogh, 2012; Lau and Dybbroe, 2012; Rose, 2014), gray reports by external consultancy agencies (Jespersen, 2015; Thomsen and Ravn-Mortensen, 2012) and local public authorities and regional researchers (Christensen et al., 2010; Husted and Erkmann, 2009; Husted and Vestergaard, 2010), dissemination reports and pamphlets (CFBU, 2010; Neighborhood Mothers, 2013) and self-reported, publicly accessible websites (https://bydelsmor. dk/english). Data consist of qualitative data collected through interviews with NM participants: project coordinators and participating women and local informants as well as a survey of NM's many partnerships and collaborating public and civil agencies.

Key Drivers

Neighborhood mothers apply three key principles and, in many senses, serve as intermediaries: (1) *dialogue:* initiated by the neighborhood mother visiting local migrant women on subjects of interest to them, listening, speaking the same mother tongue and sharing some of the same experiences; (2) *bridge building and transition makers:* between migrant women and the local community and its offerings, including civic activities and initiatives, public and health services, library-related activities, preschool programs, school cultures and demands, learning to bike and healthy living; and (3) *networking:* neighborhood mothers initiating and developing networks, gradually subjectifying migrant women in social gatherings and talks on various topics by local people, knowledge sharing and building, friendship and networking. One of the external evaluations points out that, in many ways, NM appears to be a unique organization that complements public systems in providing competent, peer-to-peer and timely support and self-help to migrant women. NM's strength relates to their ability to make and sustain contact with ethnic minority women who are often isolated and disconnected from local authorities that, for their part, would like to reach out to these women. By virtue of their own experiences and dedication, neighborhood mothers are able to create a special relationship with minority women based on knowledge, identification and confidentiality (Jespersen, 2015). Other research sees NM as using means of cultural dissemination and intercultural interaction so that NM's diverse activity portfolio encourages migrant women in learning Danish and gaining in-depth knowledge of Danish culture, the welfare state, schooling and civil society (Rose, 2014).

Institutional Structures

NM institutional structures and intersections are multiple. The organization labels itself a *patchwork model*, as illustrated Figure 3.1. This mirrors how each local NM unit interacts and collaborates with a number of different local health, social or labor market authorities, civil society or civic groups or private enterprises.

This allows great flexibility and opportunities for co-creating dynamic relations and collaboration that enables local NM units to develop co-ownership and agency. In addition, this might foster an individualized focus on agency, leading to NM's activities being sensitive toward the needs and support of individual women, contrary to what happens with standardized services. Many evaluation reports highlight this as a significant result (Christensen et al., 2010; Husted and Erkmann, 2009; Husted and Vestergaard, 2010; Jespersen, 2015). On the other hand, this leads to a problematic differentiation of local NM activity profiles and portfolios that represents a national organizational challenge. Evaluation reports document that local variations occur related to which roles and impacts are fulfilled by local municipal agents, civic society organizations and housing organizations. Three models seem to be present: in one,

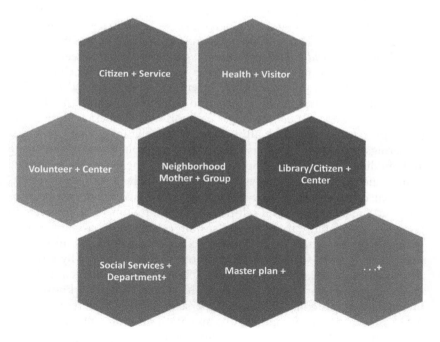

Figure 3.1 The Patchwork-Model

Source: Adapted from Neighborhood Mothers, Manual start-up (2014).

ownership lies predominantly with civic partners/civic society, in another with municipal/public partners and in the third one with larger non-governmental organizations (NGOs). This leads to quite a variation in institutional structures and collaborative formats that set boundaries for national collaboration (Christensen et al., 2010: 15). Health promotion and social housing research studies label NMs as health promotion agencies and important partners in social housing community centers that live and interact with the local population in local areas, using resourceful people as role models. Likewise, social housing and community research has long documented that planning, implementation and evaluation—as part of a local community strategic process and a long-term investment where citizens, local communities and municipal employees co-produce—lead to significantly better health, livelihoods and everyday life. Collectivity, social dimensions and a creative and citizen-driven activity profile are the main ingredients for a good outcome (Delica and Nielsson, 2012; Lau and Dybbroe, 2012: 186).

WOMEN'S COLLECTIVES AND COLLECTIVE ACTION

NM pursue a number of objectives and deliver results, as mentioned above, that clearly position their outreach within a gendered sphere, highlighting the importance of empowering and engaging isolated women in the local community. They use a variety of methods:

- Peer-to-peer learning and short-term education (Andersen and Hulgård, 2014; Barckley et al., 2005) provided to NM coordinators in order to offer networking and support to the women involved
- Self-help as an explicit learning principle provided by NM coordinators who invite participating women to take this on and replicate it by helping others
- Role modeling performed by significant women, who have been carefully singled out to become NM coordinators because they share a degree of similarity, originating from the same livelihood, having a foreign background and moving to Denmark just like the target group of women. This is followed by a strong focus on agency, urging the women involved to be actively participating in, managing and bettering their lives.
- Action learning (Pedler, 2011), situating problem-oriented everyday actions and initiatives for change and empowerment
- Self-managed action learning (Bourner, 2011), in which the women take action and responsibility, furthering their own initiative and ownership—and thereby being able to develop an independent livelihood. In many ways, this is the recipe for strong citizenship-building among individuals, families and local community, trying to bridge individual and institutional rights with legal status and potential for

action (Boje, 2015; Kabeer, 2012; Somers and Wright, 2008). Since this is an ambitious beginning, it is not surprising that evaluation findings pinpoint not only strengths but also dilemmas.

ALLIANCES AND PARTNERSHIPS

As illustrated in their patchwork model, forming and sustaining alliances and partnerships is at the heart of NM. Throughout its existence, NM has been part of a considerable number of strategic interventions and social programs, together with local authorities, national public bodies and governmental agencies and with other civil society organizations and private consultants. The organizational model of NM, being of Dutch origin and having been implemented in 40 Danish NM units, has consequently developed a solid network and partnerships that, despite leading to a certain amount of diversity, also knit NM together in a firm partnership model. This provides a high standard of cross-regional experimental work and sharing of experiences. Consequently, NM is strong on alliances and partnerships at the macro and meso level, whereas the micro level is more difficult to achieve. The individual women are on a long journey of empowerment; evaluation findings reveal that the women may become dependent on NM role models and coordinators and lean on these significantly for help and support, engaging less in developing firm relations with their own peers (Christensen et al., 2010; Husted and Erkmann, 2009).

Innovation and Implementation Strategies

The original idea of NM was developed in Germany, imported to Denmark, and largely scaled up throughout the country. The multimethod social innovation approach comprises a number of methods and ways of working, providing a synergetic patchwork (Andersen, 2016a). As mentioned, the NM approach combines dialogue, bridge building and transition makers as well as networking across different sectors, professionals and citizens. Adding to this, a strong learning and skills training dimension runs through the 14 classes that must be completed prior to serving as a neighborhood mother. It comprises a peer-to-peer learning design with citizenship, educational and professional components. Local NM units contribute to user-driven innovation, providing local welfare professionals in day-care institutions with inside knowledge on how day-care professionals could work better with bilingual mothers, resulting in a pamphlet for dissemination (Thomsen and Ravn-Mortensen, 2012: 41). In addition, open innovation seems to be in focus since local units seek to engage and motivate individual women to take an active part in developing the activity profile. However, this is a challenge since NM comes as a somewhat predesigned model and project coordinators being educated for NMs networking and bridge building naturally take on a certain responsibility and agency. Involving local women in the open innovation of activities has proved to be a demanding task—but evaluation reports suggest that this changes over time.

Potentials, Challenges and Way Forward

NM has a remarkable outreach and a rich variety of informants: the involved women themselves, the NM coordinators, local collaborators and partners, all underline the significant individual and social outcome that has been achieved throughout the years. This is well documented in the many evaluation reports.

The potentials address a number of issues. NM could profitably develop national guidelines for their project coordinators, outlining their tasks and objectives, since these have been shown to be too diffuse. The gender aspect is also addressed, and it is recommended that a similar initiative for ethnic men and fathers be included and developed (Thomsen and Ravn-Mortensen, 2012).

However, the evaluation reports also shed light on a number of finely balanced challenges and tensions. First, on one hand, NM provides guidance, self-help and networking by competent and trustworthy peer women (NM coordinators) who become the lead focus; on the other hand, NM, to a large extent, engages many local women in empowering learning and self-education activities, enabling them to act by themselves in families, local community and society in general. Second, on one hand, NM provides a confidence-building environment and network of many Danish migrant women that facilitates gradually finding one's feet, while on the other, NM should pay more attention to creating a mixed and diverse group of women of different nationalities and cultures that are able to share their similarities and their differences. Third, on one hand, NM provides a safe, local and well-known venue, but on the other, NM should gradually broaden its sphere of action and enlarge the number of locations in which neighborhood mothers can familiarize themselves on how to become citizens in Danish society. Fourth, on one hand, NM has an obligation to deliver on the needs and objectives of the public welfare state and local municipalities, and to give women the skills to accommodate these; on the other hand, NM should pay more attention to women being able to develop an empowering agency and take advantage of their power, interests and needs.

Dignity and Design in India

Introduction and Overview

The case of Dignity and Design (D&D) from India is a significant example of grassroots innovation in transforming gendered and intersectional marginalities of women in one of the most socially excluded and marginalized communities in India. D&D is one of the country's first craft and marketing social enterprises that is committed to social and economic empowerment of women who have been freed from the practice of manual scavenging, other forms of bondage and sexual violence. It strives to provide dignified livelihoods to poor and marginalized women and their families by selling an ethnic range of products. Thus, the core idea of D&D is to create sustainable and dignified livelihood options for women who have been liberated from manual scavenging, bonded labor and other caste-based oppressions.

This case is drawn from a larger research study that focused on social innovation and poverty reduction in various world regions including India, undertaken as part of the SI-Drive Project by the author. As part of this initiative, mapping of social innovation cases across various social innovation practice fields was undertaken, followed by in-depth case studies. As an outcome, the project report analyzed 13 in-depth case studies in the field of poverty reduction and sustainable development including the study of D&D from India (Millard et al., 2017). For this case study, a qualitative research design was used, and multiple data collection methods and tools were used for an in-depth understanding of the issue, including in-depth interviews and group interviews with relevant actors, key informant interviews and so on and review of additional documented materials.

Key Drivers

D&D tried to address the lack of access to alternative livelihood options for liberated manual scavengers who have been socially and economically excluded from the so-called mainstream. Society finds it unacceptable for these communities to have any new livelihood options because of the historicity of the stigma attached to them. Manual scavenging is a caste-based discriminatory practice in India. According to the Census of India 2011, this inhuman practice of manual scavenging continues in India, despite the existence of various national laws meant to eradicate manual scavenging, and which prohibit employing manual scavengers. Further, the census of India 2011 also mentions that, there are still 2.6 million dry latrines where women continue to be employed as manual scavengers, in spite of the existence of laws requiring conversion of all dry latrines. In addition to performing this humiliating task, the scheduled caste communities involved in this practice face extreme discrimination in society and have become "the Untouchables among the Untouchables". Women who are mostly employed for such work face gender- and caste-based discrimination, human rights violations, their children face discrimination at school and, hence, barriers to education, and the community faces everyday barriers to alternative employment, health services, mobility in society and so forth.

To break this cycle of oppression, economic equity was necessary along with social equity, which the organization felt was possible by generating alternative livelihood options for the oppressed, and therefore, D&D was initiated. The historicity of the cycle of oppression reveals that manual scavengers not only worked in extremely oppressive conditions for their daily living but also were not paid any money and instead were given grains once a year, roti (bread) daily and 5 rupees only at the time of festivals. The whole structure was designed in a way that makes it impossible to even think beyond one's daily meal and, therefore, about basic survival needs. Therefore, this new solution comes from women's participation in the entire initiative rather than a top-down approach.

Institutional Structures

D&D was born out of the work of Jan Sahas Development Society (an NGO) located in Dewas, Madhya Pradesh, India. Jan Sahas works for the protection of human rights and the development of socially excluded and marginalized communities. Its vision and strategy include abolishing all kinds of social exclusion, atrocities, slavery and discrimination based on caste, class, ethnicity and gender. Jan Sahas was founded in 2000, triggered by an incident where one child laborer and two dalit laborers died in a fireworks factory. The incident brought a few people together to form an organization to raise the voice of the excluded communities. *Jan* means "people", and *Sahas* means "courage". The organization believes in empowering and building capabilities of excluded communities so that they can negotiate change with courage and dignity. Jan Sahas started its work in Bhaurasa village in Madhya Pradesh, India, to eradicate the inhuman occupation of manual scavenging. To date, Jan Sahas has liberated about 21,000 people from manual scavenging in the country, of which more than 90% are women. After a few years of work for the liberation of manual scavengers and against atrocities committed against excluded communities, Jan Sahas realized that it is not enough just to liberate manual scavengers, but it is also important to rehabilitate them. D&D was thus initiated in 2014 by Jan Sahas to provide alternative livelihoods to liberated women manual scavengers. The effort was also to demonstrate an alternative model for their rehabilitation to the government. D&D is a registered company under the Companies Act and is presently active in two areas in Madhya Pradesh: Bhaurasa in Dewas District and Tarana in Ujjain District. D&D is thus a hybrid model of Jan Sahas (an NGO). Women's self-help groups (SHGs) support D&D. The innovation strategy of the organization comprises three key elements for the empowerment of the marginalized communities for which the organization works and is shown in Figure 3.2.

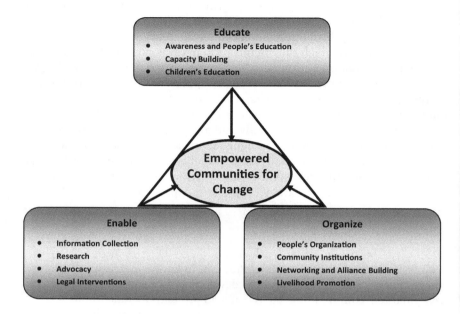

Figure 3.2 Innovation Strategy

Source: Adapted from www.jansahasindia.org.

WOMEN'S COLLECTIVES AND COLLECTIVE ACTION

Women from marginalized and oppressed and deprived communities are the primary stakeholders of D&D. Jan Sahas, the parent organization of D&D, has a long history of facilitating women's collectivization for the abolition of gender- and caste-based oppression. It started with social movements and campaigns for the abolition of caste-based atrocities like manual scavenging, in which large numbers of women participated, leading to an increased awareness that resulted in the liberation of a large number of manual scavengers. This further led to the launch of the social enterprise, D&D, whose aim was to provide alternative livelihoods for these liberated female manual scavengers who were stigmatized by mainstream society. A major strategy was to collectivize women into SHGs and focus on their capacity development based on their interests and aspirations. Thus, skills development and training of women has been widely undertaken as part of this initiative, whereby it has given initial skills training in sewing and clothes-making to about 498 women and organized about 280 women into SHGs, some of whom now work at one of the four key clothes production centers. Many other women have been given sewing machines individually to start their own enterprises.

ALLIANCES AND PARTNERSHIPS

Partnerships and collaborations have been the key components of the organization's efforts to work with marginalized and socially excluded communities. In the past, it has partnered with the government and with other rights-based organizations to strengthen the movement. Presently it is partnering with the government and commercial companies in exploring livelihood options for the community. Such a partnership with USHA Machines provides initial support, such as sewing machines and a trainer for training the women for the new world. So far, skills training has been undertaken and initial capital has been provided to 498 liberated manual scavenger women to start production units. Currently, a total of four production units are functioning in two areas, in which about 50 women work and produce garments. Women are also trained in producing clothes, home furnishings and stationary. Women working in these production units also receive knowledge support from other similar crafts-based social business organizations like Kumbaya, Rewa, Rangasutra and Women Weave. Other organizations such as the Karuna Trust, Tata Trust and other funding agencies also made contributions and supported the idea. The Tata Institute of Social Sciences, through its students' field engagements, also provides knowledge, practice and capacity-building support to the initiative. Intersectoral practice and learning are evident among NGOs/social enterprises, State, corporate social responsibility (CSR) and university.

Innovation and Implementation Strategies

The innovation is multidimensional, at one end Jan Sahas tried to liberate people from the undignified work of manual scavenging and simultaneously through the D&D initiative, aimed to provide dignified, equitable and sustainable livelihood opportunities to liberated women manual scavengers. This project also aimed to demonstrate an alternative to the failed Government efforts to rehabilitate liberated manual scavengers, where the government gave a paltry sum to them under the Pratishtha Yojana/Specific Rehabilitation Scheme for Manual Scavengers, which failed to have any impact. The aim has therefore been to socially and economically include women who have been excluded due to caste- and gender-based discrimination. Simultaneously, D&D demonstrated an alternative rehabilitation model to the government by mainstreaming gender and showing that it must invest in community capacity building and not just paying compensation to manual scavengers, which generates no long-term result.

The innovation solution evolved over time. Jan Sahas's program, Rashtriya Garima Abhiyan, the National Campaign for Dignity and Eradication of Manual Scavenging, adopts a model whereby it organizes liberated manual scavengers into community-based institutions so that they are better able to ensure alternative dignified livelihoods. In 2013–2014, Jan Sahas organized camps in 200 districts across 18 states in India for the total eradication of manual scavenging called Maila Mukti Yatra/Women's Liberation Movement (of women who were engaged in manual scavenging), in which 5,000 women freed from the practice of manual scavenging participated. Such collective action and movements aiming to collectivize women resulted in the identification of beneficiaries and gave liberated manual scavengers a platform to express their interest in pursuing new forms of livelihood. Thus, liberated manual scavengers could collectivize, and then they showed interest in clothes-making, and D&D was born. Through D&D, women were given skills training in clothes-making. Forms of collectivization and engagement of beneficiaries, community capacity building and influencing existing government policy have thus been key innovative solutions. Collectivization, awareness-raising and capacity-building processes helped women negotiate to improve their status in society. This has led to a process of progressive agency development and empowerment for women, which gave them the motivation and confidence to be part of the D&D initiative and earn livelihoods with dignity and pride.

From the initial conception of D&D to its evolution into what it is today took both time and effort. The idea of imparting a totally new skill (clothes-making) to women and then converting it into an income-generating activity took quite a long time. Women took much longer than six months to learn sewing. This also led to a considerable loss of financial and other resources for D&D. This very slow movement was a kind of barrier to immediate growth, but it has been a part of the people-centric process, which the organization adopts and helped in bringing true participation of the primary stakeholders into the entire initiative. Other challenges included bringing women to the production centers, ensuring regular attendance and getting the women to adhere to timetables, among others. Eventually, however, the women's interest increased and they started feeling more connected to D&D. A lack of knowledge of the market and market segments was another major challenge, which the organization is slowly trying to deal with through market research and creating alliances and networks.

Potentials, Challenges and Way Forward

The initiative ensures a holistic development of the women of the deprived and marginalized community on both social and economic fronts. It is a very important innovation in the daily lives of women manual scavengers. They now have new hope, a new life where they don't have to collect human excreta every morning but stitch clothes to earn their livelihoods. Collectivization of the local community and the process of raising their

awareness regarding the inhuman practice of caste- and gender-based discrimination also led to policy advocacy for liberating and rehabilitating
manual scavengers. In this context, D&D, an initiative by Jan Sahas,
works toward demonstrating an alternative rehabilitation model and
promoting livelihoods with dignity for liberated manual scavengers.

Conclusion and Discussion

What we have seen in our case analysis is that both our cases have been
quite successful in enabling marginalized women's collectives as driving forces for gendering people-centered social innovation. As we have
pointed out throughout the chapter, this is due to a patchwork of methods, approaches, temporality, funding, income-generating and voluntary
work. Both cases situate intersectional learning arenas in a multitude of
ways that have been proved to strengthen agency, empowerment and
skills training among marginalized women. The fact that intersectional
learning offers a varied number of different learning-and-doing opportunities paves the way for subjectifying the women since they themselves
are actively involved in deciding and finding their way at a pace of their
own, providing better livelihoods, better earnings, better families and better citizenship. Following from this we have also seen that empowering
marginalized women might take much longer than expected by external
bodies and funding agencies—or even founders of the enterprise and role
models. Temporality—that is time—is a significant feature when people-
centered social innovation is at stake.

Economic and societal dimensions are imperative for societal and individual change for marginalized women. Both our cases address this in a
variety of ways. NM arose to address the issue of individual women in
need who were isolated and not participating as fully fledged citizens,
despite having lived in Denmark for many years. This issue is certainly
also a significant societal matter since strengthening self-supporting and
education is a top priority in Denmark. D&D came about to tackle different issues, namely, those of livelihood insecurity, poverty and inequality of life, that are being collectivized to provide women with earnings
and a safer life.

The women's collectives explored in our case studies are able to exercise
their collective agency and power-with through the formation of collective actor networks. These newer networks are important community-
based people's institutions that are able to renegotiate inequitable structures,
values and norms in order to address marginalities. They also help in
reinstitutionalization by deinstitutionalizing patriarchal structures and
transforming livelihood insecurities. The case studies also suggest that
women's access to livelihood opportunities through participation in these
collective organizations helps them to increase their livelihood assets,
including physical, social, cultural, economic, human and other aspects,

and it simultaneously gives them better decision-making and negotiating abilities in societal, community and household spaces.

Practical gender needs and strategic gender needs are two important arenas for gendered people-centered social innovation. According to Moser and Levy (1986), practical gender needs arise from the concrete conditions of women's positioning by virtue of their gender with respect to the sexual division of labor. It is important to address such needs in order to tackle poverty, livelihood insecurity, quality of life and so on. Thus, the case studies illuminate how marginalized women collectivize to address these issues. Today we can see that the livelihood risk has forced marginalized communities to collectivize so that they are able to negotiate in the neoliberal markets (Banerjee and Shaban, 2019). In addition, Moser and Levy (1986) explain strategic gender interests as arising from the analysis of women's subordinate position in society that is derived from the identification and formulation of an alternative, more equal and satisfactory organization of society in terms of the structure and nature of relationships between men and women to replace those that exist at present.

Addressing strategic needs is more difficult within inequitable and entrenched structures of inequity, and the change strategy needs to be process-oriented and geared toward systemic change. However, through our case studies, we see that collectivization of women has the potential to address systemic changes like caste inequity. Addressing strategic gender needs would also include tackling specific gendered inequities, including gendered norms and values. NM demonstrates how, in spite of the institutional solidarity of a Nordic welfare state, it supports marginalized and isolated citizens—women who, by sharing problems, efforts and networking, can transform their livelihood. Thus, our conceptualization and the cases reveal that marginalized women's collective enterprises, which are hybrid in nature, have the potential to address the triple challenge which social innovation aims to tackle: social demands, societal challenges and systemic changes within societal complexities, deprivations and inequities. Furthermore, it helps in gendering the field of social innovation, which has so far been either gender-blind or gender-neutral, by focusing on practical and strategic gender needs and exploring the power relationships and processes of empowerment within multiple and challenging contexts of patriarchy, poverty, disempowerment and exclusion, among others. This shows a relationship as given in Figure 3.3.

As mentioned earlier, Figure 3.3 depicts the relationship between the formation of collectives by marginalized women and how this can translate into collective action and social change. As drawn from the case studies, the various processes inherent are further elaborated to include how such collectives can progressively become empowered to address

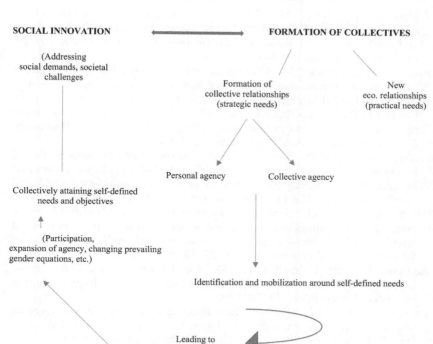

SOCIAL INNOVATION ←————————→ FORMATION OF COLLECTIVES

(Addressing social demands, societal challenges

Formation of collective relationships (strategic needs)

New eco. relationships (practical needs)

Personal agency   Collective agency

Collectively attaining self-defined needs and objectives

(Participation, expansion of agency, changing prevailing gender equations, etc.)

Identification and mobilization around self-defined needs

Leading to
COLLECTIVE ACTION

Figure 3.3 Establishing a relationship among the formation of women's collectives, collective action and people-centered social innovation: a gendered perspective

both practical needs (income generation/livelihoods, security, etc.) and strategic needs, leading to the expansion of women's agency, which was limited within specific structural and patriarchal inequities. It further highlights how the expansion of agency and collective action can attempt to address entrenched gendered inequities, leading to a pathway for people-centered social innovation from a gendered perspective.

References

Andersen, J. and Larsen, J. E. (1998). "Gender, Poverty and Empowerment," *Critical Social Policy*, 18(2), pp. 241–258.

Andersen, L. L. (2012). *Intersectional Learning: New Venues for Professional Learning in Collaborative and Transformative Formats*. Conference, Critical Perspectives on Professional Learning, Leeds University, Leeds.

Andersen, L. L. (2015a). *Intersectional Learning in Hybrid Organisations*. 5th EMES International Research Conference on Social Enterprise. Helsinki, Finland, p. 6.

Andersen, L. L. (2015b). "Micro-Processes of Collaborative Innovation in Danish Welfare Settings: A Psychosocial Approach to Learning and Performance," in *Collaborative Governance and Public Innovation in Northern Europe*. Bentham EBooks, pp. 249–268.

Andersen, L. L. (2015c). "Social Entrepreneurship and Social Innovation: Human Economy, Governance and Volunteerism Revisited," *Cursiv*, 15, pp. 35–54.

Andersen, L. L. (2016a). "Multimetodisk Social Intervention: Bromley by Bow [Multi-Methodic Social Intervention: Bromley by Bow]," in *Social Intervention. Meningsfuld indgriben i menneskers llv. [Social Intervention. Meaningful Intervening People's Lives]*. Frydenlund Academic.

Andersen, L. L. (2016b). "Social Innovation og socialt entreprenørskab [Social Innovation and Social Entrepreneurship]," in R. Posborg, H. Nørrelykke and H. Antczak (eds.), *Socialrådgivning og socialt arbejde [Social Service and Social Work]*. København: Hans Reitzels Forlag, pp. 545–560.

Andersen, L. L. (2018). "Neoliberal Drivers in Hybrid Civil Society Organisations: Critical Readings of Civicness and Social Entrepreneurism," in Masoud Kamali and J. H. Jönsson (eds.), *Neoliberalism and the Transformation of Social Policy*. London: Routledge, pp. 23–34.

Andersen, L. L. and Hulgård, L. (2014). "Social Innovation and Collaborative Learning," *Spor—Et Tidsskrift for Universitetspædagogik*. http://forsknings basen.deff.dk/en/catalog/2291731129.

Banerjee, Swati. (2015). "Framing Innovations in Policy Agenda: Convergence of NRLM and PRIs for Gendered Inclusion," in Chandrakant Puri (ed.), *Two Decades of Panchayati Raj in India*. Mumbai: University of Mumbai.

Banerjee, Swati. (2018). "Social Innovation in South Asia," in Jurgen Howaldt, Christoph Kaletka, Antonius Schroder and Marthe Zirngiebl (eds.), *Atlas of Social Innovation: New Practices for a Better Future*. Dortmund: Sozialforschungsstelle, TU Dortmund University.

Banerjee, Swati and Shaban, Abdul. (2019). "Reimagining the Social Enterprise Through Grassroots Social Innovations in India," in Philippe Eynaud, Jean-Louis Laville, Luciana Lucas dos Santos, Swati Banerjee, Lars Hulgard and Flor Dinis de Araujo Avelino (eds.), *Theory of Social Enterprise and Pluralism*. New York: Routledge.

Barckley, E. F., Cross, P. and Major, C. H. (2005). *Collaborative Learning Techniques*. New York: Jossey-Bass Higher and Adult Education.

BEPA. (2011). *Empowering People, Driving Change: Social Innovation in the European Union*. Luxembourg: Publications Office of the European Union.

Billis, D. (2010). "Towards a Theory of Hybrid Organizations," in D. Billis (ed.), *Hybrid Organizations and the Third Sector*. Basingstoke and Hampshire: Palgrave Macmillan, pp. 46–69.

Boje, T. P. (2015). "Citizenship, Democratic Participation, and Civil Society," *Cursiv, Århus University, DK*, 15, pp. 27–45.

Bourner, T. (2011). "Self-Managed Action Learning," in *Action Learning in Practice*. Gower Publishing, Ltd, pp. 113–124.

Brandsen, T., van de Donk, W. and Putters, K. (2005). "Griffins or Chameleons? Hybridity as a Permanent and Inevitable Characteristic of the Third Sector," *International Journal of Public Administration*, 28(9–10), pp. 749–765. https://doi.org/10.1081/PAD-200067320.

Buckingham, H. (2011). "Hybridity, Diversity and the Division of Labour in the Third Sector: What Can We Learn from Homelessness Organisations in the UK?" *Voluntary Sector Review*, 2(2), pp. 157–175. https://doi.org/10.1332/204080511X583832.

Cameron, J., Gibson, K. and Hill, A. (2014). "Cultivating Hybrid Collectives: Research Methods for Enacting Community Food Economies in Australia and the Philippines," *Local Environment*, 19(1), pp. 118–132. https://doi.org/10.1080/13549839.2013.855892.

Casebourne, J. (2014). *Why Motivation Matters in Public Sector Innovation*. NESTA. www.nesta.org.uk.

CFBU. (2010). *Bydelsmødre. Brobygning mellem isolerede indvandrerkvinder og samfundet [Neighborhood-Mothers. Bridge-Building Between Isolated Migrant Women and Society]*. Copenhagen: Center for Housing Development (CFBU).

Chambers, R. (1995). *Poverty and Livelihoods: Whose Reality Counts*. IDS Discussion Paper, No. 347. Brighton: Institute for Development Studies.

Chambers, R. and Conway, G. (1992). *Sustainable Rural Livelihoods: Practical Concepts for the 21st Century*. IDS Discussion Paper, No. 296. Brighton: Institute for Development Studies.

Christensen, K. O., Aner, L. G. and Frederiksen, N. (2010). *Projekt Bydelsmødre. En samlet evaluering [Project Neighborhood Mothers. Final Evaluation]*. Copenhagen: Center for Boligsocial Udvikling [Center for Housing Development].

Delica, K. N. and Nielsson, I. N. (2012). *Medborgercentre—et fremtidigt bibliotekskoncept [Community Centre—a Future Library Concept]*. Copenhagen: Kulturstyrelsen [Agency for Culture].

Evers, A. (2005). "Mixed Welfare Systems and Hybrid Organizations: Changes in the Governance and Provision of Social Services," *International Journal of Public Administration*, 28, pp. 737–748. https://doi.org/10.1081/PAD-200067318.

Evers, A., Ewert, B. and Brandsen, T. (2016). *Social Innovations for Social Cohesion. Transnational Patterns and Approaches from 20 European Cities*. Liege: EMES European Research Network.

Gibson-Graham, J. K. (2014). "Rethinking the Economy with Thick Description and Weak Theory," *Current Anthropology*, 55(S9), pp. S147–S153. https://doi.org/10.1086/676646.

Howaldt, Jurgen. and Hochgerner, Josef. (2018). "Desperately Seeking: A Shared Understanding of Social Innovation," in Jurgen Howaldt, Christoph Kaletka, Antonius Schroder and Marthe Zirngiebl (eds.), *Atlas of Social Innovation: New Practices for a Better Future*, pp. 18–22. Dortmund: Sozialforschungsstelle, TU Dortmund University.

Haugh, H. M. and Talwar, A. (2016). "Linking Social Entrepreneurship and Social Change: The Mediating Role of Empowerment," *Journal of Business Ethics*, 133(4), pp. 643–658. https://doi.org/10.1007/s10551-014-2449-4.

Humbert, A. L. (2012). *Women as Social Entrepreneurs*. Third Sector Research Centre, Working Paper 72.

Husted, M. G. and Erkmann, M. (2009). *Midtvejsevaluering af Projekt Bydelsmødre og Kommunale Kvindeambassadører i Akacieparken og på*

Bispebjerg (Midterm evaluation of Neighborhood Mothers and Municipal Women Ambassadors in Akacieparken and Bispebjerg). Copenhagen: Development and Social Service Administration.

Husted, M. G. and Vestergaard, M. (2010). *Evaluering af Projekt Bydelsmødre Akacieparken/ Bispebjerg [Evaluation of Neighborhood Mothers in Akacieparken/Bispebjerg]*. Copenhagen: Socialforvaltningen, Københavns Kommune [Social Service Administration].

Huysentruyt, M. (2014, January). *Women's Social Entrepreneurship and Innovation, OECD Local Economic and Employment Development (LEED)*. Working Papers, OECD Publishing. https://doi.org/http://dx.doi.org/10.1787/5jxzkq 2sr7d4-en.

Millard, Jeremy, Banerjee, Swati et al. (2017, January). *SI Drive*. www.si-drive. eu/wp-content/uploads/2017/03/SI-DRIVE-Deliverable-D10_3-Poverty-1.pdf.

Jespersen, M. S. (2015). *Evaluering af Bydelsmødrene [Evaluationreport: Neighborhood Mothers]*. Copenhagen: Deloitte.

Kabeer, N. (1999). "Resource, Agency and Achievement: Reflections on the Measurement of Women's Empowerment," *Development and Change*, 30, pp. 435–464. doi:10.1111/1467-7660.00125.

Kabeer, N. (2012). "Empowerment, Citizenship and Gender Justice: A Contribution to Locally Grounded Theories of Change in Women's Lives," *Ethics and Social Welfare*, 6(3), pp. 216–232. https://doi.org/10.1080/17496535.2012.704055.

Krishna, Sumi. (2007). *Women's Livelihood Rights: Recasting Citizenship for Development*. New Delhi: Sage Publications.

Krogh, M. (2012). *At blive bydelsmor. Læring og identitetsdannelse i et "frit land med regler" [Becoming a Neighborhood Mother. Learning and Identity-Building in a "free country with rules"]*. Copenhagen: Roskilde University Press, Master Program of Pedagogy and Educational Studies.

Lau, C. B. and Dybbroe, B. (2012). "Kommunal sundhedsfremme i borgernes hverdag—ud fra en settings- og empowermenttilgang [Local Health Prevention in Citizen's Everyday Life—a Settings- and Empowerment Perspective]," in *Sundhedsfremme—et kritisk perspektiv [Health Prevention—a Critical Perspective]*. Copenhagen: Roskilde University Press, pp. 177–189.

Ljunggren, E., Alsos, G. A., Amble, N., Ervik, R., Kvidal, T. and Wiik, R. (2010). *Gender and Innovation. Learning from Regional VRI-Projects*. Nordlands Forskning, NF-rapport no 2.

Mair, J., Mayer, J. and Lutz, E. (2015). "Navigating Institutional Plurality: Organizational Governance in Hybrid Organizations," *Organization Studies*, 36(6), pp. 713–739. https://doi.org/10.1177/0170840615580007.

Mair, J. and Noboa, E. (2003). *The Emergence of Social Enterprises and Their Place in the New Organizational Landscape*. IESE Working Paper No. D/523, 3(523). https://doi.org/10.1111/1467-8616.00112.

Malhotra, A. et al. (2009). *Innovation for Women's Empowerment and Gender Equality*. International Centre for Research on Women. www.icrw.org/wp-content/uploads/2016/10/Innovation-for-Womens-Empowerment.pdf.

McCall, Leslie. (2005). "The Complexity of Intersectionaltiy," *Signs: Journal of Women in Culture and Society*, 30(3), pp. 1771–1800.

Millard, J., Bannerjee, S., Cecchini, S., Ecer, S., Como, E., Tognetti, M., . . . Karzen, M. (2017). *SI Drive: Social Innovation in Poverty Reduction and Sustainable Development: Case Study Results*. EU Seventh Framework Program.

Moser, Caroline and Caren, Levy. (1986). *A Theory and Methodology of Gender Planning: Meeting Women's Practical and Strategic Needs.* DPU Gender and Planning Working Paper No. 11. London: Development Planning Unit, Bartlett School of Architecture and Planning, University College.

Moulaert and Van den Broeck. (2018). "Social Innovation and Territorial Development," in Jurgen Howaldt, Christoph Kaletka, Antonius Schroder and Marthe Zirngiebl (eds.), *Atlas of Social Innovation: New Practices for a Better Future.* Dortmund: Sozialforschungsstelle, TU Dortmund University.

Mulgan, G., Tucker, S., Ali, R. and Sanders, B. (2008). *Social Innovation. What It Is, Why It Matters and How It Can Be Accelerated. Skoll Centre for Social Entrepreneurship.* Working Paper. Oxord: Said Business School. http://eureka. sbs.ox.ac.uk/761/1/Social_Innovation.pdf.

Neighborhood Mothers. (2013). *En fortælling om BYDELSMØDRE—kvinder som bringer håb og forandring i andre kvinders liv [A Narrative About Neigborhoods Mothers—Women That Brings Hope and Change to Other Women].* Presentation Växjö, Sweden.

Neighborhood Mothers. (2014). *Neighbourhood Mothers. Manual for Start Up.* Copenhagen Neighborhood Mothers. https://bydelsmor.dk/english.

Pedler, M. (2011). *Action Learning in Practice.* Gower Publishing, Ltd.

Pestoff, V. (2014). "Hybridity, Coproduction, and Third Sector Social Services in Europe," *American Behavioral Scientist,* 58(11), pp. 1412–1424. https://doi. org/10.1177/0002764214534670.

Pines, A. M., Lerner, M. and Schwartz, D. (2012). "Gender Differences Among Social vs. Business Entrepreneurs," in Thierry Burger-Helmchen (ed.), *Entrepreneurship. Gender, Geographies and Social Context.* InTech, pp. 1–14.

Rose, M. J. (2014). "Bydelsmødre, er det vejen til integration?—en undersøgelse af fællesskabsaspektet i forhold til læring og integration i dansk kultur [Neighborhood Mothers, the Road to Integration? An Inquiry into the Community Aspect Related to Learning and Integrat]," *Reflexen, Journal for Educations at Department of Learning and Philosophy, Aalborg University,* 9(1), pp. 1–8.

Seibel, W. (2015). "Studying Hybrids: Sectors and Mechanisms," *Organization Studies,* 36(6), pp. 697–712. https://doi.org/10.1177/0170840615580005.

Sewell, W. H. Jr. (1992, July). "A Theory of Structure: Duality, Agency, and Transformation," *American Journal of Sociology,* 98(1), pp. 1–29. The University of Chicago Press. www.jstor.org/stable/2781191.

Somers, M. R. and Wright, O. (2008). *Genealogies of Citizenship: Markets, Statelessness, and the Right to Have Rights.* Cambridge: Cambridge University Press.

Thomsen, M. H. and Ravn-Mortensen, L. (2012). *Brobygning og forebyggelse på frivillig basis. Evaluering af Bydelsmødre indsatsen [Building Bridges and Prevention Voluntary. Evaluation Report: Neighborhood Mothers].* MHT Consultancy.

von Hippel, E. (2005). *Democratizing Innovation.* Cambridge: MIT Press, vol. 5. https://doi.org/10.1111/j.1540-5885.2006.00192_2.x.

Weiler, S. and Bernasek, A. (2001). "Dodging the Glass Ceiling? Networks and the New Wave of Women Entrepreneurs," *The Social Science Journal,* 38(1), pp. 85–103.

Wieringa, S. (1994). "Women's Interest and Empowerment, Gender Planning Reconsidered," *Development and Change,* 25(4).

Wijkström, F. (2011). "Charity Speak and Business Talk. The On-Going (Re)hybridization of Civil Society," in A. Wijkström and F. Zimmer (eds.), *Nordic Civil Society at a Cross-Road*. Baden-Baden: Nomos Verlagsgesellschaft.

Wijkström, F. and Zimmer, A. (2011). "Introduction: Nordic Civil Societies Beyond Membership and Movements," in F. Wijkström and A. Zimmer (eds.), *Nordic Civil Society at a Cross-Roads. Transforming the Popular Movement Tradition*. Baden-Baden: Nomos, vol. 12.

4 Genealogy and Institutionalization of People-Centered Social Innovation in Kudumbashree, Kerala, India

P. K. Shajahan and Lars Hulgård

Introduction

People-centered social innovation (PCSI) as propounded in this chapter is conceptualized as a combination of the ideas of people-centeredness in development discourse as well as an emphasis on the social relational dimensions of social innovation. Key features in this approach are participation, public sphere and plurality, which are much-neglected criteria in policy making within the interrelated areas of social entrepreneurship, social enterprise and social innovation. The chapter uses an institutional and social origin approach (DiMaggio and Powell, 1991; Salamon and Anheier, 1998; Mair and Marti, 2009) and argues that social innovation in the historic outset was people-centered. Empirical evidence for PCSI is further based on in-depth interviews with leaders of Kudumbashree (April 2013 and October 2014) that were followed by field visits, including on-site observations and group sessions with women in several places and situations of affiliation with the program. Kudumbashree, as it is better known, is the Kerala State Poverty Eradication Mission, initiated by the government of Kerala both to uproot absolute poverty from the state and to increase the level of participation of women in economic and political life. It is founded on the dynamics of three critical components that together form its specific kind of social innovation, targeting poverty eradication and political empowerment among women. The three components are microcredit, entrepreneurship and empowerment (social, economic and political). We argue that Kudumbashree is an example of PCSI based on the recognition of and solidarity with women, not as isolated individuals and entrepreneurs. Accordingly, the core of PCSI, as well as of Kudumbashree, is to understand people in their entire context and capacities and not just as individuals aiming to improve their market value. Social innovation in this sense happens only when succeeding in harvesting from the *totalities* of people's communities and everyday life (Coraggio et al., 2015). We address Kudumbashree through a perspective not so different from Patricia Wilson's when she claims that "communities that successfully build or rebuild productive social capital will be those best positioned for prosperity and adaptability in the coming century" (1997: 756). However, social capital in a noninstitutional view tends to become instrumentalized as a social technology that empowerment-oriented experts can use to address marginalities of communities. Thus, Somers (2008) claims that social capital has become a resource to be fed to marginalized communities: after years of privatization and structural adjustment to neoliberal standards, marginalized people are left with nothing but their own networks, now served to them as a resource: "Let them eat social capital," Somers argues (2008: 213). Thus, the chapter aims to offer a constructive critique of the notions of social capital as a foundation for social innovation and to provide a nuanced understanding of the same by exploring varied aspects of solidarity economy that Kudumbashree has been able to promote both at the level of local communities and at Kerala state level. The social capital foundations of Kudumbashree collectives, together with economic activities aimed at improving conditions for members from a solidarity economy perspective within a broader people-centric approach, provides a strong argument for what we would like to propose as PCSI. Finally, we argue that the three intrinsic pillars of PCSI—elaborated in the chapter as (1) a willingness to engage in large-scale combinations across multiple dimensions (relational), (2) an emphasis on process dimension and (3) an epistemic openness (Hulgård and Shajahan, 2013)—can be used to examine the possibility of a dynamic combination of (social) value orientations of social innovation and an approach putting people at the center of development discourses.

Origin of People-Centered Development

The notion of people-centered development (PCD) has several roots, but they are all concerned with the prospect of building sustainable communities and societies through participatory and multidimensional strategies. Such strategies usually depart from a deep understanding of the context in which they are articulated. The 1995 UN World Summit for Social Development in Copenhagen is a key point of reference for policy when framing the core elements of PCD. In its final declaration, the summit recommended to the General Assembly of the United Nations a people-centered sustainable development approach. The declaration confirmed by heads of states and governments highlights the necessity of concerted actions among economic, social and political strategies committed to building transparent and accountable governance as a necessary procedure for building PCD (UN, 1995). A few years later in 2003, at its 58th session, the UN General Assembly not only reaffirmed the commitment from the World Summit in Copenhagen but also specified some of the objectives for PCD. Thus, the General Assembly, with a reference to the Copenhagen summit, adopted a "pledge to eradicate poverty, promote full and productive employment and foster social integration" to build stable, safe and just societies for all (UN, 2003).

The notion of people-centeredness is relevant for two reasons that we will be addressing in this chapter: first, due to the importance of international development work with a reference to UN strategies and policies, such as the Social Development Goals (SDG) adopted by the United Nations in 2015, particularly SDG 11, "Make cities inclusive, safe, resilient and sustainable" is aimed at promoting sustainable cities and communities, and, second, due to the emergence of a people-centered way of thinking and experimenting with social innovation in the areas of the social and solidarity economy spread around the world. Thus, a people-centered paradigm of social innovation is found to have appeared during the same decades as did the PCD framework in global development policies. Through this chapter, we seek to understand the shared meaning of PCD and the framework of social innovation, thereby elaborating on the notion of PCSI. Such an approach to social innovation is explicated by discussing a large-scale innovation in poverty eradication adopted by the southern state of Kerala in India known as Kudumbashree.

PCD in International Development

The UN adoption of PCD has inspired David Cox (1998) to analyze the relevance of people-centeredness in a divided world amid growing inequalities and exclusion. Accordingly, Cox argues that the misplaced priorities and inequalities in the distribution of power in the dominant development paradigm make PCD necessary for putting people at the center of development discourse. He argues that the key to rectifying the situation of distorted development is the empowerment of those who are excluded from the development process and then to build political, economic and social structures which are more participatory in nature. To Cox, the PCD framework must rest on five critical foundations. These are (1) *awareness* among the people of the realities of their situation and their environment, (2) *social mobilization* for emphasizing the right of people to participate in their own development, (3) their actual *participation* in the development process, (4) *self-reliance* where people have maximum control over their own development and (5) *sustainability*. Taken together, these five elements in PCD form a direct link to contemporary social innovation analysis. The interrelation among the five elements further represents a challenge to the prevailing distribution of power because it aims at redistributing influence and command over resources by establishing an enabling environment aimed at emancipating and empowering people at the margins. Accordingly, Cox argues that PCD favors "process over outcomes, which is an approach that not all parties will be happy with" (1998: 519). As we shall see in the following section, critical social innovation analysis also emphasizes a strong process dimension as the single most influential feature that distinguishes social innovation from other types of innovation and change.

PCSI

Social innovation relates to the PCD framework in the sense that it is about the satisfaction of human needs by the empowerment or sociopolitical mobilization of people trying to fulfill their needs (Moulaert et al., 2013). Thus, an important strand in contemporary social innovation theory marks out social innovation from other types of innovation by insisting that it is about changing social relations aimed at improving the livelihood for those at the margins of society. The insistence of social innovation theory on uniting the fulfillment of human needs with active engagement and changes in social relations is based on two fundamental goals: creating an environment where people directly engage in the process of development and addressing issues of social justice (Hulgård and Shajahan, 2013). Actions taken within the paradigm of social innovation target "the fundamental needs of groups of citizens deprived of a minimum income, of access to quality education and of other benefits of an economy from which their community has been excluded" (MacCallum et al., 2009: 64). Thus, fulfilling needs and ensuring social justice, such as the inclusion of the excluded, necessarily demand a reconfiguration of the power dimensions of social relations. However, not all types of social innovation research and literature, in general, emphasize the reconfiguration of social relations and the role of participation as important features of social innovation. In this context Ayob et al. (2016), by emphasizing the role of relational aspects in social innovation, make the distinction between strong and weak traditions in the evolution of social innovation as an academic discipline. Accordingly, the strong tradition argues that participatory and collaborative processes target a reconfiguration of "power relations", whereas the weak tradition focuses on "the utilitarian social value of the innovation" (Ayob et al., 2016: 637). We would add to this distinction that the strong tradition, with its emphasis on process and a social change dimension, is dominant only in discussions, whereas in day-to-day operations of social innovation, the weak tradition is a more widespread vehicle for social innovation. Pundits of social innovation (SI) and social entrepreneurship (SE) usually argue that an integrated perspective on process and outcome is what marks out the SE/SI field from other types of social change. However, in reality, the policy interest concentrates on the benefit of the outcome with little or no interest in the process dimension of changing the dominant power relations (Jessop et al., 2013).

Through the Kudumbashree experiment presented in the following section, we analyze how a combination of the ideas of PCD and social innovation is in operation to bring large-scale change—social, economic and political.

Kudumbashree in the Perspective of Strong SI

Kudumbashree is a mega-scale SI with a multidimensional and explicitly articulated process approach to empowerment, and thus, a clear case of the strong social innovation tradition. The initiative was launched to promote livelihood development as a statewide initiative in the southern Indian state of Kerala in 1998. *Kudumbashree* means "prosperity of the family" in Malayalam, the language spoken in Kerala. Being a symbol of family prosperity, Kudumbashree also refers to the role of women, and hence, the name further points directly toward the primary target of the organization: to wipe out absolute poverty from the state of Kerala through pluralistically framed women-empowerment projects throughout the entire state. In the words of the Kudumbashree Mission Statement,

> [t]o eradicate absolute poverty in ten years through concerted community action under the leadership of local governments, by facilitating organization of the poor for combining self-help with demand-led convergence of available services and resources to tackle the multiple dimensions and manifestations of poverty, holistically.
>
> (Kudumbashree, n.d.a)

In comparison with many other community-oriented or enterprise-oriented projects and programs, Kudumbashree stands out both through its size and its holistic and multidimensional approach to empowerment and poverty eradication. This holistic and multidimensional character of the initiative is evident from three main types of interventions: microcredit, enterprises and empowerment (social, economic and political). These are interwoven into a complex structure where locality and territoriality are embedded in structures and aspirations of universality. While the first two types of intervention are expected to address the economic and livelihood marginalities, the third aspect of empowerment has a wide range of impact on the daily lives of women, in particular, and poor households, in general.

Concerning size and coverage, it is worth noting that Kudumbashree covers 4.3 million women members and their households through a community-based institutional structure integrated with local self-governments (LSGs)[1] for ensuring a seamless participatory development process. The following details provide a glimpse of the achievements and scaling of Kudumbashree through a "three-tier community structure"[2] with neighborhood groups (NHGs) at the lowest level, area development

societies (ADSs) at the intermediate and community development societies (CDSs) at the LSG level:

- About 277,000 NHGs, 19,854 ADS, 1,073 CDS
- INR 16.88 billion savings mobilized, INR 41.95 billion loans disbursed
- 128,000 NHGs linked with banks—INR 11.40 billion credit mobilized
- 31,000 microenterprises of women belonging to socially and economically deprived households
- 60,000 agricultural groups
- 10,000 contracting jobs
- Five producer companies
- 2015 elections covering all three tiers of LSGs together, a total of
  13,993 women contested, out of which 7,376 were elected. (This is
  against the 2010 elections when about 8,000 Kudumbashree women
  contested and 5,485 were elected.)

(Various reports accessed from www.kudumbashree.org)

In an interview in October 2015 with one of the leaders at Kudumbashree, we got a glimpse of how the economic functions of Kudumbashree are integrated into the social and political goals as an integral
feature of its organizational structure and functions with respect to wider
changes it could bring along:

> For the first time we are having a secret ballot. Before, people would
> raise their hands. It has been controversial to change this. . . . Social
> capital has been turned into political capital. Today 61% of women
> in political office in Kerala are from Kudumbashree. . . . When the
> women come together, they discuss a lot more than economic issues.
> They create social bonds. . . . One woman once said—and you will
> hear that everywhere—"Kudumbashree is my mother and I will not
> trade her for an entire empire." . . . For Kudumbashree, economy
> is just an entry point. It functions on community support, and cre-
> ates synergy with the Local Self Governments; these layers are well
> integrated into each other. Thus, we are close to the grassroots and
> there is mutual synergy between Kudumbashree and the Panchayats.[3]

In the case of Kudumbashree, the tangible outcomes of economic benefits might appear to be a predominant feature, which has contributed
significantly to addressing poverty and economic marginalities in the
state. By integrating economic actions with the formal institutional governance structures at the local level, participatory processes have major
implications for promoting a "people's democracy", which is expected to
address issues of injustice and inequality in the long run. The reconfiguration of social relations as emphasized in the strong tradition of social
innovation (Ayob et al., 2016), with its focus on processes, is found to be

at play. The analysis of this process innovation needs to be done against the overall backdrop of the social and political context in the state of Kerala, as explained in the following section.

Kerala's (Social) Development and Participatory Democracy Context

Kerala is a state in the southwestern part of India with a population of 33.3 million (2.76% of India's population) according to the 2011 census. The majority of the people (56.7%) follow Hinduism, followed by 24.7 % Islam and 19.0% Christianity. Kerala stands highest in almost all the social development indicators such as elimination of absolute poverty, education, health care and so on in comparison to the all-India average data on the same indicators and is comparable to many developed countries. Kerala became a case for discussion all over the world with its low economic indicators and high social development achievements, widely discussed as the "Kerala Model of Development". Specific indicators of this model are explained by Franke and Chassin as follows:

- A set of high-material quality of life indicators coinciding with low per-capita incomes, both distributed across nearly the entire population of Kerala.
- A set of wealth and resources redistribution programmes that have largely brought about the high material quality of life indicators.
- High levels of political participation and activism among ordinary people along with substantial numbers of dedicated leaders at all levels. Kerala's mass activism and committed cadre were able to function within a largely democratic structure which their activism has served to reinforce. (1999: 120)

According to the Human Development Report 2011,[4] Kerala stands highest in the Human Development Index (HDI) with 0.790 as against the national average of 0.477 and the lowest of 0.358.

As seen in Table 4.1, Kerala remains far above in all the three indices, thus staying significantly above the national average as far as the

Table 4.1 Components of the HDI for India and Kerala, 2007–2008

Indices	All India	Kerala
Health Index	0.563	0.817
Income Index	0.271	0.629
Education Index	0.568	0.924
HDI	0.477	0.790

Source: India Human Development Report (2011).

composite HDI is concerned. Some specific health indicators provided in Table 4.2 give a clearer picture of the scenario in the health sector, which is supported by a most elaborate public-funded health infrastructure in the state. Kerala has about 2,700 government medical institutions with 330 beds per 100,000 population, which is the highest in the country.

Literacy rate, one of the basic indicators of educational reach, provides yet another dimension to the high social development of the state. Table 4.3 shows the literacy rate of Kerala from 1951 to 2011, according to the respective census reports.

High political awareness, early introduction of progressive social policies such as Land Reforms[5] and unparalleled educational initiatives, including literacy movements, have contributed to Kerala having high social development achievements. Sustenance of high social development in the state could also be attributed to the effective functioning of democratic decentralization in the state since the 1990s. While the participatory democracy through the LSG system in India became constitutional entities through constitutional amendments, Kerala went on to make this

Table 4.2 Health Development Indicators for India and Kerala, 2007–2009

Health Indicators	India	Kerala
Birth rate (per 1,000 population)	22.80	14.6
Death rate (per 1,000 population)	7.40	6.6
Infant mortality rate (per 1,000 population)	44.00	6.7
Maternal mortality rate (per 100,000 live births)* 2009	301	40
Total fertility rate (per woman)	2.90	1.70
Couple protection rate (%)	52	62.30
Life at birth (male)	62.60	71.40
Life at birth (female)	64.20	76.30
Life at birth (average)	63.50	74.00

* The data for this item is available only for the year 2009 whereas in the case of other indicators in the table, the data is for the period 2007-09.

Table 4.3 Literacy Rate in Kerala and India, 1951–2011

Year	Literacy (National)	Literacy (Kerala)	Male (Kerala)	Female (Kerala)
1951	18.33	47.18	58.35	36.43
1961	28.3	55.08	64.89	45.56
1971	34.45	69.75	77.13	62.53
1981	43.57	78.85	84.56	73.36
1991	52.51	89.81	93.62	86.17
2001	65.38	90.92	94.20	87.86
2011	74.04	94.59	97.10	92.12

Source: Compiled from various census reports.

more people-centered in popularizing the participation of people in the affairs of the LSGs.

Democratic decentralization through the 73rd and 74th Constitutional Amendments in India paved the way for making local democratic governments in both rural and urban contexts a reality, with strict conditions for the institutional mechanisms, regular elections and social inclusion. In rural India, the constitutional amendment has mandated that there will be a three-tier panchayat system with the village panchayats at the lowest level, the block panchayat at the intermediary level and the district panchayat at the highest level through direct election of representatives at all three levels. Although such institutional mechanisms have played significant roles in bringing the development process closer to people, aspirations of a participatory democracy in aspects of decision-making and the direct implementation of development policy at the local level has been varied across the country. Such variations have been mostly attributed to two factors, one being the levels of participation by people—not only in elections of their representatives to the panchayats but also in the functioning of panchayats itself—and the second being the devolution of power and resources to the panchayats by the respective state governments. Kerala stands out among all the states in India in terms of ensuring participation as well effective devolution of three Fs (Funds, Functions and Functionaries) to these lower levels of government, making development options suit the needs of local communities. These structural alterations were coupled with a process of making participation of people in the development process a reality through a people's planning campaign started in 1996. The purpose of this campaign was to enable the LSG mechanism, with appropriate structures and processes, to ensure people's participation, awareness creation, popularization, sensitizing structures of government to people's needs and the need to debate alternatives to existing models of development.

All through the discussion about LSGs, the process of making people participate in the affairs of their own life contexts with a significant amount of control over processes by the people themselves signifies a particular model of social innovation founded on process dimensions. While the participatory democracy context puts people at the center of the development process, in general, Kudumbashree considers women as the drivers of such processes.

People at the Center, Women at the Forefront: People-Centeredness in Kudumbashree

The Kudumbashree experiment in Kerala needs to be located in the general context of participatory democracy through the LSG system in India discussed in the previous sections. We argue that both the effective operationalization of participatory democracy through the LSGs and the

Kudumbashree experiment are aimed at placing people at the center of the development process. Thus, PCD became the bedrock of a functional participatory democracy in Kerala, where development plans were evolved from assemblies of smaller communities which were linked together at LSG, district and state levels. This is based on the stronger belief that participatory democracy, in general, and PCD, in particular, cannot exist in the absence of *active citizenship* or where such an "active citizen has become the privileged object of development imaginaries"(Robins et al., 2008: 1071). In order to promote active citizenship, the idea of PCD should have mechanisms for inclusiveness of those who are generally on the margins of development policy implementations. Kudumbashree, being the state poverty eradication mission, conceived this inclusion by bringing in women from poorer households as initiators of the change they want to bring in their society.

Right from the beginning in 1998, Kudumbashree aimed to deepen the democratic process by bringing women to the forefront of this participatory democratic process. Within the existing LSG framework, Kudumbashree created further structures and processes at the local level for making this an unstoppable reality by organizing themselves under a three-tier community-based structure. At the bottom there are the NHGs composed of 20 to 40 women members selected from poor families. ADSs are formed at the ward level of local government by federating 8 to 10 NHGs. The CDS, formed at the village panchayat level or at the municipality (town) or corporation (city), is a federation of ADSs. This system works in close association with both the urban and rural LSG institutions through a network of community-based organizations working with women. By doing so, not only the women but also several marginalized groups and sections became the focus of intervention, as could be seen in the range of activities and entrepreneurial projects undertaken by Kudumbashree. Thus, although Kudumbashree was formed as a state-level mission to eradicate poverty, it went on to become a grassroots mechanism for ensuring participation and promoting active citizenship at the village or municipal levels. During one of our visits, a Kudumbashree leader talked about this in the light of social capital:

> What participation in Kudumbashree has done to the women is to build a strong social bond, a strong solidarity among them. The women who are poor and scattered have come together under one collective identity. This social capital of marginalized women has instilled confidence and encouraged mobility, not only physical mobility but also intellectual mobility. They could argue with elected representatives, bankers and bureaucrats and get their demand met. For the women, Kudumbashree is an icon, an identity.
>
> (interview with leader at Kudumbashree headquarters, October 2014)

Cox (1998) argues that people-centeredness in social work is important in a divided world amid growing inequalities and exclusion. In the preceding quotation, the Kudumbashree leader represents an approach to social work that links the people-centered view to an understanding of social capital based on social justice and civil rights. With a reference to Somers (2008), the social capital of the women in Kudumbashree moves from the level of a social technology fed to people in poverty to a structural level, where citizenship rights are stimulated and exercised with the use of social capital. As we shall see in a later section of this chapter, we suggest that PCSI is a way of linking the PCD framework to the strong tradition of SI as it has emerged during the last two or three decades on a global scale. We further argue that the strong SI approach immanent in the PCSI framework can systematically target a reconfiguration of social relations for the benefit of people at the margins of society. The misplaced priorities and inequalities in the distribution of power in the dominant development paradigm make PCD necessary for putting people at the center of development discourse. Posited in the context of social and economic inequalities, Kudumbashree works toward addressing poverty through a variety of field engagements, ensuring distribution of power and resources. In an interview in October 2014, the coordinator of social projects at Kudumbashree shared that the social projects under Kudumbashree are examples of the inclusion of the most excluded sections of society. According to him, for many of the welfare projects, whether related to housing, education or even livelihood or social enterprises, there are certain prerequisites for beneficiaries to be included in the project. Identification of beneficiaries is undertaken through a participatory and transparent system with clearly laid-down indicators of poverty and marginalization. At the same time, a large number of people who live in abject poverty, neglect and exclusion cannot draw the benefits of several welfare programs due to the conditions attached to the schemes. For example, destitute people who are homeless, beggars or terminally ill cannot get the benefit of many of the schemes. This is similar to the case of the mentally or intellectually challenged. The Ashraya project of Kudumbashree makes sure that their welfare needs are taken care of through a community-led and state-supported program. Through this project, not only basic needs such as food, shelter (including land for a home), drinking water and sanitation but also other supports, such as social security benefits, education facilities for children, skill development and employment, among others, are conceived as a comprehensive package aimed at making the life of destitute more dignified.

As we have seen in a previous section, Cox (1998) argues that PCD rests on the five critical foundations of awareness, social mobilization, participation, self-reliance and sustainability. These foundations of PCD seemed to be reverberating in the guiding approach of Kudumbashree as expressed by the executive director when the authors interviewed her in

October 2014. In the interview, the executive director highlighted how the Kudumbashree approach is a combination of four Cs, Conscientization, Collectivization, Communitization and Convergence, which are explained as follows:

- Conscientization: to generate critical consciousness about the state of affairs surrounding the people, which produces and reproduces poverty
- Collectivization: the process of bringing together people (women) who face similar conditions to create a shared platform
- Communitization (of issues): although poverty is individually experienced, communitization is to generate a collective understanding of the situation of poverty. Communitization of poverty means taking the individual experience into collective analysis and for collective action.
- Convergence: government efforts to address poverty have been fragmented. Institutional mechanisms are also fragmented. Kudumbashree is aiming at a convergence of schemes, resources and institutional mechanisms in order to have an integrated approach to addressing poverty.

While conscientization and collectivization are simple parallels of the first two foundations of PCD—awareness and social mobilization, the meaning of *communitization*, as well as the idea of convergence, encompasses Cox's combined ideas of participation, self-reliance and sustainability. He further argues that an important precondition for PCD is an enabling environment. Here the enabling environment is generated by two factors: first, the constitutional bodies of LSGs that created a broad framework of participatory democracy with 50% of the seats on elected bodies reserved for women and, second, the process of deepening democracy through the Kudumbashree network from neighborhood groups to the CDS discussed earlier. When we interviewed the executive director of Kudumbashree in October 2014, she emphasized that, although the constitutional amendment provided the immediate backdrop for Kudumbashree to become established, other factors such as high female literacy and political awareness contributed significantly to this. Furthermore, the constitutional amendment provides for only 33% of seats to be reserved for women, but Kerala and a few other states went on to extend this quota to 50%. Although this is not a direct outcome of Kudumbashree, an enabling environment was created by Kudumbashree to help women occupy these institutional positions as well. Thus, an enabling environment for women to be at the forefront of development planning and intervention not only reprioritized people's concerns but also helped to effectively address issues of exclusion. As discussed earlier, the inclusion of the most excluded has been taken up as a key strategy for Kudumbshree through projects such as Asraya, aimed at providing concerted support to people living in destitution. Identification of a person in destitution is undertaken using a 9-point scale covering aspects such as nonownership of land, house, sanitation, drinking water facilities, and employment of any person in the family, as well as women-headed family, SC/ST[6] family, presence of mentally/physically challenged/terminally ill person and an adult illiterate member in the family. The identified member or the family is supported by converging various state social security and welfare programs, as well as bringing in additional resources required. Each panchayat is required to prepare a household level plan to provide support to such families/individuals. The BUDs school for children with mental and physical disabilities run by Kudumbashree is yet another project of inclusion. There are 63 such BUDS schools registered in the state under the Persons with Disability Act. Both the Asraya Project and the BUDS school are run under the aegis of Kudumbashree and managed by women of the neighborhood. Putnam (1993), in his seminal work *Making Democracy Work*, presents the twin frameworks of social capital where (1) the existence of social capital affects individual welfare positively due to the collective engagement that individuals cannot negotiate and (2) trust and cooperation generated out of social capital make the institutions of governance more accountable and efficient. Following Putnam's approach, the link between micro-level SI, such as at the community level of Kudumbashree, and broader policy can accordingly be explored through two aspects of "effectiveness": internal versus external effectiveness. Active involvement in civic organizations "teaches" citizens how to cooperate and generate social capital. Trust, a precondition for internal organizational effectiveness, is generated and can be transferred to the broader policy through mechanisms that German philosopher Jürgen Habermas has labeled the sluice model (Habermas, 1996: 356). In the center of his argument stands the application of a sluice model of problem solving and communication that is a crucial part of his democratic theory. The legitimacy of political decisions is secured only by "communication flows that start at the periphery and pass through the sluices of democratic and constitutional procedures" (Habermas, 1996: 356). Thus, in a constitutional democracy the political system

> is internally differentiated into spheres of administrative and communicative power and remains open to the lifeworld. For institutionalized opinion- and will-formation depends on supplies coming from the informal contexts of communication found in the public sphere, in civil society, and in spheres of private life. In other words, the political action system is embedded in lifeworld contexts.
>
> (Habermas, 1996: 352)

According to Habermas and especially the sluice model, the civil, politically oriented public sphere serves as an important mediator between the citizenry and its elected officials, since the public sphere is "rooted in the communication of civil society" (Cohen, 1997). Accordingly, civic organizations of all types and kinds have the capacity to generate external effectiveness resulting from their institutional affiliation with the macro institutions of society. Society is largely to be understood as a web of institutions based on such patterns of internal and external effectiveness. According to the "Putnamian" understanding, social capital represents a kind of pool of resources and features of social life (networks, norms and trust), allowing citizens and societies to generate effectiveness when organizing matters of common concern.

Such a "sluice model" of deliberation and social capital generation is found to be clearly in operation in the case of Kudumbashree. Women members of Kudumbashree have been able to improve their conditions of vulnerability in social, economic and political realms through conscientization, collectivization and communitization, as discussed earlier. First, new forms of livelihood options promoted through microcredit and microenterprises have altered the livelihood and economic vulnerabilities in significant ways. Approximately 30,000 microenterprises of women from poor households in operation under Kudumbashree is a testimony to the impact of such collective actions on individual conditions of marginality. Furthermore, one of the officials of Kudumbashree specified during the interview that women could even enter arenas of work that were mostly male domains in Kerala, such as running taxi services and construction enterprises. Second, the large-scale collectivization and networks of women formed under Kudumbashree turned out to be a formidable force in the social and political domains of life in Kerala. As discussed earlier, the number of women holding political offices in Kerala, a large number of them from a Kudumbashree background, is testimony to that fact that the process of engagement with women through Kudumbashree has resulted in the governance process and structures being engendered. According to the official interviewed, capitalizing on the twin opportunities of women's quotas of 50% of the seats in LSG institutions and the social and political capital generated out of the collectivization through Kudumbashree, women have been able to influence governance and make it more accountable and efficient. The Women Component Plan has been introduced as an integral part of the annual plan of LSG institutions, with 10% of the total plan allocations earmarked for it (Sukumar, 2012).

While Kudumbashree attempts to undertake actions on a variety of factors contributing to poverty and marginalization, the role of women's collectives as social capital is important to sustain and institutionalize these initiatives because it ensures fulfillment of the basic needs of the community, in general, and of women from poor households, in particular, as well as enabling women to be socially and politically empowered. Conscientization, collectivization and communitization, discussed earlier, are the building blocks of such social capital generated in the process. The following section attempts to analyze Kudumbashree from the perspective of PCSI through the lenses of social capital and solidarity economy.

Kudumbashree in the Perspective for Institutionalization of PCSI

Patricia Wilson (1997) claims that "communities that successfully build or rebuild productive social capital will be those best positioned for prosperity and adaptability in the coming century" (Wilson, 1997: 756). A similar understanding of the qualities of social capital was promoted by Robert Putnam when he argued that social capital can help "neighborhoods, and even entire nations, to create wealth" (Putnam, 2000: 322). Furthermore, it was anticipated that the generation of social capital as a vehicle for community building was the task of a new type of leader—civic entrepreneurs, who "create social capital by creating opportunities for people to work together on specific projects to advance their economic community" (Henton et al., 1997: 31). Thus, social capital has been endowed with qualities that transcend time and place and can be implemented as a general tool for the regeneration of virtues that have been destroyed.

However, social capital in a noninstitutional view tends to become instrumentalized as a social technology that empowerment-oriented experts can use to address the marginalities of communities, irrespective of their factual situation. Thus, Somers (2008) claims that social capital has become a resource to be fed to marginalized communities: after years of privatization and structural adjustment to neoliberal standards, marginalized people are left with nothing but their own networks now served to them as a resource: "Let them eat social capital," Somers argues (2008). This is often the case when weak types of SI are applied to the lives of people at the margins and in situations with a sole focus on the outcome of SI, neglecting processes and relational dimensions. The constructive critique of the notions of social capital presented here provides a nuanced understanding of the same by exploring varied aspects of solidarity economy that Kudumbashree has been able to promote, at both the level of local communities and the state level of Kerala, with the social capital generated through collectivization as its base. In the social science tradition, social networks and social capital have often been employed to examine the impact of micro-level interaction on the democratic and economic performance of local communities, and even entire states. Accordingly, it has been argued that dense social networks and local trust building are causal preconditions for a well-functioning democracy and widespread economic prosperity (Putnam, 2000), and thus, social structures appear to be mere consequences of individual rational behavior.

Following the principles of a solidarity economy, we shall question the specific relations between actors and institutions involved in creating sustainable communities (Laville, 2010).

The institutional approach to social innovation applied in this chapter is inspired by the soft statism presented by several scholars who argue that it is imperative to consider social innovation in a policy context, emphasizing the government–association partnership (Moulaert et al., 2013). According to this perspective, relationships between civil society and state institutions are to be seen more as linkages than antagonisms (Hulgård, 2015). With the adoption of an institutional approach to social innovation, we have been able to reject choosing between structural and action-oriented approaches. The former claims that society primarily exists and changes through structural dynamics, while the latter holds social structures to be mere consequences of individual rational behavior. Instead, we question the specific relations between actors and institutions involved in the making of various forms of social capital and the (welfare) state policies confronting, surrounding and institutionalizing these actors. The micro–macro link becomes a question of specific institutional configurations among actors, institutions and policies instead of a priori conceptions of autonomous individuals or presocial structures (Healey, 1997: 55). Woolcock (2000) argues that the capacity of social groups to act collectively hinges on their engagement with formal institutions. Skocpol (1997a, 1997b) stresses that inclusive and "blossoming" civil societies have rarely existed in the United States without active federal government influence. Woolcock (2000) further reminds us that the narrowly defined sociological definition of social capital centered on networks within, between and beyond communities must not blind us to the institutional context within which these networks are embedded, especially the role of the state. Both in a Northern and a Southern perspective, an unadulterated bottom-up approach to social innovation and social capital fails to encompass the historical background and the evolution of the typical Nordic welfare state and the trajectory of "the Kerala welfare state", especially as it has been informed by Kudumbashree. Accordingly, the institutional discourse is based on the premise that SI must be regarded in policy contexts of changing institutional configurations. There is thus a case for top-down and state-driven initiatives when producing both bonds and bridges of social capital. The institutional perspective further holds that the need for social policy is neither withering away during the process of evolution nor merely for poor people. It is a cornerstone in the manufacture of both bonding and bridging social capital and thus strong types of social innovation.

The conceptual arguments by Wilson (1997) and Putnam (1993, 2000) hold true for Kudumbashree, where the high social capital generated through Kudumbashree collectives led to wealth creation, high prosperity and adaptability, in addition to meeting individual welfare needs of the people. Thus, the sustenance of social development in Kerala seems to have been significantly influenced by the prosperity generated out of the social capital base of Kudumbashree. Furthermore, Somers's (2008) argument of de-commodifying social capital points in the direction of institutionalization as a prerequisite for social capital to be effective beyond the mere existence of networks as resources, and is very well explained through the institutional mechanisms and processes within Kudumbashree. The Kudumbashree mechanism of NHGs, ADSs and CDS is well integrated into the LSG framework in the state and further at the government institutional level. The state-level mission is further operationalized at the district level to provide maximum state support to the functions of Kudumbashree. Thus, the institutionalization has both the government–association partnership and specific institutional mechanisms of its own in an integrated fashion. Such an institutional integration of Kudumbashree collectives with formal institutions further strengthens the argument by Woolcock (2000) that the capacity of such social groups to act collectively primarily hinges on their engagement with formal institutions. In this case, the institutionalization of social innovation is operationalized through the integral link the grassroots structures under Kudumbashree have been able to establish with the LSGIs as well as the state development planning process. Thus, the grassroots organizations of Kudumbashree, while maintaining their independent identity, could effectively foster a functional relationship with the state structures, thereby altering power relations in favor of the people, in general, and women, in particular.

Conclusion

People-centeredness in development is a way of altering the power relations between the structures and processes of development policy implementation. As stressed by Godin (2015), innovation, even stripped from the link to SI, was always related to the struggle for freedom by people and social movements. Only in more recent times did it become limited to activities narrowly related to the market economy and technological development. However, going back to the foundations of the concept in ancient Greece, when it embodied both concrete and abstract ways of imagining and experimenting with new ways of expanding the space for freedom, it had people's livelihood at the center. As argued in earlier sections, it is an approach aimed at rectifying the situation of distorted development by institutionally empowering the people. In the same vein, social innovation in its strong tradition ensures that meeting human needs is attempted not as outcomes to be achieved, but through processes of reconfiguration of social and political relations both within the community and with the structures of governance. Thus, transference or realignment of power toward the powerless is central to the political project of social innovation (Edmiston, 2016). The social capital foundations of Kudumbashree collectives, together with economic activities aimed at improving conditions for members from a solidarity economy perspective within a broader people-centric approach, provides a strong argument for what we would like to propose as PCSI. Finally, we argue that the three intrinsic pillars of PCSI, elaborated in the chapter as (1) willingness to engage in large scale combinations across multiple dimensions (relational), (2) emphasis on process dimension and (3) epistemic openness (Hulgård and Shajahan, 2013), are useful to examine the degree of PCSI and development discourses, in general. Kudumbashree networks of institutional structures are procedurally and structurally connected both with the bureaucracy at the level of district and state missions of poverty eradication and with the decentralized democratic system of LSGs. Furthermore, the market links of Kudumbashree microenterprises and other innovative livelihood and welfare initiatives establish the importance of the large-scale relational dimension of PCSI. Social and political empowerment, which is the bedrock of Kudumbashree, emphasizes the process dimension in social innovation as one significant aspect of PCSI. Last, PCSI presents a new epistemic openness which combines the political projects both of PCD, by putting the people at the center of development discourse, and of SI, by operationalizing the idea of altering power relations in favor of the people. Thus, PCSI is an approach which goes beyond the conceptions of social innovation as individual or small-group interventions to a broad-based, people-centered approach in order to address complex social developmental challenges through systemic and systematic intervention that is designed and delivered through a process of institutionalization.

Notes

1. LSGs are the lowest level of institutions of governance and came into being in 1994 in India with the 73rd and 74th Constitutional Amendments for giving constitutional status to these institutions in rural and urban contexts, respectively.
2. Kudumbashree has a locality-based approach, with NHGs formed as collectives of 20 or more women from socially and economically marginalized households in the immediate neighborhood as the lowest functional structure. Several such NHGs in the local electoral constituency, called a *ward*, are integrated into an ADS, which is further amalgamated at the LSG level as a CDS. (Kudumbashree, n.d.b). A CDS is a registered nonprofit society under relevant legislation in the state of Kerala.
3. Panchayats are the LSG institutions in rural areas. A three-tier panchayat system exists in rural areas, consisting of village panchayats at the lowest level and intermediate and district levels at the levels above.
4. India Human Development Report 2011: Towards Social Inclusion, Institute of Applied Manpower Research, Planning Commission, Government of India.
5. The first popularly elected communist government in Kerala in 1957 brought land reforms aimed at abolishing the feudal system in the state through a

legislative process amid strong opposition from the landed class. This gave tenancy rights to people who had worked on the land for generations under the feudal system.
6. SC/ST refers to Scheduled Caste and Scheduled Tribe which are historically marginalized communities in India and are notified in the Constitution of India. By virtue of their historical disadvantages, these communities have been extended positive discrimination by way of guaranteeing reservation in education, jobs and political representative system.

References

Ayob, N., Teasdale, S. and Fagan, K. (2016). "How Social Innovation Came to Be: Tracing the Evolution of a Contested Concept," *Journal of Social Policy*, 45(4).

Cohen, J. L. (1997). *American Civil Society Talk*. The National Commission on Civic Renewal. Working Paper #6. University of Maryland.

Coraggio, J. et al. (2015). "The Theory of Social Enterprise and Pluralism: Solidarity-Type Social Enterprises," in J-L. Laville, D. Young and P. Eynaud (eds.), *Civil Society, the Third Sector and Social Enterprise*. Abingdon: Routledge.

Cox, D. (1998). "Towards People-Centred Development: The Social Development Agenda and Social Work Education," *The Indian Journal of Social Work*, 59(1), pp. 513–530.

DiMaggio, P. J. and Powell, W. W. (eds.). (1991). *The New Institutionalism in Organizational Analysis*. Chicago: The University of Chicago Press.

Edmiston, D. (2016). *The (A)Politics of Social Innovation Policy in Europe: Implications for Sociostructural Change and Power Relations*. CRESSI Working Paper Series No. 32. Oxford: University of Oxford Press.

Franke, R. W. and Chassin, B. H. (1999). "Is the Kerala Model Sustainable? Lessons from the Past, Prospects for the Future," in M. A. Oommen (ed.), *Rethinking Development: Kerala's Development Experience*. New Delhi: Concept Publishing Company, vol. I.

Godin, B. (2015). *Innovation Contested. The Idea of Innovation over the Centuries*. New York: Routledge.

Habermas, J. (1996). *Between Facts and Norms*. Cambridge: Polity Press.

Healey, P. (1997). *Collaborative Planning—Shaping Places in Fragmented Societies*. London: Palgrave Macmillan.

Henton, D., Melville, J. and Walesh, K. (1997). *Grassroots Leaders for a New Economy—How Civic Entrepreneurs Are Building Prosperous Communities*. San Francisco: Jossey Bass Publishers.

Hulgård, L. (2015). "Differing Perspectives on Civil Society and State," in J-L. Laville, D. Young and P. Eynaud (eds.), *Civil Society, the Third Sector and Social Enterprise*. Abingdon: Routledge.

Hulgård, L. and Shajahan, P. K. (2013). "Social Innovation for People-Centred Development," in F. Moulaert, D. MacCallum, A. Mehmood and A. Hamdouch (eds.), *International Handbook on Social Innovation*. Cheltenham: Edward Elgar.

Jessop, B., Moulaert, F., Hulgård, L. and Hamdouch, A. (2013). "Social Innovation Research: A New Stage in Innovation Analysis?" in F. Moulaert, D. MacCallum, A. Mehmood and A. Hamdouch (eds.), *International Handbook on Social Innovation*. Cheltenham: Edward Elgar.

88   *P. K. Shajahan and Lars Hulgård*

Kudumbashree. (n.d.a). *The Mission Statement.* http://kudumbashree.org/index. php/pages/7.
Kudumbashree. (n.d.b). www.kudumbashree.org/pages/9.
Laville, J-L. (2010). "Solidarity Economy," in K. Hart, J-L. Laville and A. D. Cattani (eds.), *The Human Economy.* Cambridge: Polity Press.
MacCallum, D., Moulaert, F., Hillier, J. and Vicari Haddock, S. (2009). *Social Innovation and Territorial Development.* Farnham: Ashgate.
Mair, J. and Marti, I. (2009). "Entrepreneurship in and Around Institutional Voids: A Case Study from Bangladesh," *Journal of Business Venturing*, 24(5), pp. 419–435.
Moulaert, F., MacCallum, D., Mehmood, A. and Hamdouch, A. (eds.). (2013). *International Handbook on Social Innovation.* Cheltenham: Edward Elgar.
Putnam, R. D. (1993). *Making Democracy Work: Civic Tradition in Modern Italy.* Princeton: Princeton University Press.
Putnam, R. D. (2000). *Bowling Alone: The Collapse and Revival of American Community.* New York: Simon & Schuster.
Robins, S., Cornwall, A. and Von Lieres, B. (2008). "Rethinking Citizenship in the Post-Colony," *Third World Quarterly*, 29, pp. 1069–1086.
Salamon, L. M. and Anheier, H. K. (1998). "Social Origins of Civil Society: Explaining the Nonprofit Sector Cross-Nationally," *Voluntas: International Journal of Voluntary and Nonprofit Organizations*, 9(3), pp. 213–248.
Skocpol, T. (1997a). "Building Community Top-down or Bottom-up?" *The Brookings Review*, 15(4). http://www.brook.edu/pub/ review/oldtoc.htm# FAL97.
Skocpol, T. (1997b). *The New Majority. Toward a Popular Progressive Politics.* New Haven; London: Yale University Press.
Somers, M. R. (2008). *Genealogies of Citizenship.* Cambridge: Cambridge University Press.
Sukumar, M. (2012). "Engendering Local Development Plans: Gender Budgeting Initiative by a Local Government Institution in Kerala, India," *Universitas Forum*, 3(1).
United Nations. (1995, March 6–12). *Report of the World Summit for Social Development.* Copenhagen and New York: United Nations.
United Nations. (2003). *Implementation of the Outcome of the World Summit for Social Development and of the Twenty-Fourth Special Session of the General Assembly.* United Nations A7c 3/58L.9/Rev.1. New York: United Nations.
Wilson, P. (1997). "Building Social Capital: A Learning Agenda for the Twenty-First Century," *Urban Studies*, 34(5–6), pp. 745–760.
Woolcock, M. (2000). "Social Capital: The State of the Notion," in Jouko Kajanoja and Jussi Simpura (eds.), *Social Capital. Global and Local Perspectives.* Helsinki: Government Institute for Economic Research.

5 Ethos of Social Innovation
In Search of a Decolonizing Analysis

Adriane Vieira Ferrarini

Introduction

There have always been socially transformative and innovative processes, changing historically around causes, contexts, forms and protagonists. Social innovation was developed at the interface between different scientific disciplines and in the articulation of social actors and various operational arrangements. However, precisely these aspects linked to diversity, which are virtues of social innovation, can become a weakness. After all, who would be against social innovation? This trend for consensual and agnostic analyses of social innovation, in turn, leads to the risk of a fad or even its uncritical incorporation into instrumental rationality.

So how can one really identify what is social innovation? Is it really "innovation"? Is it really "social"? For what and for whom is innovation produced? Similar questions are found in the literature in the North (Moulaert et al., 2013; Bouchard, 2012), where studies on social innovation have been widely disseminated, but these have only recently begun to appear in sociological production on social innovation in Brazil—where studies in the fields of economics or technology predominate—and mainly in the form ofcases. Such studies provide an important contribution, but also give rise to critical reflections, especially necessary in the South.

Thinking about social innovation in the South, where social problems are more serious and the regulatory and emancipatory models have been imposed by its historically subordinated insertion into the global dynamic, requires an innovative approach to thinking about transformation and emancipation. The nefarious colonialist consequences were not extinguished with the end of colonization but have taken on new outlines as conservative ideas were recently strengthened in the globalized world. Even allegedly emancipatory practices often reproduce or are guided by contributions and recipes from developed countries and from international organizations, constituting neocolonialist positions and practices.

Hence, the need for a closer look into epistemology and methodology to produce qualifications and differentiations in order that the plurality and complexity that involve social innovation do not become eclecticism. For this, the chapter proposes a critical and decolonizing analysis of social innovation aimed at overcoming poverty in the South. The study was produced by articulating theoretical research in Brazilian and international literature on social innovation and the results of empirical research on public policies aimed at overcoming poverty in Brazil, later developed in the period from 2006 to 2016.

The chapter initially presents a field of controversies about social innovation related to its origin and inaccuracies. Subsequently, the concept of ethos is applied to social innovation, and epistemological, theoretical and methodological insights on the theme are discussed through its constituent elements (rationalities, intentionalities and intensities). Finally, the advances and limits of socially innovative practices for overcoming poverty in Brazil are analyzed, as well as some epistemological and ethical-political implications of the production of social innovation in the South.

Social Innovation: Controversies and Inaccuracies

In the last two decades, the theoretical debate and the emergence of experimentalism around what is conventionally called *social innovation* have spread significantly. Among the many causes of this dissemination, we highlight the growth of socio-environmental problems, the expansion of the involvement of multiple actors in social practices and the incorporation of interpretative and evaluative systems from the field of technology and economics in social intervention.

To the North, especially in countries of Europe, in the United States and in Canada, there is a vigorous production of knowledge about social innovation, resulting in the emergence of its theoretical-conceptual foundations. Although there are multiple definitions of social innovation, there is a recurrent link to the increase in the effectiveness of processes, services and products related to the satisfaction of social needs not met by the market, to social inclusion and to the training of disadvantaged segments, generating new and lasting solutions for social groups, communities or society, in general (Murray et al., 2010).

Social innovation is, essentially, an inter- and transdisciplinary phenomenon, since the processes and practices of innovative actors tend to cross boundaries between scientific disciplines and between regulatory frameworks of governmental structures. However, such virtues of social innovation can become its Achilles' heel. If all sectors can promote socially innovative actions, through multiple arrangements and from different perspectives, how can one identify what social innovation really is? The empirical plurality is added to the predominance of applied analyses of social innovation that may suggest a predominantly pragmatic character:

> The advantage of examining the pursuit of positive social change through an innovation lens is that this lens is agnostic about the sources of social value [. . .] social innovation transcends sectors,

levels of analysis, and methods to discover the processes—the strategies, tactics, and theories of change—that produce lasting impact.

(Phills et al., 2008: 37)

Even the discourses of political agencies refer to social innovation in a reductionist way, which does not reflect the advances made in current research programs and collective action practices (Jessop et al., 2013). From a pragmatic perspective, it is important that social innovation works well, but for what? And for whom?

Reflections of this analytic tendency are perceptible in the South. In Brazil, specifically, despite the growing interest in social innovation, it is surprising that it has little visibility in critical sociological debate and production. This does not mean the absence of socially innovative practices; on the contrary, they have spread in recent decades, especially produced within civil society and the state, but have been increasingly studied and researched in the field of business and in the form of cases.

Such studies provide undeniable contributions to the dissemination of social innovation and its virtues, but the absence of analytical depth contributes to the equalization of different practices among themselves or even to considering as social innovation practices with an ultimate purpose distinct from the production of social value. By attributing the label of social innovation to welfare practices—even in a modern guise (Ferrarini, 2016)—or for marketing purposes (Lacerda and Ferrarini, 2013), a new fad can be created which can de-characterize the transformative potential of social innovation. In this chapter, further analysis begins with a set of inaccuracies generated by the multiplicity of concepts and uses of social innovation. Such imprecisions were preliminarily identified, interpreted and grouped around three main controversies that pervade social innovation.

The first controversy concerns the fact that innovations in technology have emerged in the midst of modern science and have constituted the driving force of changes that expanded productivity and are continually generating harmful consequences for humans and nature. *Is it therefore legitimate and relevant to use innovation—applied to the social—to correct the problems that the use of innovation itself has created?* In this chapter, reflections on this controversy refer to the genesis of innovation. However, the analytical effort is not restricted to taking up the historiography of the concept but to understanding the epistemological and societal implications of the use of innovation in constituting the contemporary globalized world.

The second controversy concerns theoretical vagueness. The idea of social innovation is not new:

Other concepts that cover part of the same content have been used: for example, social invention (Weber, 1968 [1922]; Ogburn, 1922;

Coleman, 1970), social change, transformation or regulation (Weber, Durkheim), social diffusion through imitation of new practices (Tardé, 1999 [1893]) or changes in social practices.

(Jessop et al., 2013: 113)

According to not only the advance of analytical perspectives but also the simplistic use of the term, *social innovation* acquires different meanings and connotations, even to refer to a multiplicity of associated political practices, for example, to the rationalization of the social state and to the commodification of well-being (Moulaert, MacCallum and Hillier, as cited in Moulaert et al., 2013). So,*what is, in fact, the concept of transformation, change or social emancipation for which social innovation is proposed?*

Some will say that social innovation has no revolutionary claim andothers that palliative actions do not transform nor innovate and may even aggravate the social question. This is not a question of exhaustive theoretical analysis but of recognizing the substantive distinction between classical and contemporary conceptions, which allows us to identify the existence of fundamental distinctive meanings that orbit around social innovation from the epistemological dimension.

The third controversy involves methodological imprecision in research and evaluation processes of social innovation. *Given the multiplicity of contexts and subjects, what criteria are to be used? How should we adapt or build assessment systems and typological models, recognizing that they are traditionally based on certain naturalized references, coming from a hegemonic rationality (economic and political)?*

Such inaccuracies and controversies will guide further theoretical-epistemological and ethico-political exploration in order to understand, discriminate and qualify socially innovative practices. The notion of ethos is used as an analytical resource for this purpose.

Ethos of Social Innovation

Meta-theoretical reflections demand levels of analytical abstraction only possible when an abstracted reality was captured in its dynamics. Ethos—a theoretical notion with essentially practical interest—has appeared as a possibility of mediation between theory and empiricism for the analysis of social innovation because it encompasses the specificities of protagonists and contexts.

In the context of sociology and anthropology, *etho*sis used to describe the set of habits, customs and beliefs, or even behavioral traits—moral, social and affective characteristics—that define a person, group, community or nation. *Ethos*therefore takes on the meaning of social and cultural identity. In addition, it is a discursive construction of the subjects themselves, which occurs in interaction and in a given context

(Maingueneau, 2011). In the analysis of social innovation, ethos will be composed of three constituent elements, which are discussed in the next section: rationality, intentionality (ethical-political) and intensity (democratic). These elements have emerged from analyses and results of previous research seeking answers to the controversies and inaccuracies that involve social innovation.

Rationale Underlying Social Innovation

The common assumption involving social innovation as a solution to social problems hides the rationality that gives it meaning. After all, who defines what the social problem is? In the literature on social innovation, a "problem" or an "unmet need" is generally understood as the product of regulatory failures. But should not social innovation be the place for emancipation, and not for the restitution of regulatory mechanisms (and, therefore, maintainers) of a system which permanently generates inequalities and multiple social problems? Going forward, if innovation—in Latin, *innovation*—refers to an idea, method or object that is created and that bears little resemblance to previous standards, to what extent could social innovation as regulation represent something new?

This process of naturalization of concepts is not restricted to the conception of social problem and social innovation; it needs to be understood in the context of globalized Western capitalist modernity. Therefore, a historical incursion is necessary to elucidate the meanings of both the social question—and the multiple interpretations that social problems can acquire—and emancipation—as a framework to which the debate on social innovation and related concepts is linked.

Science and capitalism have become intertwined throughout recent history that constitutes modern society. Science played a fundamental role in the constitution of the world as we know it and in the search for the modern ideal of constituting a civilization free from barbarism and arbitrariness through rationalism (Ferrarini, 2008). Technological innovation was a great catalyst for changes in modernity. The technological advance made it possible to break with systems based on the subsistence economy by prioritizing the expanded production capable of a generating surplus (Polanyi, 2000). As wealth is historically inseparable from power, much of the surplus generated by the mass of workers, amid the current force correlations, was transferred to the ruling classes, in a repetitive and expansive metamorphosis (meticulously described by Marx) through which capital is manifested (Heilbroner, 1988, as cited in Ferrarini, 2008).

Capitalist accumulation is expressed through profit, which has the effect of regulating economic activity. Although profit found feverous support in modern economics as a neutral and exact science for the rigor of mathematical methods and abstracted from the moral dimension, a true revolution in religious customs and values was necessary for the legitimization of the ideology of capital (Heilbroner, 1988, as cited in Ferrarini, 2008). The "de(moralization)" of economic activity advanced decisively in the late 19th century with (1) the utilitarian philosophy, (2) Lionel Robbins's assertion (1945) about the economy as a relation between ends and scarce resources (Abramovay, 2004; Raud-Mattedi, 2005; Coraggio, 2009) and (3) the theory of rational choice. For the latter, "individuals, taken as units of analysis and positioned on the basis of social dynamics, act rationally, ponder means and ends in favor of self-interests, and maximize their individual preferences" (Gaiger and Corrêa, 2011: 37).

Such economic rationality is called "formal" by Polanyi, differently from Aristotle's "substantive" conception, in which the economy refers to the care of the home or the management of life. The modern capitalist economy disengaged itself from the purpose of satisfying human needs, reproducing life or maximizing welfare and began operating at a level of abstraction aimed at maximizing capital. This aporia is the social question itself, defined as the inequalities generated by the relation between capital versus labor and the forms of resistance built by the workers (Castel, 1998; Iamamoto, 2001).

Epistemologically, the system generated a split between economic and social dimensions with major societal implications: not only never before has so much wealth been produced in the world but also never so much poverty and global inequality. The number of hungry people in the world is growing, reaching 821 million in 2017 or one in every nine people (FAO, IFAD, UNICEF, WFP and WHO, 2018). Latin America, a continent which participates as a dependent and subordinate in the global economic race, presents the highest levels of inequality, violence and corruption in the world.

This is because the history of contemporary capitalist society is the history of a European localism that was successfully globalized by colonizing processes based on the arbitrary and violent imposition of modern ideas and on science as the only valid knowledge. This imposition meant the invalidation and decimation of knowledge and cultures of the sociological South, which have come to be considered marginal, local, savage or primitive and therefore not credible.

> If the process of exclusion is large within a given culture, it is even greater among cultures. A culture that has a narrow conception of itself tends to have an even narrower conception of the others.
>
> (Williams, as cited in Santos, 2000: 18)

Numerous social and economic indicators denounce this paradox of modernity: science produced the technical conditions for the fulfillment of the modern ideal of building an emancipated civilization free from barbarism, blind submission to religious beliefs, and servile obedience to monarchs, but it did not build the moral conditions for this. The contradiction amonguniversalist, humanist and emancipatory principles of modernity and rationalist and colonialist foundations and methods has remained invisible for centuries under the veil of Cartesian-positivist rationality—and still underlies the global dynamics of hegemonic development.

This is why the epistemological debate is necessary. For Santos (2005), colonialism—an unequal relationship between North and South—is the epistemological dimension of the social question and involves knowledge. Colonialism adds up to capitalism—the unequal relationship between capital and labor—as the societal dimension of the social question, which encompasses practices. Consequently, the analysis of the construction of alternatives to the contemporary social question also requires an epistemological bias. After all, even critical theory, in its quest for social emancipation, failed to overcome the gaps caused by determinism, materialism, and objectivism (Santos, 2003):

> The reduction of modern emancipation to the cognitive-instrumental rationality of science and the reduction of modern regulation to the market principle, encouraged by the conversion of science into the main productive force, constitute the determining conditions of the historical process that led emancipation to surrender to regulation . . . Emancipation ceased to be the other of regulation to become its double.
>
> (Santos, 2000: 56)

Social innovation, as a contemporary version that brings together concepts and practices aimed at social transformation and emancipation (Ferrarini, 2016), also involves the influence of the "commodification" and "scientificization" of the world (Santos, 2000). Even socially innovative approaches—originally developed by the third sector (social economy organizations, solidarity movements, civil society organizations, local communities, etc.)—are increasingly used as catalysts for market innovations (Jessop et al., 2013):

> It should supplement innovation and competitiveness dynamics in the global competitive economy in which the "creative destruction" process engendered by rapid technological change and the globalization of the economy requires "social measures" in order to gild the bitter pill of the problems it bears (de-industrialization and investment offshoring, structural loss of jobs, growing inequalities, etc.). This discourse has been translated into new policy approaches in which the progressive privatization of successive layers of public services (health, housing, education, social insurance, pension systems, etc.)

and the substitution of competitive logics for collective ones have created new markets and Business opportunities for the private sector.

(Jessop et al., 2013: 121)

The reduction of the functions of the welfare state leads to the aggra-
vation of the social question, an opposite effect to that sought by social
innovation. Or, under formal economic rationality, social innovation can
be utilized to reverse the damage produced by the instrumental use of
innovation itself—in its origin in the technological field. Therefore, even
if a certain action is worth innovative features or procedures, could it be
considered social innovation if it is focused on maximizing profits and
not on well-being? Could practices conceived from a formalist economic
perspective be considered social innovation? All? None? Some? What are
the limits?

Already a substantivist perspective, geared to a human development and
social emancipation paradigm, social innovation does not care about business innovation but about recognition of the diversity of human needs that
must be met for human development to materialize (Jessop et al., 2013).

It should be noted that economic rationality (formal or substantive)
is generally underpinned by social innovation. This explains many of
the misgivings about social innovation and, specifically in the Brazilian
context, labels it—perhaps at an early stage—as a cosmetic solution for
market-oriented practices. In this sense, economic rationality becomes a
watershed in the analysis of socially innovative practices, although there
is no way of stating whether it constitutes an absolute criterion for dis-
carding any and all innovation produced by the market, in any context.
This topic will still receive inputs in the next section.

Ethical-Political Intent

The second element of the ethos of social innovation is ethical-political
intentionality—resulting from the rationality implemented—and seeks to
clarify two relevant questions regarding the production of social innovation: What is innovation produced for? And for whom? Intentionality is
linked to the environment in which social innovation is produced (mercantile, social or state) and to the way in which the product is understood
and appropriated. Although it is desirable that social innovation occurs
in the articulation between different social actors and composes new
synergies, the individualities and identities are not completely diluted in
the collective. The analysis is always contextual. State and society are
complementary and interdependent (Skocpol, 1996), but they can also
be opposites since social innovation in the third sector usually happens
outside institutions and often against them (André and Abreu, 2006).

The context of the civil society, represented by social movements
and multiple forms of organizations—formal or informal—and linked

to various social causes, is a genuine *locus*of socially innovative actions in the struggles historically fought against forms of oppression and violation of rights. Often the production of social values in itself is more strictly of interest to civil society. In general, it leads to entrepreneurship from the bottom up, driven by necessity and with scarce resources and local and traditional knowledge, characteristics that often neglect social innovation, according to canonical conceptions (Ferrarini, 2016). However, civil society is also plural and contradictory; it can both constitute new paradigms of social emancipation, and forms of social regulation, in close articulation with state regulation (Santos, 1995).

The commercial business environment would create the greatest challenges for the production of social innovation because of its immersion in a mercantile rationality (already mentioned) whose key factor for increasing competitiveness is the externalization of social costs. Often business motivations for the development of social innovation are derived from public pressures and aim at minimizing the social losses of their own interventions or at improving the image of their brands in the market (Santos, 2002; Mészáros, 2002; Soares, 2004). There are progressive business segments, but the desire to innovate socially, to some extent, will be subject to the imperative of profits. On one hand, this does not invalidate the possibility of coproducing social innovation, even because there are profit margins that can finance the work of many social organizations for the creation of social value, such as poverty reduction, social justice, access to drinking water and other benefits related to collective benefits (Murray et al., 2010).On the other hand, there is the epistemological contradiction of the economic rationality already discussed.

As for the state context, innovation is associated with the transformation of public management structures as a way of including dominated interests, in addition to the traditional form of representation as well as the ability to generate synergistic processes between state institutions and civil society organizations. The state plays a prominent role in strengthening its intermediary function, without calling the centrality to itself, but guaranteeing democratic spaces of formation, discussion and deliberation guided by the principle of social justice. From this perspective, it is characterized as a state that facilitates social processes (Lacerda and Ferrarini, 2013). However, in the state there are also corporatist interests and the instrumental use of social innovation, where raising votes for governors is the equivalent of profiting from business.

In addition to the ethos of each social group, it should be emphasized that an environment must contain technical, social and behavioral aspects for social innovation, which involve ability to adapt, learn and change through creativity, questioning mental models, common vision and cultural diversity, tolerance of the risk of innovating without being penalized and democracy through the active participation of citizens (André and Abreu, 2006).

In the analysis of social innovation, although it does not consider the identity in a static and definitive form, as the practices transform the subjects that transform practices again(Hall, 2005), each individual or social group has prerogatives that impose operational formats, restrictions and priorities. The sectors also interact and transform each other, to a lesser or greater degree, in different contexts and times. Therefore, the analysis of the capacity for transformation, resilience or even maintenance of the status quo (changing to not change) acquires meaning in the context and dynamics of social life. Although some environments, due to their rationality and intentionality, are more favorable to social innovation, the use of criteria—or even of indicators—capable of measuring the intensity of innovation is complementary to rationality and intentionality in the attempt to discriminate and qualify the social innovation.

Level of Democracy in Social Innovation

The level of democracy involves the way social value is produced. It seeks to highlight the process of development of social innovation, which is characterized as the capacity to promote empowerment and alteration of power correlations. For a long time, it mattered more that the innovations generated results. The risk was that the process could be top-down in paternalistic workplaces, without links to the power structures of society. In such cases, even with community benefits, many social organizations or enterprises would not be distinguished from conventional ones in their daily practices (Hulgård and Ferrarini, 2010) and might even reinforce old power structures, making real change impossible (André and Abreu, 2006).

Defined as a process, social innovation differs from the dominant model of "closed innovation" (based on control of ideas and environment) and acquires contours similar to open innovation in which many subjects are intentionally involved. The result is the collaboration of many actors and tends to be more effective, representing a paradigm shift (Chesbrough, 2006).

Radicalization of democracy means opening up management spaces in which popular participation has a high potential to reframe the public sphere and civil society conceptions. Social innovation therefore suggests a migration from representative democracy to deliberative democracy, in which access to information, critical thinking and community protagonism make it possible to intervene in the social field. The construction of a deliberative public sphere fights rooted welfare traditions by empowering local social actors. Respect for one's neighbor, supported by the principle of social justice, is found within this radicalized democracy:

> The deliberative model is a substantive and not merely procedural conception of democracy, involving values such as egalitarianism and social justice. The decision-making process is not to choose

between alternatives, but to generate new alternatives, which would allow greater social innovation. Finally, it is expected that the decisions thus made will provide greater redistributive justice and be more sustainable.

(Fleury, 2004: 5)

Therefore, the success of the process of producing social innovation would be linked to levels of participation. In this text, four levels are suggested based on Carvalho (1995), which contribute to distinguishing between greater or lesser degrees of contribution to the practice of self-government itself.

Participatory democracy is the least advanced kind of self-governing organization. Its main objective is to force the community's problems to be considered at the state or national level. In this system, community members elect representatives as delegates at meetings held to advocate their interests in common spaces. The difficulty of this mode of organization is the possible gap between the demands of the delegate and the community.

Co-determination is the second mode of the self-governance *continuum*. In this case, the group cohesion element is the central figure of the leader and the formal power of the organization is exercised by the assembly, which prescribes the internal rules of the organization and the actions to be taken.

The third type of self-governance is the community of interests, in which all lead. Due to the high level of common interests, anyone can speak for the group. This type of community seeks to influence society, usually through the dynamics of splitting their unity into basic subunits. Generally, members derive from the same environment or community, joined together by a very strong and concrete common denominator. When the organization reaches this point, there is now a big difference: the decision-making is no longer taken by direct vote, which is decided by a simple majority, but by consensus. This ensures that everyone has a voice and gives the minority the power to veto.

The last and most favorable type of self-governance is self-management, in which all workers in a particular enterprise or actors in a particular community become leaders. Elements of other models are found in self-management. In this case, anyone can vote and become a leader, considering their skills and the demands to be resolved.

The definition of different types of participation, in conjunction with a significant number of converging efforts in the field of solidarity economy (Gaiger, 2016), can inspire the production of levels of democracy and deepening governance processes in social enterprises—empirical fields commonly recognized as socially innovative. The level of democracy—together with other reflections catalyzed by the notion of ethos—aims to contribute elements for the analysis of socially innovative practices. In this chapter, an analysis of practices aimed at overcoming poverty in the South is undertaken.

Social Innovation in Overcoming Poverty in the South: Decolonizing Practices and Knowledge

Considering the emergence of the idea of social innovation in the North, the first question to be asked is whether it would be reasonable to think about social innovation in the South. Within the scope of Ecosol (Solidarity and Cooperative Economy Research Group)/Unisinos, the analytical treatment given to social innovation has been the same as that of other concepts such as entrepreneurship, capital, technology and economy. In all these cases, when the "social" attribute is added, there is the understanding that concepts can be reappropriated by another rationality and logic, given the semantic plurality they welcome as social and historical constructions. However, there is no consensus in this regard in Brazil.

The case of social entrepreneurship is the precursor of this debate in the Ecosol Group and can serve as a base due to its strong link with social innovation. In Brazil it is common to have the type of entrepreneurship developed from the bottom up, with scarce resources, usually without technological innovation and a substantive economic rationality. While these characteristics pluralize and enrich the very concept of entrepreneurship, they increase the possibilities of legitimization and inclusion of these entrepreneurs, who would be disqualified as such in the light of hegemonic theories.

The same is true of social innovation. There are many processes of social innovation that are invisible due to socioeconomic, ethnic and regional diversity but, above all, to the condition of societal and epistemological subordination of socially innovative groups. Therefore, the epistemological debate aboutsocial innovation is essential in the South. Many criticisms of social innovation show that failure attributed to the alternatives also expresses the failure of the knowledge that guided them since knowledge and practices are indissociable:

> The poverty of experience is not the expression of a lack, but rather the expression of arrogance, the arrogance of not wanting to see, much less value the experience that surrounds us, just because it is outside the reason we can identify and value it.
>
> (Santos, 2003: 742)

In the case of practices aimed at overcoming poverty—the cruelest and most urgent expression of the social question in the South, and therefore a priority—one must avoid "the poverty of studies on poverty" (Demo, 2003). "The materiality of poverty can never be relegated, but even less can one leave aside the political maneuver involved and which is at the heart of the fabrication of misery" (Demo, 2003: 41). "The shortening of poverty to its material basis thus signifies enormous political poverty . . . because they are faces of the same whole" (p. 43).

Poverty in the South is not limited to insufficient income since economic, social, political and cultural dimensions are mutually related to one another, giving feedback and potentializing its causes and effects (Ferrarini, 2011). Among the countries of the South, Brazil can be considered a very complex and sui generiscase. Brazil is the most emblematic example of extreme and persistent inequality. In 2017, it ranked as the 10th-most unequal country in the world, close to very poor countries[1] and simultaneously ranked eighth in the world economic ranking, along with the largest economies in the world (according to International Monetary Fund data).[2] In addition, Brazil has a population of about 208 million inhabitants and a continental dimension, with regions significantly different from each other, which generates great internal inequalities. It is also worth noting that the political-institutional system is inherited from centuries of colonization and long periods of dictatorship, reproducing authoritarian and patrimonial governments, typical of the Latin American political culture. In Brazil, there was no classic trajectory of the expansion of rights (Marshall, 1967) because social rights came before civil and political rights, having been "granted" as benefits instead of being citizen conquests (Carvalho, 2001).

The Brazilian welfare state was implemented late and incompletely, behaving historically as a simulacrum of the European welfare state (Draibe, 1989; Ivo, 2001; Bresser-Pereira, 2010). Thus, the traditional forms of primary social protection have been weakened or de-characterized, without being replaced by effective secondary systems. Inequalities and authoritarianism create ruptures in the social fabric due to the difficulty of constructing a citizen identity and the feeling of social belonging.

Significant innovations in Brazilian social welfare originate in the so-called Citizen Constitution of 1988—a historical landmark at the beginning of reforms in the sense of expanding and democratizing social policies. With regard to social assistance, a significant advance was the change in the paradigm of social protection, where the beneficiary became a subject of rights and no longer a "beggar". However, the cycle of governments self-named as popular and that materialized and furthered some constitutional achievements began in 2000, having played a more significant role in the provision of essential goods and services through universal policies. In this period, there was a deep synergy between social movements and the state, which welcomed popular demands in the governmental public agenda and created innovative policies and programs in many different fields.

It is in this context that the Bolsa Família Program was created (in 2003) to address poverty in Brazil. The Bolsa Família is the largest income transfer programs in the world, with a quarter of the Brazilian population living under its coverage until 2017 (more than 50 million people) and which became world famous for promoting significant improvements and unprecedented social indicators, being replicated in several countries around the world. Brazilian poverty is historical, persistent, multigenerational and structural. In addition, poverty in Brazil refers not only to those who are losing rights, goods or services but to those who have never had or for whom they have been very precarious, undermining the physical and moral dignity of significant portions of the population. Therefore, income transfer could not be restricted to material contribution. Income is conditional on access to children's health and education, coupled with a set of social-welfare and intersectoral services (housing, sanitation, health, etc.).

The first decade and a half of the 2000s was a period marked by economic growth and optimism, which, alongside policies and programs, had a share of influence in improving social indicators. The year 2015 marked the fourth consecutive election of the left-wing Workers' Party and the sudden explosion of an overwhelming economic recession, accompanied by a serious political and institutional crisis. Since then, scandals and corruption schemes have been unveiled almost daily; they affect all powers and almost all political parties and government structures. Society is seen naked and reflected in the mirror of corruption, because it is embedded in a historically patrimonial, clientelistic and authoritarian social system, being product and producer—since government and society are not imperviously separate entities. Since the impeachment of President Rousseff in 2016, there have been cuts in social spending and policies. However, critical analysis of actions for overcoming poverty does not allow Manichean or immediatist inferences. The balance of the last "three golden decades of Brazilian citizenship" reveals that, without denying the advances already mentioned, certain fundamental and structural changes have not been geared toward the emancipatory and innovative defeat of poverty.

It will not be possible here to perform a detailed analysis of the actions for overcoming poverty through the Bolsa Família, but the main social innovations produced and their limitations will be highlighted. The Bolsa Famíliacan be considered innovative fundamentally for its design and comprehensiveness. It decentralized social protection actions in the communities, emphasized participation by entities active in the territories, advocated intersectorality, envisaged coordination among several states, unified access to income with other services and rights, emphasized the education of children and restored dignified access to food. The fact that in 2015 Brazil no longer figured on the Hunger Map indicated this advance, which was lost in 2017. A set of complex and integrated planning and social control instruments is also highlighted.

Regarding the limitations of the implementation of socially innovative processes and products, it is considered that the investment in tangible and intangible assets was insufficient. Education has achieved unprecedented success in including poor and non-white youth in higher education, but it still falls far short of repressed demand. The Bolsa Famíliasignificantly increased access and permanence in school of poor children and young people but failed to improve the overall quality of primary and second-ary education, which is among the worst in the world. Poverty cannot be overcome or inequality reduced without education, and there is also no development without education! Also noteworthy is the massive and unprecedented offer of vocational education courses to the most vulner-able populations, in articulation with the Bolsa FamíliaProgram, with a view to enabling social and productive inclusion. This initiative was innovative when proposing cross-pollination between social and eco-nomic policies, but no adequate economic opportunities were created for the public because the development matrix did not change. There was also no intersectoral articulation of policies capable of enabling the social and economic inclusion of the poorest, since policy managers and operators were not prepared to act systemically, as advocated by the policy, and the allocation model of resources and targets remained sec-torally fragmented. Consequently, innovations were identified in plan-ning but with structural limits on implementation at the municipal and local level.

With regard to bottom-up initiatives spearheaded by civil society, the solidarity economy is noteworthy. It emerged as a way of coping with unemployment but went on to acquire an emancipatory political sense and propositional character in the circumstances existing in Brazil. Solidarity economic enterprises are promoted by the workers themselves through self-management, socialization of the means of production, cooperation and sustainability. Its substantive economic rationality, internal and external level of participation and popular protagonism can make solidarity economy a case of high-intensity social innovation. How-ever, formal evaluation of solidarity economy efficiency is controversial because formal parameters and indicators do not pick up its economic effects, which use atypical combinations of redistribution, domesticity, market and reciprocity (Polanyi, 1977). The parameters also fail to pick up the "extra-economic" effects (seen in childcare, improving mental health, reduction of violence and social vulnerability, etc.).

The analysis of social innovation in overcoming poverty in Brazil in the light of the elements of ethos is hard to imagine in terms of economic rationality, that is, the possibility of overcoming poverty in the South from an economic and political substantive perspective, be it in experi-ences of civil society or in certain policies to encourage local development processes and social and solidarity economy. After all, the history of cap-italist development under the aegis of the market economy and democ-racy in its liberal representative version is the history itself of inequality and poverty imposed on the South.

With regard to ethical-political intentions, all stakeholders are welcome and necessary to strengthen the Brazilian society eroded by abysmal inequality, political anomie and the institutional disbelief plaguing the country today. However, many of the structures and public resources, under both right- and left-wing governments, continued to be treated as private property through corruption strategies, a clear modern reproduction of the old oligarchic and patrimonial forms. The brief dream of a real social security state closed its cycles and showed that the design of good social programs and the improvement of circumstantial indicators are insufficient; it is necessary to have a systemic vision and action, political will and inclusive economic outlook.

As for the market, some of the big companies—considered socially innovative—are involved in corruption scandals. Moreover, the banks—also recognized for social innovation promoted through their foundations—have never before made so much profit, even in the middle of the severe economic crisis. They take large amounts with one hand and donate crumbs with the other. Even assuming that there is social innovation in their practices, there is a need to critically spell out the criteria, dynamics and impacts in order to identify whether it can be considered social innovation and to evaluate the characteristics and the limits of innovation.

On the other hand, civil society continues to innovate because it has always needed to do so in order to survive without the support of their citizenship rights. The timing is intriguing because, while Brazilian society is experiencing an unprecedented escalation of anomie and urban violence, there is also a significant growth of associative initiatives and social innovation under the most diverse reciprocal arrangements, targeting multiple causes (environmental, ethical consumption, production, social and ethnic-racial inclusion, etc.). In abysmally unequal societies, it is understandable that different, and even contradictory, processes coexist or that the explanations about them are also still insufficient, given the permanent social instability. There is no specific public policy for social innovation in Brazil as yet, but as in the solidarity economy, the government agenda is being called on to include these issues.

Finally, on a par with an increased level of democracy, the already-mentioned activation of citizenship has generated fluid, heterogeneous and pulsating democratic initiatives. However, in Brazil there is no strong tradition of citizen participation, which demonstrates the relevance of these processes for strengthening society. As for sectoral public policies, even in the "golden decades" they generally did not achieve more effective participatory formats, reinforcing the idea of passive recipients of services.

In the case of the Bolsa Família, despite significant changes regarding the notion of social welfare as a right and a set of services offered, this led partly to insertion by consumption. The absence of participatory formats is the main limitation for the development of public awareness through public policies. For the poor population of the South, resources and government services need to be a pedagogical pretext for the activation of citizenship, not an end in themselves (Ferrarini, 2008).

Overcoming poverty in the South requires not only protective actions or compensation but also emancipation. That is, even in a perspective that intends to be decolonizing, the state cannot fail to fulfill its role in the delivery of essential services but needs to recognize the claims of citizenship and social innovation produced by society, as well as to stimulate and provide institutional support for these innovations. Instituted and instituting processes are not mutually exclusive but complementary to the creation of alternatives to guarantee rights and resources.

Final Considerations

Although many people have reservations about social innovation due to its plural character, studies and research have shown that it contributes to imagining, planning and building collectively future visions and strategies for improving quality of life through methods and epistemologies challenging conventional and outdated forms of intervention. However, commitment to transformation through solidarity and the appreciation of multiculturalism and sustainability in development are principles of social innovation that show that it is far from being a neutral field or restricted to the pragmatic application of formulas.

For this reason, theoretical, epistemological, ethical and political controversies emerge and raise thought-provoking reflections. Rather than demarcating rigid boundaries, the use of the notion of ethos as a source for the critical and decolonizing analysis of social innovation sought to contribute to the establishment of clearer permeability zones and—it might as well be said—permeability zones that are socially and cognitively fairer. This does not rule out groups from the act of producing social innovation; on the contrary;it aims to elucidate this diversity and contribute to the measurement of intensity and impact because not everything is social innovation and not all social innovation is equal. Nor does the epistemological debate aim to be Manichean and exclusionary but assign complexity to the analysis of social innovation, which does not mean that it will not provide grounds to dismiss innovations that, ultimately, do not turn to the social.

In the search for differences, the identification of the underlying rationality can contribute to preventing the risk that social innovation, on a larger scale, will reproduce the very social problems that it seeks to overcome. The primacy of the social over the economic—in a clear break with modern instrumental economics—links social innovation, epistemologically, to a substantive rationality.

However, local arrangements are always complex and the ethical and political intentionality of social innovation must be understood in the dynamics of social life. That is why the environment and characteristics of each sector and each social actor who innovates need to be considered. If the increasing interconnection among thestate, the market and civil society is clear, it is also true that these sectors have conditions, ideals and different resources thatmay be concurrent, complementary, competing or contradictory.

The level of democracy, in turn, highlights the importance of the process of social innovation through the quality of participation, empowerment of the individuals involved and the change in power relations. In this sense, the migration of representative democracy to more participatory forms is desirable, and ultimately, it will move the power actions of the current state or private structures to the organized public sphere.

If the critical epistemological debate about social innovation has been shown to be necessary in the North, it is essential in the South. Due to the colonial process of Westernization of the world, social innovation in the South is not restricted to solving social problems but to retrieving knowledge and building power since social justice in this context requires cognitive justice. Therefore, participation is essential in both the process and the results (Lacerda and Ferrarini, 2013) with the prerogative of triggering more or less intense changes in power relations (André and Abreu, 2006), establishing autonomy in the population involved and providing sustainability of the results (Ferrarini, 2008). The epistemological dimension also proved necessary for the recognition and valuation of innovative efforts and capabilities in seemingly anachronistic or disqualified settings that require rationality and substantive concepts able to explain and measure the multiple forms of plural economy and direct participation.

Taking into account that the field of social innovation is still undergoing systematization and is not much discussed in Brazil, this chapter does not aim to produce conclusive statements, but share reflections and experiences from typical realities of extreme material and immaterial inequalities. The chapter is also intended to formulate new questions in order to contribute to the North–South dialogue and to complex analyses. Despite the known differences between North and South, the study allows one to grasp that there are also many similarities when the genuine principles and objectives of social innovation are considered since, in a globalized world (and in the systemic vision required for innovation), problems are interconnected—and solutions as well. Therefore, the challenge to differentiate without excluding (or even to include without making it equal) has proved exciting and stimulating for further research and analysis with a view to encouraging socially engaged practices and to enhancing epistemologies that have historically been rendered invisible.

Notes

1. Data from the Human Development Report (HDR), prepared by the United Nations in 2017.
2. Available in www.imf.org/external/datamapper/datasets/weo.

References

Abramovay, R. (2004). "Entre Deus e o Diabo: Mercados e Interação Humana nas Ciências Sociais," *Tempo Social*, 16(2), pp. 35–64.

André, I. and Abreu, A. (2006). "Dimensões e Espaços da Inovação Social," *Finisterra*, 41(81), pp. 121–141.

Bouchard, M. (2012). "Social Innovation, an Analytical Grid for Understanding the Social Economy: The Example of the Québec Housing Sector," *Service Business Journal*, 6(1), pp. 47–59.

Bresser-Pereira, L. C. (2010). "A Construção Política do Estado," *Lua Nova*, 81, pp. 117–146.

Carvalho, J. (2001). *Cidadania No Brasil: O Longo Caminho*. Rio de Janeiro: Civilização Brasileira.

Carvalho, N. V. (1995). *Autogestão: O Nascimento das ONGs*. Brasiliense: São Paulo.

Castel, R. (1998).*As Metamorfoses da Questão Social: Uma Crônica do Salário*. Rio de Janeiro: Vozes.

Chesbrough, H. (2006). *Open Innovation: Researching a New Paradigm*. Oxford: Oxford University Press, Comeaus.

Coleman, J. (1970). "Social Inventions," *Social Forces*, 49(2), pp. 163–173.

Coraggio, J. (ed.). (2009).*¿Que és lo Económico? Materiales para un Debate Necesario Contra el Fatalismo*. Buenos Aires: Ciccus.

Demo, P. (2003). *Pobreza da Pobreza*. Rio de Janeiro: Vozes.

Draibe, S. (1989). "As Políticas Sociais do Regime Militar Brasileiro: 1964–84," in G. Soares and M. D'araújo (eds.),*21 Anos de Regime Militar: Balanços e Perspectivas*. Rio de Janeiro: FGV Editora, pp. 271–309.

FAO, IFAD, UNICEF, WFP and WHO. (2018). *The State of Food Security and Nutrition in the World 2018. Building Climate Resilience for Food Security and Nutrition*. Rome: FAO.

Ferrarini, A. (2008). *Pobreza: Possibilidades de Construção de Políticas Emancipatórias*. São Leopoldo: Oikos.

Ferrarini, A. (2011). "Multidimensionalidade da Pobreza e a Integração de Políticas: Concepções e Metodologias para o Desenvolvimento Social," *Caderno de Pesquisa Interdisciplinar em Ciências Humanas*, 12(101), pp. 48–72.

Ferrarini, A. (2016). "O *Ethos* da Inovação Social: Implicações Ético-Políticas para o Estudo de Práticas Produzidas em Diferentes Ambientes," *Revista Contemporânea*, 6(2), pp. 477–466.

Fleury, S. (2004). *Democracia com exclusão e desigualdade. Report prepared for the United Nations Development Programme (UNDP) about democracy in Latin America, Brasília*. Available in: http://app.ebape.fgv.br/comum/arq/PNUDsoniafleury.pdf (last accessed 6 June 2019).

Gaiger, L. (2016). *Empreendimentos de Economia Social e Solidária: Um Estudo em Perspectiva Internacional. Projeto de Pesquisa*. São Leopoldo: Unisinos.

Gaiger, L. and Corrêa, A. (2011). "O Diferencial do Empreendedorismo Solidário," *Revista Ciências Sociais Unisinos*, 47(1), pp. 34–43.

Hall, S. (2005).*A Identidade Cultura na Pós-Modernidade*. Rio de Janeiro: DP&A.

Hulgård, L. and Ferrarini, A. (2010). "Inovação Social: Rumo a uma Mudança Experimental na Política Pública?" *Revista Ciências Sociais Unisinos*, 46(2), pp. 256–263.

Iamamoto, M. (2001). "A Questão Social no Capitalismo," *Revista Temporalis*, 2(3). Brasília: ABEPSS.

Ivo, A. (2001). *Metamorfoses da Questão Democrática: Governabilidade e Pobreza*. Buenos Aires: CLACSO.

Jessop, B., Moulaert, F., Hulgård, L. and Hamdouch, A. (2013). "Social Innovation Research: A New Stage in Innovation Analysis?" in F. Moulaert, D. Mac-Callum, A. Mehmood and A. Hamdouch (eds.), *The International Handbook of Social Innovation*. Cheltenham: Edward Elgar.

Lacerda, L. and Ferrarini, A. (2013). "Inovação social ou Compensação? Reflexões Acerca das Práticas Corporativas," *Polis*, 35(1), pp. 1–16.

Maingueneau, D. (2011). "A Propósito do *Ethos*," in A. Motta and L. Salgado (eds.),*Ethos discursivo*. São Paulo: Contexto, pp. 11–30.

Marshall, T. (1967). *Cidadania, Classe Social e Status*. Rio de Janeiro: Zahar Editores.

Mészáros, I. (2002). *Para Além do Capital*. Campinas: Editora da Unicamp.

Moulaert, F., MacCallum, D., Mehmood, A. and Hamdouch, A. (2013). The International Handbook of Social Innovation. Cheltenham: Edward Elgar.

Murray, R., Caulier-Grice, J. and Mulgan, G. (2010). *The Open Book of Social Innovation*. London: NESTA, The Young Foundation. www.nesta.org.uk/sites/default/files/the_open_book_of_social_innovation.pdf (Accessed on 21 April 2017).

Ogburn, W. F. (1922). *Social Change with Respect to Culture and Original Nature*. New York: B. W. Huebsch.

Phills, J., Deiglmeier, K. and Miller, D. (2008). *Rediscovering Social Innovation*. Stanford: Stanford Social Innovation Review, Fall. www.ssireview.org/articles/entry/rediscovering_social_innovation/ (Accessed on10 April 2017).

Polanyi, K. (1977). *The Livelihood of Man*. New York: Academic Press.

Polanyi, K. (2000) [1944]. *A Grande Transformação: As Origens da Nossa Época*. Rio de Janeiro: Campus.

Raud-Mattedi, C. (2005). "Análise Crítica da Sociologia Econômica de Mark Granovetter: Os Limites de uma Leitura do Mercado em Termos de Redes e Imbricação," *Política & Sociedade*, 6(1), pp. 59–82.

Robbins, L. (1945).*An Essay on the Nature and Significance of Economic Science*. London: Macmillanand Co. Limited.

Santos, B. (1995). "Sociedade-Providência ou Autoritarismo Social?" *Revista Crítica de Ciências Sociais*, 42. Maio. www.boaventuradesousasantos.pt/media/pdfs/Sociedade_Providencia_ou_Autoritarismo_Social_RCCS42.PDF (Accessed on 21 April 2017).

Santos, B. (ed.). (2000).*A Crítica da Razão Indolente—Contra o Desperdício da Experiência. Para um Novo Senso Comum: A Ciência, o Direito e a Política na Transição Paradigmática*. São Paulo: Cortez, vol. 1.

Santos, B. (ed.). (2002). *Produzir para Viver: Os Caminhos da Produção Não Capitalista*. Rio de Janeiro: Civilização Brasileira.

Santos, B. (ed.). (2003). *Conhecimento Prudente para uma Vida Decente: Um Discurso sobre as Ciências Revisitado.* Lisboa: Afrontamento.

Santos, B. (2005). *Classroom Notes.* Universidade de Coimbra.

Skocpol, T. (1996). "Unravelling from Above (Unsolved Mysteries—The Tocqueville Files),"*The American Prospect*, 25, pp. 20–25.

Soares, G. (2004). "Responsabilidade Social Corporativa: Por uma Boa Causa!?" *RAE-Eletrônica*, 3(2), pp. 2–15.

Tardé, G. (1999[1893]). *La Logique Sociale.* Paris: Synthélabo.

Weber, M.(1968[1922]). *Economy and Society.* Berkeley, CA: University of California Press.

6 Informal Entrepreneurship as Adaptive Innovation

Strategies Among Migrant Workers in Indian Cities

Sunil D. Santha and Devisha Sasidevan

Introduction

This chapter is based on a larger study that commenced with the leading question, "How do vulnerable, migrant populations in cities survive amid high-risk conditions?" It discusses the adaptation strategies of migrant workers in the informal sector to diverse risks and uncertainties amid their day-to-day livelihood struggles in three Indian cities, namely, Kochi, Surat and Mumbai. This chapter illustrates the livelihood adaptation strategies of migrant informal workers in cities from a social innovation lens. It further elaborates on the characteristics of informal entrepreneurship as adaptive innovation. This effort is also an attempt to demonstrate the agency and creative potential of informal migrant workers as active subjects in innovations and making appropriations of their own (Smith et al., 2017).

Adaptive Innovation Among Migrant Informal Workers

Adaptive innovations are social innovations that are context-specific, developmental and always committed to the values of social justice and environmental sustainability. In the context of this chapter, it involves the processes by which local actors (such as informal migrant workers) understand the political economy of the larger city system and apply their knowledge, networks and skills to shape or modify these city systems to adapt to diverse risks and uncertainties and secure their livelihoods. Such a conceptualization of social innovation within the context of social justice and people-centered development has become increasingly important, as any discourse on the subject should have the intent and effect of equality, justice and empowerment for those who are disadvantaged or vulnerable in society (Curtis, 2014). This chapter presents the view that adaptation strategies of migrant informal workers need to be seen as a social, economic and political process and not as a mere technical exercise (Tol et al., 2008). In this regard, we need to engage substantively with the notion of justice as recognition of vulnerable and marginalized groups (Bulkeley et al., 2014).

Adaptive innovation processes need to be relatively flexible, long-term and incorporate access of vulnerable groups to social, economic, political, physical, human and natural assets (Moser and Satterthwaite, 2010). Moser and Satterthwaite (2010) assert that the asset portfolios of individuals, households, and communities are a key determinant of their adaptive capacity. Adger et al. (2005) have observed that elements of effectiveness, efficiency, equity and legitimacy are important in evaluating the success of adaptation strategies. However, in the context of migrant workers in informal sectors in Indian cities, such indicators may not be always successful in qualifying adaptation strategies. The informal sector is more complex and fluid. In addition, the implications of adaptation strategies need to be studied further.

Advocacy documents have referred to informal workers as "green entrepreneurs" and have cited examples of how their way of work has a lower carbon footprint (WIEGO, 2012; Arora, 2014). In addition, the informal sector exhibits several characteristics of urban resilience, mainly those related to flexibility and resourcefulness (Brown et al., 2014). For instance, street traders source their goods locally, use far less packaging and produce less waste, rely on reuse and recycling, and often use little or no electricity (WIEGO, 2012). In a similar vein, home-based workers depend on minimal transport, use less space and utilities and are more cautious about consuming excess electricity (WIEGO, 2012). However, the potential role of informality in contributing to urban resilience is poorly understood (Brown et al., 2014). There is an urgent need to study how informal workers resist and respond to shocks and stresses, including those that will be caused by environmental risks and uncertainties (Brown et al., 2014).

At the beginning of the 20th century, informal entrepreneurship was considered traditional and backward when compared to formal entrepreneurship (Williams and Nadin, 2010). However, in later years, structuralist thought looked on informal entrepreneurs as those marginalized groups who are exploited by a global economic system and are pushed into the informal economy due to their inability to find formal work (Castells and Portes, 1989; Williams and Nadin, 2010). From a neoliberal perspective, informal entrepreneurs are those who reject and resist the forces of an overregulated state as well as an overregulated market (De Soto, 1989; Williams and Nadin, 2010). Recent scholarship from a poststructuralist perspective, however, contests the representation of informal entrepreneurs as economic actors and instead considers them as primarily social actors (Williams and Nadin, 2010). Informal entrepreneurship provides an alternative space in which participants can transform their work identity and reveal their true selves (Snyder, 2004;

Williams and Nadin, 2010). Interpreting the works of a few other scholars, Williams and Nadin write,

> Rather than portray informal entrepreneurs as unfortunate pawns in an exploitative global economic system, or as voluntarily exiting the formal realm because of overregulation, post-structuralists thus again ascribe agency to informal entrepreneurship, but emphasize how it is a livelihood practice chosen for social, redistributive, resistance or identity reasons.
>
> (2010: 370)

It is in the context of the preceding quote that we need to consider informal entrepreneurship among migrant workers as an innovative, agency-induced adaptation strategy to deal with diverse risks and uncertainty in the city.

Methodology

The findings of this chapter are inferred from data collected through qualitative interviews with 45 migrant workers in the three cities. During the interviews, we understood that for more than 50% of respondents in each city, it was extremely difficult to unearth the diverse adaptation strategies within the given temporal-spatial dimensions. This was mainly because of the fact that most of these migrant workers were deeply rooted in their vulnerabilities, and there were no inherent manifestations of successful adaptation strategies. It was also difficult to theoretically outline some of their immediate responses to crisis situations as adaptation. Our observation was that many of these migrant workers were falling from one vulnerability spiral into another, leaving less scope for adaptation as such. Thus, we filtered out those 45 cases that seemed to be successful in dealing with diverse livelihood risks and uncertainties in the cities.

Adaptation strategies could be understood in terms of mobility (pools risk across space), storage (pools and reduces risk across time), diversification (pools risk across the assets and resources of households and collectives), communal pooling (meaning the pooling of risk across households that involves joint ownership of assets and resources; sharing of wealth, labor, or incomes from particular activities across households; and/or mobilization and use of resources that are held collectively during times of scarcity) and market exchange (Agrawal, 2010: 183). Migration thus becomes an important adaptation strategy in terms of pooling risk across space. This adaptation framework as proposed by Agrawal (2010), which considers the factors of mobility, diversification, storage, communal pooling and market exchange, guided our initial discussions with migrant workers. However, we decided to keep the interactions open as we felt that adaptation strategies of migrant workers in a postmigration scenario in cities are quite different from adaptation strategies that have their genesis in rural settings. The qualitative data collected through interviews were then thematically coded and the emerging patterns were analyzed. The diverse adaptation strategies that were categorized thematically are discussed in the following section.

Common Livelihood Adaptation Strategies of Informal Workers

Interactions with migrant workers revealed adaptation strategies through mobility, livelihood diversification, risk pooling, asset conservation, storage and enhancement, self-remedy, market exchange, structural adaptation and informal entrepreneurship. This section discusses each adaptation component in detail, while Table 6.1 summarizes the specificities within each of these adaptation strategies.

The observed adaptation strategies are discussed in the following sections.

Mobility

Mobility refers to adaptation across space in the postmigration scenario. Some of the mobility-specific strategies are reverse migration, shifting to new worksites and seasonal migration. Studies have shown that migration may not be always the first choice of households to deal with risks and uncertainties (Gilbert and McLeman, 2010). Migration as an adaptation strategy might follow after a series of successive strategies (Gilbert and McLeman, 2010). Factors such as the social and economic endowments of households and communities, ecological contexts, social and institutional networks, accessibility and availability of resources and power do influence the decisions to migrate (Gilbert and McLeman, 2010). Our study shows that migration, as an adaptation strategy, need not always be induced due to climatic events and uncertainties at the migrants' villages of origin. Thus, migration as an adaptation strategy need not always be understood as mobility from the village to the city. Instead, a key finding of our study is that, due to their heightened vulnerability contexts in the city (Santha et al., 2015), migrant workers are forced to shift from their place of work or residence in the city to other places during times of extreme climatic events and natural hazards. Thus, irrespective of the spatial contexts (urban or rural), the poor and most vulnerable groups are forced to migrate during extreme climatic events.

Reverse migration is an important response of interstate migrant workers in the three cities to deal with livelihood risks and uncertainties. One common strategy that is observed among interstate migrant workers in Kochi is that they return to their respective places of origin at the onset of a health crisis such as malaria or tuberculosis. The reason they give for such a reverse migration is that treatment is affordable in their native

Table 6.1 Adaptation strategies of migrant workers in Indian cities

Mobility	Informal Entrepreneurship	Livelihood Diversification	Asset Conservation, Storage and Enhancement	Market Exchange	Risk Pooling
Reverse migration	Setting up business enterprises and scaling them up	Shift from one occupation to another due to climate and health factors	Savings	Barter exchange	Relatives and family members helping one another
Shift to new worksites	Skills enhancement	Shifting from one subsector to another	Circulating money	Credit-based buying and selling	Insurance
Seasonal migration	Opportunity seeking behavior	Occupational shifts	Remittances	Selling assets	Shared accommodation
	Maintaining strategic relationships	Two or more members of the family working in multiple sectors	Restricting expenditure		Affiliating oneself to a political association
	Innovating new designs		Restrict credit lending		Borrowing money from relatives
	Product diversification		Technology		Informal chit-funds
	Maintaining parallel value cum supply chains		Stocking grains and other food materials		Family members as workers
	Establishing and controlling key segments of a value chain				Equated monthly installments
	Product selection				Strategic relationships
	Innovating sales strategy				Self-help groups
	Record-keeping				
	Use of internet services and knowledge				
	Working overtime				
	Skills enhancement				

Source: Fieldwork by the authors.

place, communication with health care professionals is easier due to the familiarity of language and culture and the presence of family members to take care of the sick. The hostility of the resident host population and sensational reporting by the media also forces many migrant workers to move back to their places of origin immediately after being diagnosed with an infectious disease. It was observed that migrants from Odisha used to return immediately after a flood or heat event in Surat. Usually, they return when the floodwaters reside or when the heat incidences come down. We also found that *seasonal migration* was common among migrant workers in Mumbai. Some migrant workers returned to their village to work as agricultural laborers during the lean season of their work in the cities. In most cases, the lean season coincides with the onset of monsoons in the city. In this regard, we came across some migrant workers who have been sustaining their practice of seasonal migration for the last 25 years.

Shifting worksites or keeping oneself mobile is a common adaptation strategy among those migrant workers such as street vendors. This practice is mostly observed in Mumbai, although it is picking up in Kochi and Surat. This is a strategy mainly to evade exploitative agents such as monitoring officials of the municipal corporations or the police. Migrant workers also prefer to move from one place to another, depending upon the income opportunities that one would have when compared with staying in one particular place. For instance, small-scale vendors who sell products like small toys, balloons and jute bags find mobility a better income-earning strategy than always standing at the same place. Switching worksites also helps them to avoid paying bribes to municipal officials and the police. They also avoid paying monthly rents as other shopkeepers do. Also, in a highly competitive space, there is always an opportunity to attract a greater number of customers than being in fixed locations. People also shift their worksites permanently if they were not able to improve working relationships in their neighborhood, such as with shopkeepers and the host resident population. Some women migrant workers, who are single, mentioned that they shift their worksites if they feel that they are exploited or abused by their employers. We also came across some migrant vendors who were forced to shift their worksites, as the owners of the buildings around these sites did not allow them to place their stalls permanently in that particular location.

The previously mentioned strategy of shifting worksites may not be always due to the structural and/or exploitative factors that migrant workers face in their day-to-day livelihood struggles. Our significant finding was that this practice of shifting worksites is very common among those migrant workers whose type or site of work is exposed to hazards induced by extreme climatic events. Yet another corresponding finding of this study is that adaptation strategies of migrant workers to climatic events and natural hazards are deeply embedded within those adaptation strategies that help them to deal with the day-to-day livelihood risks and uncertainties such as varying market conditions, opportunities and social relations. For example, people shift from one worksite to another if the site is prone to extreme climatic events such as floods and waterlogging. Experienced migrants in the city have developed capacities to find alternative livelihood spaces prior to the onset of hazard seasons. Usually, however, this will be a temporary arrangement. In such cases, leaving one worksite does not mean that migrants will abandon the worksite completely. They will return after the hazard event has subsided. Some migrant workers in Surat and Kochi mentioned that they have shifted their workspaces due to a rise in the mosquito menace. Our observations of the respective worksites hinted that these places were prone to waterlogging and accumulation of urban waste.

Shifting to a new occupational site is a coping strategy that has its own risk factors as well. The initial investment will be high, and it will take some time to ensure the security of the space and restore business as usual. We also found that in Mumbai and Surat, migrant workers with experience and skills tend to *shift from one subsector to another* during crisis situations such as flooding or health problems. This was specifically relevant to those migrant workers in the textile and food industry. However, as mentioned earlier, this particular coping strategy is embedded within their larger responses to their day-to-day livelihood struggles. For instance, such subsector shifts also happen when they find a better income-earning opportunity in a particular segment of a value chain, say, when there is a greater demand for embroidery works rather than for handloom products. However, during times of crisis induced by climatic events, they tend to follow the same adaptation strategies.

Livelihood Diversification

Livelihood diversification refers to migrant workers maintaining more than one occupation, sometimes involving multiple family members in income-generating activities. Studies have shown that livelihood diversification is a predominant adaptation strategy among migrants in slums. This implies that, in many instances, they maintain more than one occupation, and multiple family members could be seen to be involved in income-generating work (Parvin et al., 2013).

Livelihood diversification is an important strategy for migrant workers, which includes *occupational shifts* at regular time intervals. In Mumbai, we noticed that some migrant workers employed in the construction industry as semiskilled laborers discontinue their work during the monsoons. Although construction work is available during monsoons, these migrant workers consider the job to be hard, difficult and risky. Migrant workers such as semiskilled workers in the construction industry have to work outdoors even during the rainy season. With an increase in the intensity of rainfall and waterlogging events in the city, these workers find it extremely difficult to work outdoors. Remaining wet throughout the day makes them vulnerable to fever, cold and other illnesses such as rheumatism, which, in turn, affect their capacities to earn a regular income. The chances of meeting with accidents such as falling from slippery surfaces are also very high during the rainy season. Due to this, during the monsoons, they shift to their traditional, skilled occupation such as making and repairing shoes and umbrellas. In a similar vein, in Surat, some migrant workers have shifted from their jobs as they felt that they were more prone to infectious diseases like typhoid, dysentery and diarrhea. These migrant workers attribute the prime cause of the illness to the poor water quality and pollution at the worksite. In addition, they observe that such instances are very high following certain hazard events like waterlogging, heavy rain or heat events. For instance, we came across four migrant workers who had shifted from the textile sector to driving auto-rickshaws in the city after the 2006 floods for the previously mentioned reasons.

Yet another dimension of livelihood diversification was that *siblings and other family members were encouraged to work simultaneously in different sectors* or to take up different skilled/semiskilled jobs in the city. This is a common strategy to ensure that there is a sustainable inflow of livable household income amid all the risks and uncertainties. For example, if the father worked as a dyer in the textile industry of Surat, his son worked as an auto-rickshaw driver in the same city. We also noticed that some migrant workers tend to bring their friends and relatives who are in the productive age group to the city to take up diverse jobs, such that they are able to supplement one another's income. For instance, a migrant worker in Surat comments that he brought his wife and brother to the city. While he himself works as a security guard, his wife works as a casual laborer with the municipal corporation and his brother has also taken up a job in the city.

Some migrant workers *take up multiple jobs* to deal with the risks and uncertainties. We came across a migrant worker in Surat who used to rear cattle during the day and work as a security guard at night. In a similar vein, a woman migrant worker used to sell vegetables and later in the day used to work as a domestic maid in the nearby residential apartments. These multiple jobs are done to supplement their livelihoods with additional income. Some of the migrant workers, who did not have a place to stay, used to engage in multiple jobs during the day and night, respectively. For instance, in Mumbai, a man was found to sell balloons in the evening and used to work in bakeries or clothes shops during the daytime. We need to understand that it is the lack of access to basic livelihood assets that force migrant workers to take up multiple jobs in the city. Our observations show that this not a healthy trend. In the future, with a rise in disruptions caused by climatic events, the number of urban poor who will be forced to take up multiple jobs for a living will also increase.

Seasonality, migration and rural–urban livelihood linkages are key determinants of adaptation among most of the migrant workers who participated in our study. With variations in seasons and climatic conditions, these migrant workers have crafted their livelihood strategies in both the city and their village. Earlier studies on rural livelihoods and climate change adaptation have referred to seasonal migration as an adaptation strategy (Deshingkar, 2006; Tacoli, 2009). However, we also need to look at seasonal migration and climate change adaptation through an urban lens. Such an approach also emphasizes the need to study the interlinking of diverse adaptation strategies. There is a strong interface between livelihood diversification and mobility as adaptation strategies. None of the adaptation strategies act in isolation, and they are deeply embedded in the rural–urban–rural milieu. The adaptation strategies of migrant workers in the city are the subset of a certain larger set of adaptation strategies that most migrants adhered to at their places of origin. We have to contextualize seasonal migration and climate change within this larger spiral of the rural–urban–rural milieu. This can be illustrated further through some of our own observations.

We came across a few migrant workers in Kochi who were skilled in floral decoration. They had migrated to the city due to drought conditions prevailing in their village in Tamil Nadu. On the other hand, their floral business in the city also had a lean phase during the monsoons or during days of heavy rains. Thus, their income-earning strategy was neither sustainable during the summer in the village nor during the monsoons in the city. Subsequently, these workers have devised a strategy to optimize the maximum income-earning potential both at the city and in the village. Accordingly, they have blended mobility with diversification. During the lean agricultural season in the village, these workers worked at the floral enterprise in the city. As soon as the agricultural season set in with the arrival of monsoons, they returned to the village as farm-based laborers. However, they made arrangements such that their younger siblings replaced them at the floral shops in the city. Such a strategy helps to draw an assured income during lean and peak seasons irrespective of the spatial contexts. It also ensures the availability of sufficient food stock (rice, wheat and cereals produced on their farms) for them in the city. This helps to reduce their food expenses in the city.

In a similar vein, seasonal migration was a strategy among some migrant workers in Mumbai. Forecasting climatic variations and the associated reduction in income-earning opportunities, these workers used to return to their villages to work as agricultural laborers. Our observation also shows that most of the migrant vendors in Mumbai and Surat, who did not have a secure and safe worksite to engage in their business, used to return to their villages during times of flooding or, most prominently, during the monsoons (June–November). This is because they felt that the intensity and unpredictability of rains affected their access to safe vending spaces, pushing their sales margin below the desired threshold level, preventing them from sustaining themselves in the city.

Risk Pooling

Risk pooling as an adaptation strategy involves the pooling of risk across migrant workers or their households and networks through joint ownership and sharing of assets and resources. It is the sharing of wealth, labor, or income from particular livelihood activities. These include friends and relatives helping one another in a particular enterprise or work, benefiting from sharing insurance, accommodation practices, affiliating oneself to a political association, borrowing money from relatives, organizing informal chit funds, stimulating an EMI (Equated Monthly Installment) economy, being part of self-help groups and maintaining strategic relationships.

We also noticed that in Mumbai, in order to control expenses, siblings and their families of migrant households stay together as a joint family. Though each person earns individually, they have a common kitchen so that groceries, vegetables and grains can be bought in bulk at cheaper prices. Moreover, these migrant workers believe that communal cooking is cheaper than cooking in nuclear families. Also, they believe that there are enough human resources to share during times of crisis such as hospitalization and loss of one's job. Moreover, migrant workers who are involved in their own ventures cannot afford to hire personnel for their support. To reduce expenses on human resources, they accept help in the form of labor from their own families.

Association memberships also help to reduce risks. However, this trend of associating oneself with a collective was only seen in Mumbai and not in the other two cities. We observed among the intrastate migrants in Mumbai that they were members of associations such as the Ambedkar Study Centre and the Buddhist Society, which largely work on the empowerment of dalits and neo-Buddhists. These associations are supposed to be active during times of floods and waterlogging in the city, providing relief materials and shelters to the affected population. In this regard, we have also come across some studies that have found that such association memberships act as social capital during times of floods and waterlogging in migrant settlements of the city (Mishra, 2009).

Asset Conservation, Storage and Enhancement

A prominent strategy among interview participants was *asset conservation* and enhancement over time. As part of the larger study, we had described the range of tangible assets that migrant workers have access to, namely, natural, physical and financial resources and intangible assets, including human and social assets (Santha et al., 2015). *Saving money* is an important means of asset conservation. It is not necessary that all the migrant workers save money through a bank account. Some do vest the responsibility with their employers. Others send it as remittances to their families, who are supposed to save the money. Apart from investing their savings in agriculture back in their village and spending for marriage ceremonies and festivals, most of the migrant workers aim to enhance them through some enterprise. Nevertheless, our inquiry revealed that saving earned income has come in handy for many migrant workers to survive in the city and to compensate the loss of livelihoods during extreme weather events. It has also helped them to rebuild their enterprise following extreme climatic events such as the 2006 deluge in Mumbai.

In Kochi and Mumbai, we have come across a few migrant workers, especially women, who *loan out their savings* to other known people with an assured interest rate. Thus, they earn the interest as a supplementary income to their savings. Apart from savings, *controlling expenses* during extreme weather events and associated seasons is an important strategy. Family members control expenses on tobacco products or limit their spending for festivals, clothing and traveling during times of crisis.

Storing perishable goods is an important strategy for migrants staying in waterlogging areas of Surat. They hang the goods from the roofs, such that these products are not affected by floodwater. We noticed that perishable goods such as onion, potato and lemon are hung from the ceilings to preserve them from both heat and floodwater. Also, during monsoons, people tend to shift their produce and work equipment from the worksite to their homes. Prior to the onset of monsoons, some of the migrant vendors in Mumbai notice that the price of their products such as dry fish becomes expensive. Therefore, to be on the safe side, they dry and stock dry fish in their home. They sell their fish when there is a high demand and high price in the market. Some well-off migrant workers used to store their perishable goods such as fruits and vegetables in cold storages owned by known shopkeepers.

Market Exchange

Extreme weather events and climate variability can result in distress selling of basic livelihood assets. Thus, market exchange strategies such as distress selling during climate crisis may not be always supportive for the urban poor in the long term. Immediately after the 2006 floods in Surat, *selling assets* turned out to be an important strategy among some of the most marginalized migrant workers in the city. They sell their key assets for money to meet expenses to rebuild their workspace or to deal with the health issues that followed the floods. There was an instance in which a cobbler had to sell his stock of shoes to another cobbler to get some money for his malaria treatment. People also mentioned that they had to sell their livestock assets such as cows and goats to deal with their health problems. On the other hand, *credit-based buying arrangements* on many occasions offer support to migrant workers of Surat and Kochi during lean seasons. They have arrangements with shopkeepers to borrow groceries and vegetables from *kiranas* stores on monthly accounts, which they repay at the beginning of every month. Some migrant vendors who run mobile eateries and cold drink stalls were found to have established informal networks with distributors of raw materials, which helped them to borrow products on a credit basis.

The preceding descriptions were of generic adaptation strategies. However, this chapter suggests that it is also important to consider informal entrepreneurship as an innovative form of adaptation.

Informal Entrepreneurship as Adaptive Innovation

The most visible and direct adaptation strategy has been one of *informal entrepreneurship*. Williams and Nadin (2010: 363) have defined informal entrepreneurship as

> involving somebody actively engaged in starting a business or is the owner/manager of a business that is less than 42 months old who participates in the paid production and sale of goods and services that are legitimate in all respects besides the fact that they are unregistered by, or hidden from the state for tax and/or benefit purposes.

During our fieldwork, we observed that migrant workers excel in finding appropriate opportunities to *establish and scale up business enterprises*. This is specific to the case of skilled and semiskilled migrant workers. For instance, a migrant worker in Kochi, who had tailoring skills, established two shops, exploiting the opportunity available for unique fashions in the city. The second shop specializes in stitching jeans as well. He has employed many tailors under him. Moreover, the stitching looks different from that of his native peers, such as placing zippers on both sides of men's pants and thus making them a unique fashion garment. He had migrated to the city due to unpredictable flood and drought situations in his village in Odisha. In a similar vein, a migrant worker in Surat, after initial years of struggle, was able to establish his eatery business at two sites, namely, Chowk Bazaar and Delhi Gate. This was a strategy he devised to deal with the uncertainties related to flooding every year. His business is affected when the water level rises in Chowk Bazaar. However, he is able to sustain his livelihood by working in his store at Delhi Gate. As mentioned earlier in the subsection on Asset Conservation, Storage and Enhancement, *lending money at a high interest rate* to known networks is yet another entrepreneurial strategy used by a few migrant workers.

In yet another instance, the entrepreneurial skills of imitation jewelry workers in Mumbai need to be appreciated. These are people who do not have their own place to sell their jewelry. They are at the mercy of the gold and silver merchants who permit them to sit in front of their shops. During the rainy season, their business is worst affected, as no customer will be ready to purchase items standing in the rain. Instead of viewing this as a crisis, there were two imitation workers who studied the imitation jewelry value chain in detail and established assemblage units in the outskirts of the city. During the rains, they increase production in these units and export products to other states. *Establishing and controlling key segments of a value chain* are thus other important entrepreneurial characteristics.

We found out that vendors in Mumbai and Kochi do not sell their goods on credit during lean periods such as the monsoons. Moreover, they purchase very little quantity to sell so that the capital invested will not end up in a loss. In the words of a fish seller in Mumbai,

> [i]f required, we purchase very little fish from the wholesaler. During the lean season, it is better to reduce the quantity of fish to be sold, rather than increase the price. When our customers realize that the product's price has been raised, then they will not buy from us. Instead, we reduce the quantity rather than increase the price.

Some vendors do increase the price in one segment of a value chain when there is loss in another segment, while others work overtime to compensate losses.

Looking at the nature of their customers—be they children, women or the elderly—they market their products using different fancy names or innovative designs. For example, a shoemaker and his family members made shoes and sandals out of pure leather. But, as the prices of leather increased for various reasons, there has been a decline in local demand for leather footwear. One shoemaker also observed that the demand for leather footwear has declined in the past few years due to the unpredictability of monsoons. With a rise in the intensity of rainfall and waterlogging events in the city, the durability of leather footwear has considerably reduced. Therefore, customers prefer footwear made of synthetic material. Therefore, they shifted to manufacture footwear from synthetic materials such as Rexine. They also changed the product design, taking cues available from the Internet. And they began to market the latest products by associating them with celebrity names or cartoon characters that are very popular among children and their parents. Thus, *customized, innovative designing* is yet another entrepreneurial strategy of migrant workers.

Product diversification is an important entrepreneurial strategy that is designed according to changing cultural tastes, climatic and market conditions. For instance, some vendors in Mumbai and Kochi sell jute bags during summer and sell umbrellas during rainy seasons. Migrant workers running food stalls sell diverse products such as snacks like bread sandwiches, *chats* and *bhel* (spicy crunchy snacks) during the summer. During the rainy season, they sell *idli* (steamed rice cakes) along with batter and chutney. These entrepreneurial strategies are characterized by a set of *opportunity-seeking behavior*. In this regard, people see climate variability as an opportunity as well. Heavy rains are seen as occasions where one could increase sales of umbrellas. In a similar vein, they shift to the sale of lemonade and *gola* (shaved ice) in the summer or during times of extreme heat. Opportunity-seeking behavior thus enhances the adaptive capacities of migrant workers.

Maintaining strategic relationships with other actors not only helps in reducing risks but also aids in enhancing their entrepreneurial opportunities. There were instances where we observed that migrant workers maintained strategic mutually beneficial relationships to reduce their insecurities. For instance, a balloon seller had secured his livelihood space in front of an apartment by informally acting as a watchman to the apartment as well. This helped him to continue his occupation of selling balloons every day, irrespective of the vagaries of the weather. In a similar manner, fruit vendors and imitation jewelry workers in Mumbai were able to secure shelters during heat events and monsoons in front of certain shops by agreeing to deal with their customers at peak times. In yet another instance, a shoe polisher in Surat had managed to stay at the basement of the police quarters, thus securing not only occupational space but also residential space. He polishes the shoes of police personnel in the building, and he is excused from paying rent. Moreover, unlike other migrant workers, he does not face the threat of being evicted by the police or other officials. In a similar vein, shoe polishers in Mumbai were found to maintain a strategic relationship with railway station staff or the police to ensure a livelihood space. These spaces also provide them shelter from rains and the scorching sun.

Skill enhancement is an important requirement to sustain in a competitive field. For instance, we came across a migrant youth in Kochi who had picked up flower decoration skills very fast, so he is now in demand in other cities like Haridwar, Hyderabad, Delhi and Bangalore as well. We also sensed the entrepreneurial spirit in a migrant Dalit woman from Tamil Nadu. In the words of the woman,

> I came to Kochi to work as [a] laborer. I had no other skills. However, after coming here, I learned to stitch both men and women's garments. In my village in Tamil Nadu, nobody is ready to stitch

dresses for people from the Dalit community. I will return to my village and open a tailoring shop specifically for Dalits.

This is also a demonstration of the fact that, though a migrant worker comes to the city for the first time with limited skills, they quickly pick up the essential skills to survive in the city.

Concluding Observations

We need to be cautious that the adaptation strategies mentioned earlier should not give the impression that migrant informal workers are always capable of overcoming their livelihood challenges, climatic and health uncertainties on their own without the support of the state, civil society or the market. We need to remind ourselves again and again that, out of a very small sample of 50 migrant workers in each city, we were able to unearth concrete adaptation strategies used by only 15 migrant workers. This is mainly due to the fact that the adaptive capacities of the rest of the migrant workers were very limited, and most of them were still bonded to their rooted vulnerabilities. They lacked access to basic livelihood assets, entitlements and choices. Nevertheless, the assumption of this study was that the strategies outlined earlier could stimulate a future research framework to understand and conceptualize people-centered innovations.

Adaptive innovations among migrant informal workers emerge in complex systems. It showcases the agency of these actors to innovate and adapt in diverse challenging circumstances in the city and, at the same time, raises crucial questions about the factors that enable migrant workers to design their livelihood assets and strategies and on what terms. These are some important questions that the literature on mainstream social innovation or adaptation has seldom addressed. These questions involve a politics of knowledge that challenges the distribution of resources and power in knowledge production, technology and entrepreneurship development (Smith et al., 2017). Migrant informal workers are true social innovators, though their motivation to develop informal entrepreneurship may be born out of sociocultural and economic vulnerabilities and necessities. As a kind of grassroots innovators in the city, these migrant workers have established a vast social network and are capable of developing discourses and mobilizing supportive resources (Smith et al., 2017). The spaces of innovation among migrant workers in the city are characterized by negotiation and struggle with incumbent powers and entrenched practices that might otherwise close down such spaces (Smith et al., 2017). Social networks also play an important pathway in innovation. Informal social relations and associations play an important role in sustaining basic assets for livelihood promotion (Eriksen and Selboe, 2012; Rodima-Taylor, 2012). Migrant social networks can help to increase social resilience in the communities of origin and trigger innovations across regions by the transfer of knowledge, technology, remittances and other resources (Scheffran et al., 2012).

It is very interesting to see how migrant informal workers understand the larger context of their market or the behavior of their consumers and embed these perspectives in their own knowledge systems. This is specific to the context of adaptive innovation, where macro and external knowledge is built into self-knowledge, as per the context-specific designs, often as a knowledge bricolage (a mix of external and internal knowledge systems). Adaptive innovations have imperfect beginnings. This implies that many innovators begin to work without insufficient advance information. However, they build it through their own forms of action and reflection, trial and errors and building social networks. This is how subsystems of knowledge boundaries and their interrelationships emerge in people-centered innovations. An adaptive innovation framework that blends the agency of migrant workers within the dynamics of an informal-formal, urban socioecological system still needs to be evolved and deliberated. Future research could examine these opportunities.

Acknowledgments

The larger study was supported by International Institute for Environment and Development (IIED), London. We are grateful to Dr Diane Archer, IIED, for her guidance and comments in this research process.

References

Adger, W. N., Arnella, N. W. and Tompkins, E. L. (2005). "Successful Adaptation to Climate Change Across Scales," *Global Environmental Change*, 15, pp. 77–86.

Agrawal, A. (2010). "Local Institutions and Adaptation to Climate Change," in R. Mearns and A. Norton (eds.), *Social Dimensions of Climate Change: Equity and Vulnerability in a Warming World*. Washington, DC: World Bank, pp. 173–197.

Arora, K. (2014, August). "These 'Green Entrepreneurs' Are Our Saviours in the Climate Emergency," *Youth Ki Awaaz*. www.youthkiawaaz.com/2014/08/green-entrepreneurs-saviours-climate-emergency/.

Brown, D., McGranahan, G. and Dodman, D. (2014). *Urban Informality and Building a More Inclusive, Resilient and Green Economy*. IIED Working Paper. London: IIED.

Bulkeley, H., Edwards, G. A. S. and Fuller, S. (2014). "Contesting Climate Justice in the City: Examining Politics and Practice in Urban Climate Change Experiments," *Global Environmental Change*, 25, pp. 31–40.

Castells, M. and Portes, A. (1989). "World Underneath: The Origins, Dynamics and Effects of the Informal Economy," in A. Portes, M. Castells and L. A. Benton (eds.), *The Informal Economy: Studies in Advanced and Less Developing Countries*. Baltimore: John Hopkins University Press.

Curtis, A. (2014a, December 9). "Money or Meaning: What Is Driving Social Innovation Today?" *Pioneer's Post.* www.pioneerspost.com/news-views/2014 1209/money-or-meaning-what-driving-social-innovation-today (Accessed on 13 June 2017).

Deshingkar, P. (2006, March 6–7). *Internal Migration, Poverty and Development in Asia.* Paper presented at the conference, Asia 2015: Promoting Growth, Ending Poverty. London.

De Soto, H. (1989). *The Other Path: The Economic Answer to Terrorism.* London: Harper and Row.

Eriksen, S. and Selboe, E. (2012). "The Social Organisation of Adaptation to Climate Variability and Global Change: The Case of a Mountain Farming Community in Norway," *Applied Geography*, 33(1), pp. 159–167.

Gilbert, G. and McLeman, R. (2010). "Household Access to Capital and Its Effects on Drought Adaptation and Migration: A Case Study of Rural Alberta in the 1930s," *Population and Environment*, 32, pp. 3–26.

Mishra, N. (2009). *Social Capital Among Flood Affected Communities of Mumbai.* Dissertation. Mumbai: Tata Institute of Social Sciences.

Moser, C. and Satterthwaite, D. (2010). "Toward Pro-Poor Adaptation to Climate Change in the Urban Centers of Low and Middle-Income Countries," in R. Mearns and A. Norton (eds.), *Social Dimensions of Climate Change: Equity and Vulnerability in a Warming World.* Washington, DC: World Bank, pp. 231–258.

Parvin, A., Alam, A. F. M. A. and Asad, R. (2013, September 9–10). *Climate Change Impact and Adaptation in Urban Informal Settlements in Khulna: A Built Environmental Perspective.* International Workshop on Living in Low-income Urban Settlements in an Era of Climate Change: Processes, Practices, Policies and Politics. University of Manchester.

Rodima-Taylor, D. (2012). "Social Innovation and Climate Adaptation: Local Collective Action in Diversifying Tanzania," *Applied Geography*, 33(1), pp. 128–134.

Santha, S. D., Jaswal, S., Sasidevan, D., Datta, K., Khan, A. and Kuruvilla, A. (2015). *Climate Change, Livelihoods and Health Inequities: A Study on the Vulnerability of Migrant Workers in Indian Cities.* Asian Cities Climate Resilience Working Paper 16. London: IIED.

Scheffran, J., Marmer, E. and Sow, P. (2012). "Migration as a Contribution to Resilience and Innovation in Climate Adaptation: Social Networks and Co-development in North-West Africa," *Applied Geography*, 33(1), pp. 119–127.

Smith, A., Fressoli, M., Abrol, D., Arond, E. and Ely, A. (2017). *Grassroots Innovation Movements.* London: Earthscan, Routledge.

Snyder, K. A. (2004). "Routes to the Informal Economy in New York's East Village: Crisis, Economics and Identity," *Sociological Perspectives*, 47, pp. 215–240.

Tacoli, C. (2009). "Crisis or Adaptation? Migration and Climate Change in a Context of High Mobility," in J. M. Guzmán, G. Martine, G. McGranahan, D. Schensul and C. Tacoli (eds.), *Population Dynamics and Climate Change.* New York: UNFPA; London: IIED, pp. 104–118.

Tol, R. S. J., Klein, R. J. T. and Nicholls, R. J. (2008). "Towards Successful Adaptation to Sea Level Rise Along Europe's Coasts," *Journal of Coastal Research*, 24(2), pp. 432–442.

WIEGO. (2012, June). *Urban Informal Workers and the Green Economy*. Fact Sheet. http://wiego.org/sites/wiego.org/files/resources/files/WIEGO_Urban_Informal_Workers_Green_Economy.pdf.

Williams, C. C. and Nadin, S. (2010). "Entrepreneurship and the Informal Economy: An Overview," *Journal of Developmental Entrepreneurship*, 15(4), pp. 361–378.

7   Buen Vivir as an Innovative Development Model

Andres Morales, Roger Spear,
Michael Ngoasong and Silvia Sacchetti

Introduction

This chapter examines the development of indigenous community organizations (ICOs) in Colombia. These ICOs may be seen as a social innovation supporting a process of social change which addresses the needs of marginalized indigenous communities. It links with people-centered social innovation perspectives by critically examining northern understandings of development with Buen Vivir—a community-centric, ecologically balanced and culturally sensitive development model which challenges the dominant market-based model of capitalism that has been adopted by Latin American countries in postcolonial times.

More specifically, this chapter examines the experiences of the transformation of indigenous peoples' organized groups (IOGs) into ICOs within the social and solidarity economy (SSE) and linked to the Buen Vivir (BV) development model in Colombia. Although there is not yet a Colombian development model that embodies key tenets of the BV model, Morales (2019) has achieved a conceptual clarification of BV, on which this chapter is based.

Findings from the multiple case study showed that ICOs are transformed through a hybridization process, influenced by their indigenous cultural practices and shaped by SSE institutions and standards, which provide some institutional protection but, at the same time, can be a vehicle for legitimizing dominant Western forms (mimicry).

The approach adopted here draws on the work of Jackson (2011) to build a bridge between institutional and cultural approaches while bringing insights from postcolonial theory. In the institutional approach, the roles of agency and power tend to be ignored, while the cultural approach (values) develops an understanding of agency. Bhabha's (2012) *mimicry* and *hybridity* approach is used to capture both institutionalist and culturalist schools of thought. The mimicry and hybridity approach, in the context of cultural hegemony, is complemented by the use of institutional isomorphism to depict how organizational models can be subject to three forms of isomorphism: *mimetic, coercive* and *normative*, which underlie the processes of institutional change (DiMaggio and Powell, 2000). Post-colonial theory provides a basis for understanding power—since ICOs are constituted by indigenous people, who are considered as the "other", in a subordinate position (Spivak, 1988) and voiceless as a consequence of colonialism.

The legacy of colonialism is characterized by a binary relation between the colonizer (self) and the colonized (other), and although physical colonization is supposed to have ended with independence, a cultural hegemony is inherited in most liberated societies. Postcolonial[1] studies analyze the relationship between the center and the periphery by building on the concept of the hegemony (or domination by consent; Said, 2004, 2012).

There are moments of contestation (*resistance*) when the colonizing power interacts or clashes with the colonized groups (Spivak, 1988). Those moments of contestation (or resistance) offer a space that Bhabha (2012) calls the *third space* (interstitial or in-between space), where the colonized subject can and does articulate and negotiate his or her own identity. This third space generates hybridity (Bhabha, 1984), from the contested interpretations (resistance) of what constitute indigenous values and the traditional responses of accommodation and resistance to forces of historical change by these indigenous societies (Bhabha, 1984, 2012). In other words, the colonized subject negotiates and articulates his or her identity by creating a new point of view or perspective from the clashing (resistance) and/or blending (negotiation) of the worlds of the subordinate and of the cultural hegemony.

Mimicry (Bhabha, 1984) goes beyond simply mimicking the colonizer's culture, and reveals the ambivalent effects of domination and cultural hegemony. It is a metaphor for a process of acculturation and adaptation of imposed cultural concepts and patterns by the colonizer, but at the same time, the strategic adaptation by the colonized subject can be seen as a subtle act of resistance (Lye, 1998, 2017). Thus, domination and hegemony are never complete. In this study, *mimicry* is considered as the process of internalization and *hybridity* as an expression of creative resistance (moments of contestation).

By drawing on insights from postdevelopment (BV) and postcolonial theories (Bhabha's mimicry and hybridity), this chapter uses a multilevel model for understanding the development of ICOs in Colombia—where IOGs at the micro level formalize into ICOs in the context of SSE structures and values at the meso level, shaped by BV at the macro level.

This research draws on evidence from a multiple case-study approach with five organizations and five indigenous communities (Curripaco, Puinave, Yanacona, Misak and Wayuu) in three geographic regions (Amazonas, Cauca and Guajira). The methods of data collection used are secondary data sources, video focus groups and semistructured interviews, observations and field notes.

Introducing BV

Buen Vivir, translatable as "living well" or "good living", is considered, in its purest sense, as an ancestral-spiritual phenomenon inspired by indigenous peoples' philosophy (Cubillo-Guevara et al., 2014; Hidalgo-Capitán and Cubillo-Guevara, 2016, 2017). *Buen Vivir* is the Spanish translation of *Sumak Kawsay* or *Suma Qamaña*, an ancestral philosophy exercised by the Quechuas and Aymaras (indigenous peoples located in the Andes) since pre-Columbian times, involving a spiritual harmony and balance between nature and community (Albó, 2009; Guandinango Vinueza, 2013; Huanacuni, 2010; Pilataxi Lechón, 2014; Simbaña, 2012). The idea of what *community* is and how it is perceived by the Andean indigenous people rests on the fact that society is horizontally bound with nature. Thus, for them, nature, in the broader sense, is considered an inseparable interconnection between every being—men, women and nature—that is part of Pachamama (Mother Earth) and Cosmos (Father Earth). Hence, *community* has an added spiritual dimension, as there is a communion and dialogue based on a common rituality that claims nature as a sacred being (Acosta, 2013; Albó, 2009; Huanacuni, 2010; Prada Alcoreza, 2012; Simbaña, 2012).

BV comprises a collective approach to well-being that engenders principles of reciprocity, solidarity and complementarity and promotes collective rights and a localized, community-based model of production (Gudynas, 2011). With this in mind, BV is, in effect, the institutional, socioeconomic and political appropriation of the *Sumak Kawsay* or *Suma Qamaña*. It is an ongoing project to build a different society sustained by the coexistence of human beings in their diversity and in harmony with themselves (identity), society (equity) and nature (sustainability) and influenced by the diverse cultural values existing in each country and worldwide (Acosta, 2013; Gudynas, 2011).

Although there is no explicit evidence of the existence of *values* and *pillars* in the current literature, Morales (2019) identifies the BV values and pillars based on an extensive and in-depth review of more than 300 bibliographical references of BV literature—based on the work of Cubillo-Guevara et al. (2014), Hidalgo-Capitán and Cubillo-Guevara (2015, 2017), and Vanhulst (2015). Three values—(1) *community*, (2) *solidarity and reciprocity* and (2) *harmony and complementarity*—and six pillars—(1) *rights of nature*, (2) *community well-being*, (3) *decolonization*, (4) *plurinational state*, (5) *economic pluralism* and (6) *democratization*—were identified. Ecuador and Bolivia are used to depict BV implementation in policy. This helps establish a sound basis for the study of BV in Colombia.

BV has been conceptualized in the work of Cubillo-Guevara et al. (2014) and Hidalgo-Capitán and Cubillo-Guevara (2015, 2016, 2017) with three traditions: (1) the *indigenist* approach, (2) the *socialist/statist* approach and (3) the *ecologist/developmentalist* approach.

First, in the indigenist approach, the ancient indigenous thought is the core of BV, particularly the thought of the Andean indigenous people. This tradition prioritizes indigenous identity and aims for a more plural and inclusive society in which indigenous people legalize self-determination in their territories and propose a transformation from nation-state to plurinational state (e.g., Dávalos, 2011; Huanacuni, 2010; Pilataxi Lechón, 2014; Simbaña, 2012).

Second, in the socialist/statist approach, societal equity is prioritized and is strongly influenced by neo-Marxism. This tradition is led by the intellectuals involved in the institutionalization of BV in Ecuador and Bolivia (e.g., Coraggio, 1994, 2011; García-Linera, 2010; Ramírez-Gallegos, 2010, 2011; Santos, 2010). Through *citizen revolution* in Ecuador and *democratic and cultural revolution* in Bolivia, these intellectuals propose to implement a new development model that essentially seeks to improve equity.

Third, in the ecologist/developmentalist approach, development theory and praxis are strongly criticized and biocentrism is the final objective (e.g., Acosta, 2013; Escobar, 2010; Gudynas, 2011; Walsh, 2012). This BV tradition relates to the ecological and postdevelopment thinking linked to the critique of development, and different social movements (for example, indigenous, environmentalists, feminists, workers, peasants, pacifists and/or solidarity groups) are important in defining and implementing BV. Civil society is important, through local processes of social participation, so each community can define its own BV (Cubillo-Guevara et al., 2014).

Despite the differences among these approaches, BV can be seen as an alternative or neo-development model for establishing a completely different set of societal living standards to achieve human well-being.

Prior to exploring and discussing the Colombian BV model, it is crucial to understand that the BV interpretation is based on the indigenous communities studied. In a broad perspective, there is a tendency to categorize indigenous people in the same group, ignoring their heterogeneity and plurality (Agrawal, 1995; Gros, 1991). The plurality of indigenous people in Colombia is rooted in factors such as culture, view of the world (beliefs, values and pillars), historical contexts and geographical location, amongst others (e.g., Agrawal, 1995; Gros, 2000; Ulloa, 2004). Thus, BV needs to be interpreted in relation to each indigenous community studied, as they are all very diverse. Research findings indicate that there are five interpretations of BV interlinked to each selected indigenous community: (1) the Misak's *Latá-Latá,* (2) the Yanacona's *Sumak Kawsay* (a post-Inca indigenous community, with their language rooted in Quechua), (3) the Curripaco's *Noapaca Opicio,* (4) the Puinave's *Muriutún* and (5) the Wayuu's *Anaquai.*

The following diagram provides an overview of the relevant values and pillars. The six-dimensional structure of pillars comprises two groups of three. Members of the first group is influenced by their view of the world—*protection of nature, cultural reinforcement* and *community cohesion*—and the second one is driven by a series of negative actions (externalities) historically faced by indigenous communities—*territory, self-education*, and *autonomy (self-determination)*. All of them are bound by indigenous values including *respect* toward indigenous culture, *equality* for all in the indigenous community and *solidarity* and *reciprocity* as a vehicle that drives their BV. Moreover, the five BV notions, *Latá-Latá, Sumak Kawsay, Noapaca Opicio, Muriutún* and *Anaquai*, appeared to be solely ubiquitous dimensions that influence indirectly the development of the BV space.

Among all indigenous communities, the protection of nature appeared to be a fundamental principle for the development of their society, as it is considered a spiritual entity. Nature, in the indigenous context, is the source of life and well-being; its protection and conservation were fundamental for accomplishing BV. Cultural reinforcement was claimed to be one of the backbones in the pursuit of BV. It is the process in which the community is involved in traditional and customary practices. A third pillar, community cohesion, emphasizes that indigenous communities

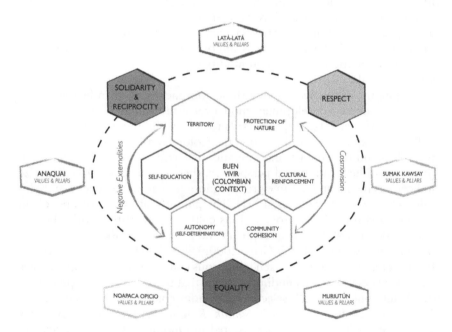

Figure 7.1 The BV model in Colombia based on the selected indigenous communities

Source: Morales (2019)

have a common vision and a sense of belonging to their indigenous culture and were strongly driven by the collective willingness to cooperate with each other in order to survive and prosper.

The second cluster of pillars was seen as externalities that either impede or slow the path toward BV. These included the dispossession of ancestral lands, the lack of autonomy to operate and manage their own resources and the need to deploy ethno-education programs to encourage the youngest indigenous generations to reembrace their culture, aiming to strengthen indigenous identity. Regarding autonomy and territory, community members highlighted the importance of recovering or holding their ancestral land to exercise their own power and management. Self-education was reported as an important pillar to maintain indigenous culture.

There have been a number of criticisms of the BV theory (Bretón, 2013; Caria and Domínguez, 2016; Lalander, 2016), which is regarded as rooted within different traditions and logics (Cubillo-Guevara et al., 2014; Hidalgo-Capitán and Cubillo-Guevara, 2017). BV can be seen as a polysemic concept that is evoked depending on different positions (Bretón, 2013; Caria and Domínguez, 2016; Vanhulst, 2015).

Drawing on Cubillo-Guevara et al. (2014) and Hidalgo-Capitán and Cubillo-Guevara, (2017), the three approaches of BV discussed earlier also face criticisms. The indigenist approach supporters are described as *pachamamistas*[2] (Stefanoni, 2010, 2011).

Supporters of the socialist/statist approach are considered practitioners of orthodox or GN approaches to development (Lalander, 2016; Svampa, 2011, 2012), creating a socialist version of development (Acosta, 2015; Caria and Domínguez, 2014, 2016). Finally, the supporters of the ecologist/postdevelopmentalist approach are accused of lacking political pragmatism, of being trapped in a discourse of romantic *ecologism* (Correa, 2007, 2008).

The strongest criticisms are the ones concerning the implementation of BV (e.g., Acosta, 2015), which is seen as very distant from the principles of the *Sumak Kawasay/Suma Qamaña*. Lalander (2016) sees deep contradictions between the BV-oriented Ecuadorian 2008 constitution (SENPLADES, 2009) and the praxis of law protecting natural resources.

Other criticisms are concerned with the idealization of indigenous communities (Correa, 2007, 2008) since the indigenous world is not free of problems, conflicts and various forms of domination and asymmetries.

From Mimicry to Hybridity: The Transformation of IOGs into ICOs

Having established the raison d'être of the IOGs to formalize as ICOs (at the meso level), the following key characteristics were identified amongst the CSEs, in order to understand the ICOs within the SSE sector in

Colombia. Drawing on Bhabha's mimicry and hybridity (1984) and bringing some insights from institutional theory (mainly institutional isomorphism of DiMaggio and Powell, 2000), the evidence suggested that ICOs (i.e., a hybrid form) result from creative resistance and/or negotiation of the two worlds (indigenous and Western), in which the IOGs emulate (adopt and adapt) external variables (i.e., the SSE standards and/or other variables) within the process of mimicry in order to be formalized.

The following subsections will discuss the transformation of the IOGs (at an informal level) into ICOs (at a formal level) by looking at the process of mimicry through analysis of local and external variables that led to the current hybrid forms (ICOs). Four themes were identified in the hybridization process: (1) *legal status, ownership and organizational structure*; (2) *production of goods and services*; (3) *decision-making*; and (4) *organizational strategies*.

Legal Status, Ownership and Organizational Structure

The ICO constitution is best understood as an interweaving of three institutional elements: *legal status, ownership* and *organizational structure*, which all jointly shaped the IOGs as they formalized. The hybridization process of the organizational constitution is based on a process of mimicry in which IOGs comply with external standards (the SSE standards) influenced by Western dominant discourses in order to secure an official and formal status (i.e., *mimetic isomorphism*). SSE standards established as guidelines for organizational behavior generate isomorphic organizations. IOGs do not need official registration in the *resguardo*[3]—local groups gather spontaneously and collaborate voluntarily to solve issues or accomplish tasks which are allocated evenly; there is a cultural sense of collectiveness. ICOs represent a hybrid form in which informal practices of the IOGs deviate from the formal SSE standards through acts of resistance to manage the tensions created by the combination of the two ecosystems (i.e., the indigenous institutions shaped by their view of the world and the SSE institutions and standards).

Almost all of the ICOs were unanimous in reporting that their constitutions were subjected to the standards established by the SSE authority (Supersolidaria) and that the chosen legal status shaped the ICOs' ownership and organizational structures—see the following three quotes. And they can draw support from many institutions that encourage and finance SSE forms at the national level (i.e., cooperatives, friendly societies or associations).

> By choosing a specific legal status, in our case, an association, we agreed on particular ways to organize and operate our entity . . . rules are established internally but follow the SSE guidelines and,

should we fail to comply with those, we might lose our formal status.

(General Manager, VICU2, CS3)

We decided to develop a cooperative because it was the only way to get access to a loan and recover our lands, we tried first to formalize as a trade union but it did not work, we received training in cooperativism and decided that was the best collective option.

(General Manager, VIMK1, CS1)

And: "We are registered as a for profit business but our aim is collective" (Accountant, YAFG1, CS2). "As a registered NFP association, we had to appoint a board of directors, although we all collaborate in any task when is needed, it is an organizational obligation" (President, VICU1, CS3).

The SSE authority (Supersolidaria) divides SSE organizations into two groups: *solidarity economy organizations* (SEOs) and *development solidarity organizations* (DSOs), which must comply with the rules and regulations set by the SSE authorities including ownership and organizational structure frameworks (DANSOCIAL, 2010; Serna Gómez and Rubio-Rodríguez, 2016; Valderrama, 2005). Three of the ICOs in this study fell into the DSO category, and one came under SEOs. The missions of DSOs and SEOs are dissimilar; DSOs are established legally to benefit internal and external actors and are NFPs, while SEOs are registered to benefit only the internal actors involved and are generally FPs. Accounts by research participants about the creation of their entity's statutes show that, by complying with external standards as they become formalized, ICOs are becoming isomorphic with each other, losing the distinctiveness they had when they were IOGs. "The objective of our association is the well-being of our members and our community, this is something that we have clearly stated and is part of our rules . . . that is why we created this association" (District Attorney, VICU3, CS3).

From a postcolonial perspective, it can be argued that such narratives are a perfect illustration of the spread of the colonizing ideology of managerialism founded on Western rationality and scientism being imposed on local systems (i.e., *coercive isomorphism*).

Although there is a range of motivations in formalizing IOGs, once the ICOs are constituted, they must comply with the standards established by the SSE authorities and are encouraged to improve their division of labor and put special emphasis on professionalization. This leads to more or less homogenized forms of organizing and regulating organizational life. As a co-founder commented,

Within the current economic sector, it does not matter whether we are indigenous or not . . . there are standards that we must comply with . . . you know, for them [non-indigenous people] there is no difference between our organizations and others established by white men.

(Co-founder, V1MK2, CS1)

The lack of social enterprise legislation in Colombia may have excluded other forms of entities sharing similar objectives from the SSE sector. Finca Lechera El Paraíso (CS2)[4] was legally registered as an orthodox venture with the aim of benefitting the entire Yanacona community (31 communities). Although a socially and environmentally oriented venture, it was not recognized under the SSE umbrella. One of the CS2 board members commented: "Our venture is not as any other conventional one . . . our objective is collective . . . of course, it is profit-oriented but distribution and benefits are collective, we are 31 communities and all must obtain a benefit from it".

(Public Administrator, VIYA2, CS2)

This example shows how a hybrid form may deviate from formal practices to manage the tensions of establishing a more collective organization. This also illuminates the disadvantaged position of the indigenous people (subordinate group) as their practices are recognized neither in the SSE sector nor in another sector (see Calvo and Morales, 2017). Although Finca Lechera El Paraíso (CS2) was formalized with a different legal status, it is considered a collectively owned venture. The development of ICOs was strongly influenced by the pursuit of the mutual benefit of all its members and the whole community. This could explain the rationale behind choosing a collective ownership approach. As one of the interviewees pointed out,

[t]he cooperative and the association was created to benefit the whole community, hence is owned by the whole community. We all put our contribution and have worked here since its foundation . . . the collective well-being is our purpose and that is why the cooperative is owned by our members and our community . . . we are spiritually bound.

(Co-founder, V1MK2, CS1)

Although Supersolidaria stipulates that SSE organizations must be owned collectively by their members, collective ownership appears to be embedded in the DNA of each organization. This links with the traditional view for most cases where territory belongs to everybody in the community and has a spiritual dimension. Indigenous territory is ruled and governed by local authorities who are elected by the entire community.

However, research showed that ownership in indigenous people's terms exhibits conceptual tensions between *the ownership of an entity* and *the ownership of the place in which the entity activities are taking place*. A couple of examples illustrate this. First, a member of the board of directors mentioned how the association's actions co-depended on the rules of their *resguardo*, and although the association was legally owned by its registered members, the venture was at the disposal of the entire community.

The second example comes from a community member who pointed out how ownership in local terms had different connotations in comparison with the Western view of land tenure and property rights, arguing that their land did not belong to people in the community, as land and natural resources are regarded as sacred and land is part of their past, present and future. Across all five CSEs, ownership was referred to as a *white men* or *foreign* practice, and it was related to the idea of individual property that was imported by the colonizers (i.e., coercive isomorphism). Land was claimed to be part of the community rather than being possessed by an individual or a few, and this form of ownership has been one of the indigenous peoples' struggles in Colombia: *land rights* and *territoriality* were two of the main motivations for setting up formal organizations (Morales, 2019).

In almost all the ICOs, in which business activities were land-based, land belonged to the *resguardo* that the members of the ICOs were part of. Activities including agriculture, cattle, floriculture and ethno-tourism seemed to be interdependent on the rules of the *resguardo* where the activities were taking place. In this respect, conceptual tensions arose because, while ownership of the ICOs was legally bound to regulations imposed by external institutions, giving the power of property to their registered member over the organization, at the same time the ICOs were culturally bound by the rules established by their community, particularly when the business activities were taking place in the *resguardo*. Thus, ICOs seemed to be caught between external and internal regulations.

For example, in the Cooperativa Las Delicias (CS1), members' main objectives were to develop a formal organization to generate income and be able to buy the lands that historically were taken away from them. Some of the Misak leaders and authorities never agreed with the strategy of legally buying Misak territory, arguing that the ancestral land should be given back for free. Such discord has led to the separation of the Cabildo[5] of Guambia from the current Cabildo San Fernando, where the Cooperativa Las Delicias and its members are located—coercive isomorphism generating conflict among members of the community when formalization occurs. And to manage the tensions (resistance), indigenous members adopt informal practices that deviate from formal requirements.

A second stream of evidence showed that the organizational structure of the ICOs is a hybrid deviation from SSE standards for both types of organizations, DSOs and SEOs. Although SSE standards require that SSE organizations must be structured according to their legal form (e.g., having a board of directors), two types of organizational structure were identified among CSEs in which external regulations adapted their forms (through negotiation). First is the *autonomous form*, which operates as a *flatarchy* organization, where responsibilities and tasks are allocated evenly and internally among members, and even though members of the board of directors play managerial and senior roles, they tend to be actively involved in company operations, although periodically the board of directors must be renewed and elected. Second is the *quasi-autonomous form*, which functions as a combination of *flatarchy* and hierarchical organizations at the internal and external levels, respectively, when ICOs were interdependent on an external entity or entities (i.e., usually the cabildo or the community).

The collective dimension can also be seen in the way that planning and organizing were at times either performed or directed by the indigenous authorities for the collective benefit of the community, independently of the ICO's autonomy. This can be linked with the indigenous literature, which suggests that indigenous communities tend to be organized in horizontal structures where the authority is chosen by the community, and the governor of the *resguardo* plays a community role working on a voluntary basis. Some ICOs have flat organizational structures with the board of directors elected by members, but board members also play team roles at an operational level. Similarly, nonregistered members were also involved in the operations of the ICOs, following cultural values of solidarity and collaboration:

> Despite the fact that tasks are allocated evenly amongst the members of our association . . . our community sometimes is also involved . . . it is necessary, because we need to outsource some of the services . . . that was the commitment with the people here in the *resguardo*. Everybody wins . . . also, sometimes we need to report to the cabildo and inform the community of any activity.
>
> (Treasurer, VIPU3, CS4)

To summarize, with regard to organizational structure, the ICO process of internalizing organizational structures, based on SSE standards, is moderated by an emancipatory practice that creates a hybrid version (*creative resistance* in postcolonial terms) through the implementation of cultural practices at an organizational, but informal, level (i.e., deviating formal practices; Claeyé and Jackson, 2012).

Production of Goods and Services

The production of goods and services varied among all CSEs. Evidence suggested that the ICOs' process of production was determined by IOGs adopting external business practices (process of mimicry) that were transformed into hybrid forms of production. Some of the challenges faced may be summarized as follows:

- Developing farming practices combining local and external knowledge
- Managing operational strategies strongly influenced by Western dominant discourses (i.e., management, business operations)
- Exploiting the land sustainably to protect Mother Earth
- Exploitation of natural resources for sustainable floriculture
- Managing marketing strategies for both community advocacy and commercialization
- Commercialization of ancestral products, indigenous medicine, and traditional cuisine
- Improving weaving and handicraft by external methods (i.e., technology or assembly-line strategy)

Two examples of the latter include "We understood that the only way to be competitive was to improve our handicraft production by implementing an assembly-line strategy, breaking the work into small deskilled tasks" (President, VIWA1, CS5) and "We tried to implement technology in our ancestral ways of production; we depended on demand, so we need to adapt to improve our production costs" (Accountant, YAFG1.5, CS2).

Research identified some similarities at the informal level to establish the nature of the ICOs' modus operandi in order to illustrate the hybridization process. The resulting hybrid forms are determined by an element of innovation in which traditional practices are enhanced (or transformed) to meet organizational objectives and improve organizational practices. For instance, the Cooperativa Indígena Las Delicias very often uses the traditional practice of bartering as a strategy to manage production surpluses (the goods that could not be sold). Bartering also enables the exchange of products between regions within the Misak community. Generally, products that are produced in cold areas are exchanged for products produced in hot areas.[6]

ICOs' informal activities may be differentiated between two types: *land-based* production of mainly agricultural goods and *culture-based* production of goods and services (including traditional handicrafts production, traditional medicines, local cuisine, fishing and hunting), both complemented with other mainly collective types of activities, as well as by external variables that influence the process of production. For example, Akayu (CS3) commercializes an ancestral product called *mañoco* (Amazonian yam). Traditionally, *mañoco* is cooked fried or is eaten in soups, but Akayu transformed it into a crisp form and commercializes it as a snack product. There were similarities and differences among ICOs during the hybridization process when emulating external methods. Similarities can be found between ICO practices at the formal level and the informal practices influenced by their indigenous culture and by exploring the mimicry process and creative resistance to strengthen identity and how this leads to a hybrid form. A member of an ICO commented,

> We currently offer services that involve the ancestral practices of our culture. The role of our Shamans as healers in our community has existed for centuries; we have clients who are interested in trying alternatives to heal themselves from different illnesses, particularly cancer.
>
> (Member, VIPU4, CS4)

A community member explained: "There is no way to understand indigenous organizations, but to understand where our organizational practices come from, in all our organizational practices there is a cultural feature" (Member, MKFC1.7, CS1).

ICO participants reported that there were advantages and disadvantages to combining both local indigenous and external knowledge. There is an intrinsic dilemma between mimicking or disregarding external practices (influenced strongly by Western managerial and entrepreneurial dominant discourses). As one participant said,

> We acknowledge that, by making our dairy production more efficient, we have to embrace both worlds, the Western one and our knowledge to improve our productivity . . . we bring in professionals that support us for the operation of the *finca* and, so far, results are quite good.

But, during the production of videos (participative video research approach), some of the participants were reluctant to highlight the advantages of appropriating Western practices that could benefit their organizational activities; instead, they wanted to report the importance of bringing local cultural aspects into the process of production and how by reimplementing ancestral knowledge (e.g., agroforestry, crop rotation, polyculture and water harvesting), production processes could be improved (i.e., by countering normative isomorphism).

Tensions in emulating external practices were observed in those CSEs that conducted land-based activities (in three of the cases) when production processes either followed local knowledge or used a combination of both Western and local. With the objective of enhancing farming processes, achieving sustainable agricultural methods and improving income generation, some of the ICOs implemented external farming methods using all or most of the following: high-yield varieties of seeds, chemically derived fertilizers, pesticides and herbicides, irrigation and mechanization. For example, there was community concern about how the land was used and how the use of pesticides and genetically modified seeds were having a negative impact on the well-being of the environment and their families. A community leader noted,

> There are many issues with implementing white men's methods of farming production . . . with them [these methods], cancer and other types of illness appeared . . . the excessive use of pesticides and other chemicals on our lands is producing some health issues and affecting the well-being of the community.
>
> (Accountant, YAFG1.8, CS2)

Similarly, regarding modern business practices (marketing, economies of scale, professionalization), one participant said, "We realized that, in order to be more productive, we have to be professionalized, we learnt a lot of strategies that could be useful for our business" (District Attorney, VICU3, CS3).

Thus, not all members were unenthusiastic about appropriate external farming methods or knowledge; on the contrary, not only were they willing to use them; they also partnered with other institutions to improve agricultural production (an innovative approach in indigenous practices). For example, Cooperativa Las Delicias partnered with a local university to conduct research to use the land sustainably, free from pesticides, and improve organic seed production. A partner researcher from a local university pointed out the importance of working in partnership with the indigenous communities to enrich scientific knowledge with the indigenous one (i.e., hybridization arising from innovation, to counter isomorphism). She stressed:

> We came here to conduct research on an onion plague that was affecting local production . . . we are now working hand in hand with them and the results have been amazing . . . their knowledge is unique and I have learnt so much from them . . . we work in a really horizontal way . . . I think many universities should stop patronizing them and appreciate what they have to offer.
>
> (Researcher, V1MK3, CS1)

Here, the evidence showed that hybrid models of production emerged from seeking sustainable and productive agricultural methods (resistance). Although many participants often blamed external approaches for agricultural problems and environmental catastrophe, many others acknowledged the advantages of combining both types of knowledge.

Two other important aspects of the hybridization transformation process, from informality to formality, should be mentioned. First, there is pressure from the regulatory environment: "There are standards that we have to comply with according to the tourist industry of the country" (Treasurer, VIPU3, CS4). And second is how collective traditional work complements the modern production of goods and services; this includes bartering to manage overproduction; and the importance of indigenous *minga* (collective work when labor is needed to manage high demand). In almost all the ICOs, *collectiveness* was an innovative approach for improving the production process. Since the ICOs' capital resources (tools, equipment, buildings, and machinery) were scarce, their key assets were human resources capabilities. Indigenous collectiveness, particularly the *minga*, was seen as crucial in developing more participative, proactive and engaged work practices. In this context, indigenous people perceived work as a cultural tradition rather than an organizational duty:

> The collective work that the 31 communities did to start the Finca El Paraíso was crucial in order to be at the stage that we are today . . . this land belongs to all of us, thus we have to protect it and preserve it. . . . When a big job is needed, we put out a call for work *mingas*. . . . And people have to come . . . it is a cultural duty . . . we cannot simply outsource the labor that we need knowing that we've got such community commitment.
>
> (Accountant, YAFG1.5, CS2)

This also shows how collective practices provided the motive power to organizations, particularly, when the organizations faced economic challenges or were in great need and increased labor was required. Thus, collectiveness amongst indigenous people not only is a cultural feature but also nurtures social cohesions and benefits the ICOs. However, this could also mean that collective work was seen as more of a communal duty than voluntary. In some CSEs, it was reported that by not participating and getting involved in collective activities, individuals were disrespected and sometimes punished:

> Collective work is something that is embedded in our community and is part of our DNA, it is a collective responsibility . . . the cooperative belongs to everybody . . . thus everybody has a duty to contribute to it. . . . People who do not collaborate disrespect their family and their community . . . we have to honor our people on an everyday basis.
>
> (Member/Co-founder, V1MK2, CS1)

The indigenous entrepreneurship literature suggests that volunteerism and collectivism are common characteristics amongst indigenous groups (R. B. Anderson et al., 2006; Giovannini, 2012; Peredo, 2001; Vázquez Maguirre et al., 2017, 2016).

Although *volunteerism* appears in the literature on SSE as an organizational strategy to enhance internal practices (e.g., Coraggio, 2007), indigenous collectiveness appears as an embedded cultural element in the mimicry and hybridity process. Irrespective of geographical location, the *minga* practice (referred to as *mingao* in the Guainía region) was commonly used by the majority of the ICOs and is one form of indigenous collectiveness frequently arising spontaneously. For instance, during the participatory video process, many participants who were not members of the ICOs joined the video activity to collaborate with the other members of their community—strengthening social bonds and reinforcing social cohesion.

Governance: Decision-Making Process

In order to understand the informal-to-formal organizational transformation within the process of mimicry and hybridization, it is important to recognize that precolonial ancestral practices have influenced postcolonial present-day practices which contextualize the SSE and its hybridization. These are diverse and include elements of the following:

- Community governance subjected to the rules of the *resguardo*
- Governors of each *resguardo* (evolved from the chief-led *cacicazgos*)
- General assembly (from all *resguardos*)
- Substantial degree of autonomy with self-determination rights
- Cabildo authority (sometimes ruling over the clan)
- The council of traditional authorities
- Some Indigenous Councils as part of the territorial government
- Some clan-led bodies, with board of members
- Morning and afternoon community meetings, age-led, with unanimity amongst the members
- Some hierarchical systems led by *Abuelo* (the eldest), shaman (*Payé*) and the chief (captain)

Two types of forms of governance were identified as hybrids arising from the transformation process: *autonomous* and *quasi-autonomous decision-making* processes. Similar to the ownership theme described earlier, some of the ICO's decision-making processes were internal to the ICO, and some external—influenced by the indigenous authorities (cabildo) and the community (in the *resguardo*). Informal modes of governance complement the formal organizational practices conforming to SSE standards and strengthen the resulting organizational practices.

Findings indicated that *governance* was a neology introduced to the indigenous communities by external bodies, such as the Supersolidaria. The term *decision-making* was widely used when referring to the collective process of selecting a course of action amongst different options to reach a goal or goals. While the Supersolidaria required that all SSE types, SEOs and DSOs, should adopt democratic governance approaches giving legal rights to their members, ICOs were, in fact, culturally bound to governance by their communities. And similarly indigenous communities tend to prioritize common ends over private ones (including for local organizations). For example, CS4 is legally registered as an association, but organizational power is extended to the *cabildo* and the community in the *resguardo*. This resulted in a hybrid form of governance:

> The objectives of our associations are ruled by the statutes that the members created . . . However, the statutes are ruled by our indigenous authorities. . . . The interest of our organization simply cannot override the interest of our people.
>
> (Vice-President, VIPU2, CS4)

Formally, the new organizational practice (hybrid form of governance) can be understood as the organizational response in the interplay of local and external variables internalized in the process of mimicry. This response is the act of resisting external forms of governance and strengthening indigenous culture by complementing formal practices with informal ones. The paradox of ICOs in complying with SSE governance standards and following the rules of local institutions can be seen as Bhabha's (2012) *third space*, where subordinate groups resist and negotiate their local and external variables, so creating a hybrid form.

Despite the fact that different forms of governance were adopted by each ICO, there was evidence of high community engagement, particularly when general assemblies were taking place (as it creates social cohesion). Collectiveness was a common feature that became an important part of decision-making. Associates' families may also be owners, and tasks may be distributed among all members of the community. The fact that 24% of the participants were community members (all the ICO's associates are community members,[7] but the 24% are non-associates of the ICOs) indicated the level of engagement with ICOs. A community member who is actively involved in the activities of the organization reported,

> Although we are not registered as members [referring to his family], we feel that we are part of the organization . . . we participate in the *minga* that they announce and we come to the assemblies, our friends and relatives are part of the organization . . . thus, so are we.
>
> (Teacher/Community Member, WAFG 1.19, CS5)

This corroborates the work carried out by Peredo (2001), Peredo and McLean (2013) that suggests that trust and community ties are both key elements of decision-making processes in indigenous entrepreneurship. The role of the community in any entrepreneurial activity is crucial, as wider participation generates a system of trust that facilitates decision-making processes when large numbers are involved.

The transformation process with regard to governance and decision-making shows how the SSE may accommodate a community hybrid (Peredo, 2001). But at the same time, formalization processes may distort community practices by being more selective of key community stakeholders, and by introducing conventional democratic practices (one person, one vote).

Thus, hybrid forms are developed when the decision-making process combines local and external variables; that is, decisions are made not only collectively following cultural traditions but also made democratically (one person, one vote) complying with external standards. For instance, in one of the ICOs, children were encouraged to be part of the decision-making process by participating in general assemblies from the age of 13. In other cases, organizational unanimity was widely practiced and decisions were made collectively and usually with a high degree of participation. Thus, decisions were not made on a majority basis but, rather, when there was not a convincing argument to block a decision. Some ICOs reported making decisions while doing a thinking *minga*, that is, when a group extensively discusses the same topic:

> General assemblies are really important for us . . . there, we have the opportunity to meet and discuss topics . . . Sometimes we take hours to make decisions because it is really important for us that everybody agrees or there is not enough reason to stop doing things. We make decisions unanimously. . . . That's why it is so important to hold thinking *mingas*.
>
> (Member, MKFG1.1, CS1)

Several factors enabled good governance practices among ICOs. First, in almost all CSEs, members shared the same conditions of being affiliated to the same indigenous community. Participants shared in (inter)personal relationships, culture, political affiliation, traditions and rules, history, social and economic conditions and common interest. This sense of homogeneity among members enabled better governance practice. In both forms of governance—autonomous and quasi-autonomous—collective practices were linked to shared community conditions, and wider participation was apparent. It was also seen as important to increase participation outside their ICOs to set an example for similar initiatives:

> We always seek to widen participation, as it legitimizes the process of decision-making and makes the process much easier when implementation is taking place. We all have common goals as we share the same socioeconomic and historical conditions . . . we need to have our ducks in a row to ensure that there is a general consensus at implementation level.
>
> (District Attorney, YAFG1.3, CS2)

> Our decisions are made by the 31 community Yanacona, they are their owners, it is their right. We do also invite our clientele to be part of the assemblies, it is important to include our stakeholders.
>
> (District Attorney, YAFG1.3, CS2)

Nevertheless, organizational issues emerged when participation was widened and inclusive governance took place. A number of ICOs reported having had a hard time during general assemblies and saw the disadvantage of grouping associates and community members, as some community members lacked information about their organizations, and there was a degree of slowness in the process. However, by implementing inclusiveness and democratic governance, ICOs improved implementation processes in the organization. Nonetheless, some weaknesses were highlighted:

> Gathering and making decisions together is great because it creates community cohesion, as our assemblies take place in community celebrations . . . but sometimes . . . we [the board of directors] struggle to please everybody . . . there is a very fine line between the social and the economic outcome.
>
> (General Manager, VIMK1, CS1)

The ICO's good practice in decision-making was subject to their capacity for effectively integrating and managing the tensions of local and external forms of governance. These cases show that informal governance practices (shaped by their view of the world) were implemented to improve the formal ones, and so this *complementarity* extends classic ideas of SSE forms of governance. This corroborates Peredo and McLean (2013), who argued that indigenous entrepreneurship revises and extends not only the concept of entrepreneurship in terms of decision-making but also the ideological basis on which these decisions are made. All ICOs (including the autonomous ones) drew on their cultural values in the decision-making process, which led to the majority of them including the wider community in their decision-making.

Organizational Strategies: Grant Seeking, Diversification, Capacity Building, Networking and Partnerships

A range of strategies were used by the ICOs to achieve short, medium, and long-term goals of the organization. All CSEs adopted external methods, combining them with informal practices as a hybrid strategy to enhance organizational practices. By emulating external methods (process of mimicry), the ICOs generated a bricolage of strategies with indigenous cultural elements that enhanced their repertoire of actions to meet capital, institutional and organizational objectives.

The analysis divided organizational strategies into different categories, grant seeking, capacity building, diversification, networking and partnerships, to examine how ICOs and their managers are influenced by external dominant discourses to overcome organizational challenges. Financial issues were the main obstacle identified in the five cases and may be seen as one of the main drivers of mimicry. *Grant seeking* was most reported by the board of directors[8] of ICOs as a key strategy to address this. Grant funding issues were more common at start-up but were also important during later development, although in some of the ICOs, initial funding was complemented by members' inputs, either in kind or in money. Only one of the ICOs used financial credit or a loan to start up and develop its business:

> Grant seeking had helped and may help us to meet our economic needs . . . sometimes it's really hard to cope with our financial responsibilities . . . and money is something that we always need . . . it is not crucial, but sometimes infrastructure is needed and we don't have enough financial resources. . . . In fact, I applied for a national award called *mujer Cafam* and I won, with the money that we got we reinvested everything into the organization. . . . Also, we have received some help from national and international institutions . . . we applied for different grants and we got some of them . . . we planned to seek those opportunities as we demonstrated that we could manage it perfectly.
>
> (President and Co-founder, CUFG1.1, CS3)

However, some tensions arose from the strategy of grant seeking. Attracting financial aid and other resource contributions (e.g., equipment, infrastructure and information technology) from external bodies could lead to high levels of aid dependency and contribute to organizational idleness and lack of managerial productivity:

> The problem in relying on grant seeking and aid so much is that the members of the organization may become a little lazy; if one only thinks of seeking aid, one tends to forget how to improve the business through other strategies.
>
> (President and Co-founder, VICU1, CS3)

On the other hand, dominant discourses may be imposed on ICOs since, typically, grants, funding and donations are subject to certain conditions and agendas that legitimate the colonized versus colonizers subjectivity among indigenous people. As a result, ICOs are obliged to change because of this (coercive) isomorphic pressure:

> Aid and external support are the disguises of neocolonial forms of power; by falling into these strategies, our communities are doomed to extinction . . . everything has an agenda behind it, I remember in here before, they [national entities] gave us financial help for local development and later they were privatizing our natural resources in our territory.
>
> (General Manager and Co-founder, V1MK6, CS1)

Additionally, in the majority of the ICOs a key aspect for tackling economic issues was business diversification, which enhanced economic performance, allowing the surplus to be reinvested in the organization and the community. For example, in Cooperativa Las Delicias (CS1), its main activity was agriculture; nonetheless, it identified that there was a lack of transport in the area where it was located and saw the opportunity to improve its income generation by operating a bus service from Guambia to Silvia. Similarly, Akayú Association (CS3) started as an association providing recycling services, but in order to include the rest of the members and improve economic performance, three more business activities were developed: retail, education and floriculture:

> We started with the recycling business and it went really well, but other things were also needed for the association, that's why we developed the other three services that today are really important for the economic performance of the organization . . . we have to admit also that, when we started, we had something different in mind for the other three services, but we improved them according to the necessities of our organization and public demand.
>
> (President and Co-founder, VICU1, CS3)

ICOs that diversified their businesses reduced the risks of relying on sales of only one type of product and ensured the survival of the company—by cost cutting while increasing their level of production in other businesses—if one of their markets collapsed, particularly in agriculture, a sector with the most difficulties in the Colombian context.

An example that illustrates a hybridity strategy in business diversification was Cooperativa Las Delicias (CS1), which diversified their businesses by using informal ancestral practices—bartering—to reduce wastage and manage food overproduction. This resulted in CS1 controlling the entire supply chain, not only producing goods with their own seeds but also commercializing them in their local store in Silvia (where they also sell other products):

> Bartering helps us to connect with our culture, plus helps us to reduce wastage and manage the surplus of production of some products . . . also, it is a really good strategy because we have access to products that we do not produce over here, our Misak community in the hot areas of Guambia also operates similarly . . . thus we complement each other.
>
> (District Attorney, MKFG1.5, CS1)

This can be linked with the BV pillar of plural economy, in which both economic practices (ancestral and orthodox) can complement each other and deliver a more efficient outcome (Hidalgo-Capitán and Cubillo-Guevara, 2016, 2017). It also shows hybrid models of production, where informal indigenous practices complement Western ones.

Capacity building was also important. The majority of ICOs tried to improve their competitiveness by embracing professional training and education[9] for their members—*normative isomorphism*, to use DiMaggio and Powell's (2000) terms. "We have seen the advantages of professionalizing our members, I myself am educated and I know how much I can contribute to the organization" (Assistant General Manager, CUFG 1.3, CS3).

The majority of respondents (focus groups) highlighted the benefits for the ICOs of having members with different educational backgrounds and skills. Although they stressed the importance of education and professional training, they asserted that ethno-education also strengthened capacity building. And in all the ICOs, members were associated with ethno-education, either as teachers or as students:

> If, for example, we have the model of collective milk production . . . and there are already 31 communities that are already benefiting from it here in Cauca . . . despite having many things that are adopted from the West, such as the technique of milking, shepherding management and operation of the equipment, we are creating an ecosystem and an eco-working space in which our young people can learn and develop other techniques to enhance our performance . . . the oldest are in charge of educating the youngest in our ancestral techniques.
>
> (Educator, YAFG1.7, CS2)

Another important aspect was that, by appropriating Western education, indigenous people could guard against being deceived. One of the oldest members and a co-founder of the CS1 stressed the following:

> When we started, we knew that we had to be educated . . . our parents and grandparents were deceived by the white men because they did not know anything about land rights and even the language . . . they [the landowners] befriended the indigenous people and then they made them sign documents assuring them that this was part of the process of buying and getting rights over the land . . . they did know the language, they didn't know what a contract was and they lost everything . . . that is why it is so important to compete on their own terms.
>
> (Member/Co-founder, V1MK2, CS1)

These findings seemed to reflect the hybridization process where internal and external knowledge is appropriated to enhance the performance of the ICO. By appropriating indigenous knowledge, local education is reinforced, leading the organization to better practices:

> The combination of ethno-education with Western education has been fundamental for the improvement of our products. At the end of the day we commercialize our art, so it is important that most members know how to make our art while thinking about business.
>
> (Treasurer, VIWA2, CS5)

Capacity is also enhanced through community collaboration to reduce labor costs, such as through work *minga*s or seed swapping.

The majority of the ICOs studied reported that two other aspects improved strategic planning and performance: *partnerships* and *networking*. The ICOs networks were constituted by internal and external actors including local and regional authorities, international entities, local businesses, the local community, local suppliers, educational institutions, cabildos and indigenous people's advocates. ICOs in the study highlighted the importance of widening their venture's networking and identifying key partnerships to enhance their organization's performance.

> Our objective is to generate an alliance with other tourist agencies, to create a tourist chain here in the region . . . we have done it already here in the *resguardo* . . . the association is in charge of finding the tourists and we connect them with other services here in the community . . . we do offer traditional medicine . . . thus we have a network of shamans here in the *resguardo* . . . they do not actually work with us . . . but we outsource the work.
>
> (Treasurer, PUFG 1.3, CS4)

> Our objective is to reinforce our culture by investing time and economic resources to research . . . How we operate and how we could work the land and treat the livestock sustainably, with our traditional knowledge . . . That is why we partner with the local agricultural schools here in the *resguardo* to encourage students to come to la Finca Lechera el Paraiso and do some fieldwork. . . . At the end of the day, this enterprise belongs to all of us.
>
> (Public Administrator, VIYA2, CS2)

Concluding Remarks

This chapter has provided original evidence about the hybrid characteristics of the selected ICOs and how they remain strongly affiliated with their indigenous values. The approach has been to examine the interplay between local and external variables influencing the development, nature and operations of ICOs in the Colombian context. The first step was examining the ICOs' raison d'être as a combination of internal and external motivations that led IOGs to formalize their initiatives where the community played a strong role.

Next, by drawing on Bhabha's (1984, 2012) mimicry and hybridity and bringing some insights from culturalist and institutional theory (e.g., DiMaggio and Powell, 2000), this chapter illuminates the characteristics of the ICOs at meso level. The CSEs explore the extent to which ICOs' hybrid forms are the result of creative resistance and/or negotiation of the two worlds (indigenous and Western), in which the IOGs adopt and adapt external variables (i.e., the SSE standards and/or other variables) within the process of mimicry as they become formalized. At meso level, despite some similarities, ICOs cannot be considered an isomorphic organization and be compared with any other SSEs; instead, ICOs' characteristics are shaped by the set of values and practices of each organization's ecosystem and the adaptation of foreign practices into their business persona.

Four conceptual categories encapsulate how the tensions and conflicts inherent in hybrid forms are managed. First are deviant informal practices, which differ from formal ones to enhance organizational praxes. Ownership was one of the examples that illuminate this phenomenon, where one of the CSEs adopted cooperativism to recover the land that was taken in colonial times. Second is the transformation of informal practices through innovation that helped ICOs to meet their organizational objectives and improve formal praxes. Many CSEs improved their production of goods and services by commercializing indigenous products. Most saw a business opportunity to diversify their offer while strengthening their indigenous culture. Third, complementarity, where informal ancestral praxes enhance formal practices. SSE forms of governance were enhanced by widening participation to the community, and similarly, complementary processes enhance organizational productivity. Fourth is the implementation of informal practices as a strategy for enhancing the repertoire of actions to meet the needs of the organization. Many CSEs implement traditional practices to achieve organizational goals. For example, CS1 implemented bartering in order to manage wastage and reduce production cost.

The formalization process to meet legal requirements has led to organizational struggles to balance the needs, values and interests among ICO members, the ICO's affiliated community, and the internal and external institutions (cabildos, local and national state authorities and SSE-related institutions). This is in line with a study conducted by Vázquez Maguirre et al. (2017) that identified a conflict of interest between managers and other members of indigenous social enterprises in Mexico and Peru. However, the internal and external values of each entity appeared to be drivers for setting organizational objectives and goals. But external institutional standards may push ICOs to follow organizational standards that lead to an eventual transformation of their indigenous values. None-theless, there remain some gaps that require further investigation concerning the influences of Buen Vivir on each ICO.

Notes

1. Postcolonialism is the total sum of all the social, political, cultural and economic changes brought about by the impact of colonialism (Claeyé and Jackson, 2012).
2. *Pachamamismo* is referred to, generally negatively, as an indigenous political discourse that only relies on indigenous peoples' view of the world and is considered populist because it is not consistent with the existing conditions in society (Stefanoni, 2010).
3. The indigenous landholdings.
4. This CSE can be defined as an SE (e.g., Giovannini, 2012).
5. Local government council.
6. See the importance of bartering for the Misak community in the following link: https://youtu.be/CroUSFEzRiE.
7. Community members: individuals who are part of the indigenous community.
   Associates or Members: individuals who are part of an indigenous association or cooperative.
8. NB: 32% of the participants were either part of the board of directors or were directly involved in the management process.
9. Remarkably, 58% of the participants were either professionally trained (vocational or technical courses) or educated in universities.

References

Acosta, A. (2013). *El buen vivir: sumak kawsay, una oportunidad para imaginar otros mundos*. Barcelona: Icaria Editorial.
Acosta, A. (2015). "El buen vivir como alternativa al desarrollo," *Revista Política y Sociedad*, 52(2), pp. 299–330.
Agrawal, A. (1995). "Dismantling the Divide Between Indigenous and Scientific Knowledge," *Development and Change*, 26(1), pp. 413–450.
Albó, X. (2009). "Suma Qamaña, el Buen Convivir," *Revista OBETS de Ciencias Sociales*, 4, pp. 25–40.
Anderson, R. B., Dana, L. P. and Dana, T. E. (2006). "Indigenous Land Rights, Entrepreneurship, and Economic Development in Canada: 'Opting-in' to the Global Economy," *Journal of World Business*, 41, pp. 45–55.
Bhabha, H. K. (1984). "Of Mimicry and Man: The Ambivalence of Colonial Discourse," *Discipleship: A Special Issue on Psychoanalysis*, 28, pp. 125–133.
Bhabha, H. K. (2012). *The Location of Culture*. London: Routledge.
Bretón, V. (2013). "Etnicidad, desarrollo y 'Buen Vivir': reflexiones críticas en perspectiva histórica," *Revista Europea de Estudios Latinoamericanos y del Caribe*, 95(1), pp. 71–95.
Calvo, S. and Morales, A. (2017). *Social and Solidarity Economy: The World's Economy with a Social Face*. Studies in International Business and the World Economy. London: Routledge.
Caria, S. and Domínguez, R. (2014). *El Porvenir de una Ilusión: La Ideología del Buen Vivir*. Quito: Abya Yala.

Caria, S. and Domínguez, R. (2016). "Ecuador's Buen Vivir: A New Ideology for Development," *Latin American Perspectives*, 43(1), pp. 18–33.

Claeyé, F. and Jackson, T. (2012). "The Iron Cage Re-Revisited: Institutional Isomorphism in Non-Profit Organisations in South Africa," *Journal of International Development*, 24(5), pp. 602–622.

Coraggio, J. L. (1994). "La construcción de una economía popular: vía para el desarrollo humano," *Revista de Economía y Trabajo*, 2(3), pp. 1–50.

Coraggio, J. L. (2007). *La economia social desde la periferia: contribuciones Latinoamericanas*. Buenos Aires: Altamira.

Coraggio, J. L. (2011). *El Trabajo antes que el capital*. Quito: Editorial Abya Yala.

Correa, R. (2007, January 15). *Discurso posesión del presidente de la República, Rafael Correa Delgado en la mitad del mundo*. www.presidencia.gob.ec/wp-content/uploads/downloads/2013/09/2007-01-15-Discurso-Posesión-Presiden cial-Mitad-del-Mundo.pdf (Accessed on 25 October 2018).

Correa, R. (2008, July 25). *Intervención del president de la república, Rafael Correa en la ceremonia de clausura de la Asamblea Nacional Constituyente*. Montecristi. www.presidencia.gob.ec/wp-content/uploads/downloads/2013/10/2008-07-25-Intervención-Presidencial-Clausura-Asamblea-Constituyente.pdf (Accessed on 25 October 2018).

Cubillo-Guevara, A. P., Hidalgo-Capitán, A. L. and Domínguez-Gómez, J. A. (2014). "El pensamiento sobre el Buen Vivir: entre el indigenismo, el socialismo y el posdesarrolismo," *Revista del CLAD Reforma y Democracia*, 11(1), pp. 1–35.

DANSOCIAL. (2010). "Dansocial, Construyendo un Pais Solitario," *Revista Solidario*.

Dávalos, P. (2011). "Sumak Kawsay: La vida en plenitud," *Convivir para Perdurar: Conflictos Ecosociales y Sabidurías Ecológicas*. Icaria Publisher, pp. 201–214.

DiMaggio, P. J. and Powell, W. W. (2000). "The Iron Cage Revisited: Institutional Isomorphism and Collective Rationality in Organizational Fields," *Economics Meets Sociology in Strategic Management*, 17, pp. 143–166.

Escobar, A. (2010). "Latin America at a Crossroads: Alternative Modernizations, Post-Liberalism, or Post-Development?" *Cultural Studies*, 25(1), pp. 1–65.

García-Linera, A. (2010). "El socialismo comunitario," *Revista de Análisis*, 3(5), pp. 12–22.

Giovannini, M. (2012). "Social Enterprises for Development as Buen Vivir," *Journal of Enterprising Communities*, 6(1), pp. 284–299.

Gros, C. (1991). *Colombia indígena-identidad cultural y cambio social*. Bogotá: CEREC, 2nd edn.

Gros, C. (2000). *Políticas de la etnicidad: identidad, estado y nodernidad*. Bogotá: Instituto Colombiano de Antropología e Historia.

Guandinango Vinueza, Y. A. (2013). "Del Sumak Kawsay al Allin Kawsay Relaciones Socioculturales en los Sistemas Familiars Comunitarios una Mirada desde las Comunidades Kichwas," in C. Von Barloewen, M. Rivera and K. Töpfer (eds.), *Desarrollo Sostenible en una Modernidad Plural: Perspectivas latinoamericanas*. Quito: Abya Yala.

Gudynas, E. (2011). "Buen Vivir: germinando alternativas al desarrollo," *America Latina en Movimiento*, 462(1–20), pp. 25–36.

Hidalgo-Capitán, A. L. and Cubillo-Guevara, A. P. (2015). "La trinidad del Buen Vivir en Ecuador," *Política Exterior Latinoamérica Análisis*, 14(9), pp. 40–53.

Hidalgo-Capitán, A. L. and Cubillo-Guevara, A. P. (2016). *Transmodernidad y transdesarrollo: el decrecimiento y el Buen Vivir como dos versiones análogas de un transdesarrollo transmoderno.* Huelva and España: Ediciones Bonanza.

Hidalgo-Capitán, A. L. and Cubillo-Guevara, A. P. (2017). "Deconstrucción y genealogía del Buen Vivir Latinoamericano: El (trino) Buen Vivir y sus diversos manantiales intelectuales," *International Development Policy*, 9(9), pp. 45–66.

Huanacuni, F. (2010). *Buen Vivir/Vivir Bien: filosofía, políticas, estrategias y experiencias regionales Andinas.* Lima: CAOI Coordinadora Andina de Organizaciones Indígenas.

Jackson, T. (2011). "From cultural values to cross-cultural interfaces: Hofstede goes to Africa", *Journal of Organizational Change Management*, 24(4), pp. 532–558.

Lalander, R. (2016). "The Ecuadorian Resource Dilemma: Sumak Kawsay or Development?" *Critical Sociology*, 42(4–5), pp. 623–642.

Lye, J. (1998). *Some Issues in Postcolonial Theory: The Literature(s) of the Colonized.* Available at http://www.brocku.ca/english/courses/4F70/postcol.php (Accessed 23 October 2018).

Lye, J. (2017). *An Introduction to Post-Colonialism, Post-Colonial Theory and Post-Colonial Literature.* Available at http://www.decolonize.org/wpcontent/uploads/2015/05/anintroduction-to-postcolonialism.pdf (Accessed on 25 October 2018).

Morales, A. (2019). "Indigenous-Hybrid Organisations in Colombia: A Multi-Level Analysis within the Buen Vivir Model," Unpublished PhD Thesis, Milton Keynes, Open University.

Peredo, A. M. (2001). *Communal Enterprises, Sustainable Development and the Alleviation of Poverty in Rural Andean Communities.* Calgary: University of Calgary.

Peredo, A. M. and McLean, M. (2013). "Indigenous Development and the Cultural Captivity of Entrepreneurship," *Business & Society*, 52(4), pp. 592–620.

Pilataxi Lechón, C. (2014). *Sumak Kawsay organización comunitaria y emprendimiento productivo: el caso de San Pablo Urku, Cayambe.* Quito: Abya Yala.

Prada Alcoreza, R. (2012). "El Vivir Bien como modelo de estado y modelo económico," in M. Lang and D. Mokrani (eds.), *Más allá del desarrollo.* Quito: Editorial Abya Yala, pp. 227–263.

Ramírez-Gallegos, R. (2010). *Socialismo del Sumak Kawsay o biosocialismo republicano.* Quito: Secretaría Nacional de Planificación y Desarrollo.

Ramírez-Gallegos, R. (2011). *La felicidad como medida del Buen Vivir en Ecuador.* Quito: Secretaría Nacional de Planificación y Desarrollo.

Said, E. W. (2004). *Humanism and Democratic Criticism.* New York: Columbia University Press.

Said, E. W. (2012). *Culture and Imperialism.* New York: Vintage.

Santos, B. de S. (2010). "Hablamos del socialismo del Buen Vivir," *Camino Social*, 9(1), pp. 4–7.

SENPLADES. (2009). *Plan Nacional para el Buen Vivir 2009–2013: Construyendo un Estado Plurinacional e Intercultural.* Quito: Talleres Gráficos Calle. www.planificacion.gob.ec/wp-content/uploads/downloads/2012/07/Plan_Nacional_para_el_Buen_Vivir.pdf (Accessed on 23 October 2018).

Serna Gómez, H. and Rubio-Rodríguez, G. A. (2016). "Governability in the Field of Cooperative Organizations: A Reflection on Its True Implementation," *Revista Virtual Universidad Catolica Del Norte*, 48(1), pp. 239–256.

Simbaña, F. (2012). "El Sumak Kawsay como proyecto político," in M. Lang and D. Mokrani (eds.), *Más allá del desarrollo*. Quito: Editorial Abya Yala, pp. 219–226.

Spivak, G. C. (1988). *Can the Subaltern Speak? Reflections on the History of an Idea*. New York: Columbia University Press.

Stefanoni, P. (2010, May 4). "Indianismo y Pachamamismo," *Rebelion*. www.rebelion.org/noticia.php?id=105233 (Accessed on 24 October 2018).

Stefanoni, P. (2011). "Adónde nos lleva el pachamamismo," *Tabula Rasa*, 1, pp. 261–264.

Svampa, M. (2011). "Extractivismo neodesarrollista y movimientos sociales: un giro ecoterritorial hacia nuevas alternativas," *Más Allá Desarrollo*, 1(1), pp. 185–218.

Svampa, M. (2012). "Pensar el desarrollo desde America Latina," in G. Massuh (ed.), *Renunciar al bien común. Extractivismo y (pos)desarrollo en America Latina*. Buenos Aires: Mardulce, pp. 17–58.

Ulloa, A. (2004). *El Nativo ecológico. complejidades, paradojas y dilemas de la relación de los movimientos indígenas y el ambientalismo en Colombia*. Bogotá: Icanh.

Valderrama, E. (2005). *La Gobernabilidad: Factor en Desarrollo en las Entidades Solidarias*. Bogota: Superintendencia de la Economia Solidaria.

Vanhulst, J. (2015). "El laberinto de los discursos del Buen Vivir: entre Sumak Kawsay y socialismo del siglo XXI," *Polis (Santiago)*, 14(40), pp. 233–261.

Vázquez Maguirre, M., Portales, L. and Velásquez Bellido, I. (2017). "Indigenous Social Enterprises as Drivers of Sustainable Development: Insights from México and Peru," *Critical Sociology*, 44(2), pp. 323–340.

Vázquez Maguirre, M., Ruelas, G. C. and Torre, C. G. D. L. (2016). "Women Empowerment Through Social Innovation in Indigenous Social Enterprises," *Revista de Administração Mackenzie*, 17(6), pp. 164–190.

Walsh, C. (2012). "'Other' Knowledges, 'other' Critiques: Reflections on the Politics and Practices of Philosophy and Decoloniality in the 'other' America," *Transmodernity*, 1(1), pp. 11–27.

8 Indian Diasporic Communities

Exploring Belonging, Marginality and Transnationalism

Rashmi Singla, P. K. Shajahan and Sujata Sriram

The Indian diaspora, primarily in the Scandinavian[1] countries along with a comparative perspective in the United States, is the focus of this chapter. It is a result of a transnational collaboration among colleagues.[2] The chapter attempts to address some of the stereotypes about Indian diasporic communities by focusing on both *here* and *there—the country of residence* as well as *the country of origin* for diaspora members (*diasporics*) through a people-centered social innovation approach.

In line with the major approach of this book, we perceive people-centered social innovation as a process of social change, new ideas and actions that address unmet social needs, especially within the context of marginalization, which can be experienced by diasporics in the country of residence as well as the country of origin. This approach is an exploration of the ways in which the mobility of individuals, goods and ideas is reshaping both the countries, with a focus on reproduction, alteration and challenges to the subjectivities of diasporics (Hulgård and Shajahan, 2013). Thus, the first-person voices and interests of the diasporic form the central aspect of the chapter, illustrating the people-centered approach as a methodological orientation, where the state *integration* provision is also covered. At the same time, historical and policy-related aspects are also briefly presented in order to contextualize people's experiences in the two cases of Denmark and the United States. Members of diasporic communities are conceptualized as active *agents* who can transform society and confront marginalization rather than being seen as just clients or patients whose well-being commands attention (Drèze and Sen, 1989).

The Indian diaspora, as a transnational community, is one of the world's largest, most heterogeneous and dynamic across the globe. It comprises approximately 30 million individuals who claim Indian origin and who have contributed to global economic, cultural and psychosocial interconnections over the past few decades (Convert PIO, 2017). Globalization and liberalization of the global economic system, coupled with the rapid advancement of transport and communication technologies that have radically altered our experience of time and space, have intensified their socioeconomic, political and cultural ties with their countries of origin. Eventually, they emerge as an inevitable link between their home and host lands, which brings major political and economic implications for both sides (Mahalingam, 2017). Thus, diaspora actors and communities are increasingly recognized as a resource in international relations, for economic and sociocultural collaborations, as well as domestically, in their country of origin. India has topped the remittance chart for 2017, pulling in US$69 billion from its global migrant workforce. China follows with US$64.14 billion, with the Philippines and Mexico behind (Times of India, 2018). The diasporic communities are undergoing transformations in various life domains through interconnections between the country of origin and country of residence; consequently, new senses of belonging and marginality are being created.

While migration from India has always been present historically, the term *diaspora* used to refer to people of Indian origin living in various parts of the world was not conventionally used. The terms commonly used were *Overseas Indians*, or *People of Indian Origin*. It was first used in academic discourse in 1994, at an International Conference on the Indian Diaspora at the University of Hyderabad (Raghuram and Sahoo, 2008), and a Center for the Study of Indian Diaspora at the University of Hyderabad was established in 1995 (Jayaram, 2005).

With the concept of diaspora and transnationalism as a point of departure, this chapter focuses on the Indian diaspora in Denmark and the United States, briefly covering policies related to the diaspora in India. The next section considers qualitative empirical studies based on first-person experiences illuminating psychosocial aspects, followed by some suggestions for promoting interconnections, communication and links between the country of origin, that is, India, and its diaspora within the people-centered approach.

In accordance with the central idea of this book, the focus on the voices of the persons involved as the major aspect of the method illustrates explicitly how a people-centered social innovation approach is not a theory but a methodological orientation aimed at giving actors a voice, along with covering state provision for dealing with the diaspora, which involves differences, similarities and belonging (Hulgaard, L. and P.K. Shajahan, 2013).

The Concept of Diaspora and Transnationalism Processes

Although the *Diaspora* historically refers to the dispersal of the Jews after the Babylonian exile in 586 BCE, in contemporary modernity it is applied to any group of people who are dwelling far from their country of origin. From a social psychological perspective, a core issue in being diasporic is how to reconcile individuality with community, a constant need to clarify one's position in relation to the power holders, to one's own identity and to what is right and wrong—issues of power, identity and ethics (Dencik, 2014). Diaspora is also about dispersal from a referent origin, maintaining connections and managing distance (Dufoix, 2008), which directs our attention to the process of transnationalism. Being diasporic today implies *transnationalism*,[3] defined as a social process of inhabiting two worlds simultaneously, through the attachment and commitment to two or more nations at the same time. Transnational families are defined as families that live some or most of the time separated from each other yet hold together and create what can be seen as a feeling of collective welfare and unity, namely, *familyhood*, even across national borders (Bryceson and Vuorela, 2002: 3). The recent proliferation of a wide range of affordable communication technologies is central to important transformations in our social and intimate lives, as it also affects transnationalism.

Transnational networks and links between India (*desh*) and the Indian diaspora abroad (*videsh*) are a part of this process. These have led to a reevaluation of the self—*identity* and exercise of *power* in the virtual space. This is illustrated in the study of Indian transnationalism online (Sahoo and Kruijf, 2014; Bhatia, 2018) and in the present chapter.

Historically, there has been migration from the Indian subcontinent that goes back hundreds of years. After the abolition of slavery in the British colonies in 1833–1834, there was a need for labor for plantations in the Caribbean, Malaya and Mauritius. *Indentured labor* from India by colonial governments and plantation owners filled this deficit, wherein the emigrant had to work for a specified employer for three to five years. This essentially highlights the importance of early recognition of *belonging* as one of the central features of emigration and the lives of immigrant communities.

A few migrants served as clerks and teachers as part of the colonial expansion to the Middle East, East Africa and South Africa, along with some petty traders and shopkeepers, referred to as the 'old diaspora'. They had very little contact with their country of origin, with many of them losing touch with the language but retaining aspects of the culture (Bhat and Bhaskar, 2007; Kapur, 2003).

The period after the Second World War heralded another movement of people of Indian origin. This was the *movement of twice-migrants*— people of Indian origin who had moved to countries in Africa and the West Indies, who saw the opportunity to move to the United Kingdom, Canada and Australia and some later to the United States (Bhachu, 1999). Many of these individuals were compelled to leave behind a greater part of their savings and wealth in their flight out of East Africa. Very rarely did these individuals return to India.

Indians in Denmark and the United States

Denmark, a Scandinavian country, along with Sweden and Norway, is characterized by the welfare state model, which emphasizes egalitarian and extensive benefit levels, wealth redistribution, and promotion of gender equality and maximization of labor force participation (Guribye and Overland, 2014). There are also processes of exclusion, xenophobia, inequality and poverty, among others. It is one of the regions where highly skilled migrants (and their families under the *green card scheme*)[4] are invited to fill gaps in the labor market, mainly since the 2000s. In the late 1960s and early 1970s, there was a demand for unskilled labor leading to the first wave of the Indian diaspora, followed by a formal halt to non-Nordic migration in 1972. Since the 1970s, immigration has consisted mainly of refugees and family reunification from Middle Eastern and Asian countries. However, these diasporic communities are under-explored academically, almost totally absent from any mapping of the Indian diaspora[5] (Jayaram, 2005).

According to the Indian Embassy in Denmark (2017), Indians in Denmark number 11,200 in total. There has been a steady rise in numbers among the Indian diaspora due to the arrival of information technology (IT) professionals, doctors and students in recent times (CPH India, 2016; Singla and Varma, 2019).

We add a comparative perspective using research by one of the authors (Sriram, 2014) about the issues of acculturation and cultural identity among the Indian diaspora in California in the United States. Sriram studied Indian American (as they like to call themselves) adolescents and families. The Indian diaspora in the United States constitutes the largest growing ethnic minority group in the United States but has a relatively short history of about 50 years. The National Origins Act of 1924, also referred to as the Johnson–Reed Act, limited the immigration of people from India and Asia into the country. The present Indian diaspora in the United States consists largely of post-1965 migrants, who have shaped themselves into a socially, politically and economically powerful minority group.

The first post-1965 wave of migration from India resulted in the movement of urban, middle-class, educated individuals to the United States for better opportunities for education and work. The growth of the IT sector in Silicon Valley further facilitated the move of Indians in the software industry. Many who went to the United States for education or work eventually settled there. These migrants had good knowledge of English and often had aspirations for upward mobility. Their access to social capital ensured the rapid growth of the population as one of the wealthiest migrant groups in America. Many of them married in India and took their spouses back to the United States with them (Hickey, 2006; Kapur, 2003; Sheth, 2001; Kurien, 2001).

Many of the Indian migrants who entered under the family reunification policy were older individuals—often the parents of first-wave migrants—who played an important role as child-minders and caretakers (Sheth, 2001).

At about the same time, there was the movement of the Indian diaspora from parts of Africa (Kenya, Tanzania and Uganda) and the West Indies, generally known as *the twice-migrants*. Many Indians moved to Britain from Africa with the rise of independence movements in the 1960s and then moved to Canada and the United States for better prospects, as mentioned earlier.

Simultaneously, the presence of the Indian diaspora in Denmark and the United States and their connections with India are also related to the diaspora policy changes taken place in India, which are covered next.

Indian Diaspora and Policies in India

Diasporic relations have taken a significant shift with economic liberalization, especially in the global South. In the pre-liberalization phase, when highly skilled and educated Indian citizens migrated to other countries for better job prospects, they were seen as *doing a disservice* to the nation, contributing to the brain drain. Overseas Chinese were portrayed as "bourgeois capitalists" and their relatives were persecuted (Lum, 2012). With economic liberalization, India and many other countries have started realizing the importance of the diaspora and the need for recasting the diasporic relations in the framework of *emotional citizenship* and *flexible citizenship*. India has established an extensive diasporic infrastructure (such as the diaspora ministry, the Ministry of Overseas Indian Affairs, in 2004). This is combined with policies designed to attract investment as well as emotionally bind the diaspora to the motherland, including people who had acquired citizenship of other countries but wanted to keep their ties with India (Lum, 2012). There have been categories of PIO, or Persons of Indian Origin, who are those currently holding citizenship of another country (except that of Pakistan, Afghanistan, Bangladesh, China, Iran, Bhutan, Sri Lanka and Nepal) who at some time held an Indian passport or had ancestors, including parents, grandparents and great grandparents, who were or are Indian citizens. A spouse of a citizen of India or a PIO is also considered a PIO, barring those nationals mentioned earlier.

In 2005, the government of India introduced the category of Overseas Citizen of India (OCI), limited to those whose parents or grandparents once had or were eligible for Indian citizenship on January 26, 1950; an OCI is granted a lifelong visa (Noujoks, 2009).

A merger of PIO and OCI was affected in which all existing PIO cardholders were deemed to have the status of OCI, being granted enhanced benefits with effect from January 9, 2015. General benefits of this merger were that the categorizations of non-citizen overseas Indians as PIOs and OCIs were scrapped. OCIs were freed from procedural requirements such as registration and reporting and were allowed visa-free travel to India, rights of residency and participation in business and educational activities in the country. OCI cards are more inclusive, as spouses of OCI-card holders are made eligible for becoming OCI themselves, where the marriage is registered and has lasted at least two years (Merger of PIO & OCI, 2017).

Several welfare and support provisions were also introduced over the years. The Indian Community Welfare Fund for meeting contingency expenditure on welfare activities for the Indian diaspora, the Social Security agreements and labor memoranda of understanding with various countries to ensure better protection and welfare of emigrants, and the Overseas Workers Resource Centre for providing information on all aspects of overseas employment and related matters to intending migrants and overseas workers are a few such welfare measures. Simultaneously, the Know India Programmes, Study India Programmes and Overseas Indian Youth Club, among others, were aimed at attracting youth to their ancestral land through specifically focused educational and recreational opportunities. Considering that overseas Indians constitute a significant and successful economic, social and cultural force in the world, their potential economic contribution to achieving strategic outcomes in an increasingly globalized world has been channeled by relaxing the norms for foreign direct investment in a variety of sectors.

While the entry relaxations could be seen as procedural easing for overseas Indians, psychosocially they created a reinvigorated sense of belonging, which earlier used to be non-facilitating and ambiguous in nature. Coupled with a series of welfare and supportive provisions, this made it easy for overseas Indians to relate to, and even engage in, economic activities like any Indian citizen could do. We can conclude that the policies have sought to expand and de-territorialize the concept of *Indian* in an attempt to promote their economic and social development (Lum, 2012).

Recent Indian policy reforms make it possible for members of the Indian diaspora to engage with India in social and economic activities like any Indian could do, barring political rights. The following section presents empirical studies about the Indian diaspora, dealing with psychosocial aspects of belonging and marginality in the context of Denmark and the United States.

Exploring Belonging Empirically

The theoretical framework driving the discussions and analysis here includes subjective processes of dispersal, connectedness (Vertovec, 2000; Dufoix, 2008) and processes of identification, as well as inclusion in/exclusion from the notion of belonging, especially in the country of settlement (Kalra et al., 2005). Multiple *identifications* (rather than identities) as argued by Bauman (1998) as an open-ended activity in which we are all engaged, whether by necessity or by choice, are part of the framework. These, along with simultaneity of belonging, are seen as possibilities in transnational social spaces. The postmodern celebration of mixed race has brought in the consideration of multidimensional models, allowing the possibility that an individual can have simultaneous membership and multiple fluid identities with different groups (Root, 2001; Aspinall and Song, 2013).

We also focus on some macro processes related to nation-states here because nation-states have entered the diaspora field, reimagining the relationship between domicile, citizenship and belonging since the 1980s: from exclusion to the recognition that diasporics may be *mobilized to invest* in the territories they and their ancestors left behind (Raghuram and Sahoo, 2008). The postcolonial multilayered history of the Indian diaspora, Scandinavian *benign colonialism* and self-perceived innocence when it comes to colonialism and racism are also included in the framework (Poddar, 2013).

In the first case, qualitative in-depth interviews are used, based on themes focusing on Indian diasporics—youth, diasporics in endogamous marriages and exogamous marriages with a Danish spouse (ethnically intermarried/mixed couples), in empirical studies of Indians in Denmark (Singla, 2008, 2011, 2012) during the period between 2006 and 2010. The first author's Indian background (being a part of the Indian diaspora in Denmark); ability to speak Hindi, Punjabi, Danish and English; professional position as a university researcher; and middle age contributed to a balance between an insider and an outsider perspective with regard to the participants. The research participants were given a choice of languages for the interviews. Most chose English or Danish, some chose Hindi or Punjabi and a few a mixture of these.

The analytical strategies adopted were that of meaning condensation combined with post hoc categories grounded in the narratives of the participants. Temporal changes, as well as a metaphorical framework of pull and push, were also used for analyzing diasporic relations. The major themes covered here concern diasporic processes and contacts. Other themes relating to family relations, job trajectories and experiences of psychosocial intervention are covered elsewhere (Singla, 2008, 2010).

Some issues of acculturation and cultural identity emerge from the exploration of belonging among adolescents and families of Indian origin living in Southern California (Sriram, 2014). A qualitative approach using ethnographic methods was used for the study to understand the stories that the participants recounted regarding their experiences of living in the United States. As members of a particular culture, there is an understanding of the nuances, cultural activities, routines, rituals and beliefs that accompany such membership. This understanding had to be derived by the researcher in order to appreciate what membership to a group entails. The interviews and observations allowed the researcher to access participants' stories in their own voice. An interview guide was used, which allowed for investigation into aspects of perceptions of being Indian in the United States: the influence of the family and community, religious and cultural practices followed, awareness about and following of identity markers, awareness about Indian culture and its practice, interactions with other Indian communities and perceptions of discrimination by the majority community. Each interview was conducted over a session of about two hours, in English. Data collection took place over a period of eight months between October 2010 and May 2011, with the researcher entering into the life of Indian Americans living in the area. Participants were also observed at community gatherings, during religious festivals, and at cultural events. Additionally, interviews were conducted with music and dance teachers who were purveyors of Indian culture for the diaspora youth.

The results of the empirical studies show a nuanced understanding of belonging and marginality of Indian diasporics in Denmark and the United States, focusing on different analytical levels: personal, group and structural (Singla, 2008, 2015; Sriram, 2014).

Some Paradoxes in the Danish Situation

There are paradoxes about a minority's situation in Denmark. Suurpää (1998) notes that accentuation of hierarchical differences between Danes and ethnic minorities coexists with a pursuit of equality. For Indians, there are several cultural associations that organize cultural programs during festive seasons, as well as engage with the expat community (CPH India, 2016). In addition, there are cyber-networking activities such as IID (India Internet Day) 2017, along with isolation for some. Another paradox is the partial racial exclusion of Indians from Danish society, in general, but their inclusion in the educational arena and labor market, indicated by their high level of education and income compared to other ethnic minorities and even Danes. The average income of Indians before tax was 389,300 DKK (62,887 USD), which was the highest among the non-Western immigrants (Statistics Denmark, 2017: 69). One reason for the educational aspirations can be attributed to the Danish welfare regime, which affects the transition to adulthood. Completion of education can be accomplished without experiencing overwhelming financial difficulties due to a combination of extensive state provision with some assistance from the family (Singla, 2004, 2005).

Another paradox is indicated in the psychosocial understandings of the young adults in the empirical study (Singla, 2008). Consider the young Indian woman, Mita, who was born and raised in Denmark; she keeps in close contact with her ancestral country, related probably to her marriage to an Indian and their business relations with a major city in India,[6] and has a critical, positive link to Denmark. She has been to India eight times in the past decade and mentions her vague dream of returning to

India as a possibility in the distant future: "Tomorrow my dream is to work in India. To give myself such a status in the company that I can go and live there forever. . . . The Danish culture is very restricted . . . not very open to foreign cultures."

She is a frequent user of the Internet for business and social purposes. Her social contacts are between "here" and multiple "theres"—India and Britain, where some of her extended family members reside. Mita's narrative lucidly illustrates that globalization,[7] through transnational business and knowledge exchange, directly influences diasporic identity processes. Furthermore, it illustrates that diasporics may be mobilized to invest in the territories they and/or their ancestors left behind (Naidoo, 2005; Raghuram and Sahoo, 2008).

On the other hand, Rajiv, an Indian in an ethnic intermarriage with a Danish wife (Singla, 2015), indicates another pattern of intense transnational connection. He had lived for three years in Denmark and has frequent contact with his parents in India, illustrating the concept of transnational social spaces, referring to two or more national states that become a part of a single new social space (Faist and Kivisto, 2010). Rajiv travels once or twice a year to India, sometimes with the objective of providing financial advice to his father, in line with the Bryceson and Vuorela (2002) conceptualization of a transnational family—strong and sustainable ties between the person and a network of family and relatives based in other countries, consisting of regular communication, sharing resources and family burdens and decision-making processes that take into account the welfare and interest of other relatives.

> We have to figure out the situation and someone has to take all that over, because they [parents] are getting old and want to simplify their life, you know they have a big house, which they are taking care of all the time.
>
> (Rajiv)

It is noticeable that Rajiv mentions no experiences of exclusion in Denmark and has close emotional ties with the extended family in India and in the United States where some of his relatives live, through the Internet and Skype.

These narratives illustrate how close emotional relationships can be maintained with family members illustrating the previously mentioned term *emotional citizens* in the country of origin and other countries by visiting and through the Internet and social media. This is also confirmed by the narratives of Indians in Britain (Charsley, 2012; Williams, 2010), twice-migrated Indians from Uganda (Bachu, 1999), newer migrants and newly arrived skilled migrants (Raghuram, 2008).

However, it would be too simplistic to conclude that transnational marriage implies intense, frequent relations with extended family in the country of origin. For highly educated Raaka from India, married to Danish husband Klaus for the past eight years, there is just limited contact with family members in India. Raaka is aware of her responsibilities toward them and fulfills her duties, not only when a sister was widowed and invited to stay in Denmark for a period but also with regard to her parents' residence. She explains about the financial support she has offered through purchasing a couple of apartments for her family in India. Her husband Klaus is co-owner of the apartments, which indicates his supportive stance toward her family:

> What we did was, I had a necessity to find a place to my parents, because they lived with me, and I got married and I moved out and I knew that they need a place to live. Therefore, we bought two apartments, Klaus and me actually, we settled our parents in one of them and in the new apartment, my brother lived so that he could take care of them . . .

An analysis of Raaka's narrative indicates her filial duty through her responsibility toward her parents. Thus, there can be transnational ties in particular domains of life, without frequent ongoing communication and high emotional involvement.

Her narrative challenges media-driven stereotypes of marriages in which there is an asymmetry of rights and resources in the relationship between genders, with women having a lower position, although she underscores her experiences of racism and discrimination, especially in relation to getting a job in Denmark in keeping with her qualifications.

These relationships across borders confirm that transnationalism implies reciprocal sharing of the joys and sorrows across borders. This is seen in other groups, for example, Turkish women in Denmark, who provide care and economic support to their families in their country of origin (Mirdal, 2006).

The narratives from Rajiv and Raaka—who can be structurally positioned as reunified spouses with India as country of origin—documents the differing patterns of transnational relations, which, for some, include economic contribution to the family in India and experiences of exclusion. Bucieck and Juul (2007) discuss how remittances contribute both to *the feeling of being included* and to possession, which is an important aspect of belonging and is perhaps one of the reasons for India's ranking as the highest remittance-receiving nation, as mentioned at the beginning of the chapter. In spite of these differences, all participants in the study underscored their belonging to the country of origin in varied forms. However, we cannot generalize about the nature of transnational contact on the basis of structural categories, such as type of migration, gender and socioeconomic belonging only, as the intersection of these factors with subjective aspects, such as the nature of relationships, the agency of the persons involved and the choices made, is important. Consequently, our understanding of a simplistic definition of transnationalism is challenged through a people-centered social innovation approach when we focus on the persons involved in these transformation processes. Not all migrants can be considered diasporics and as having ties with the parental country of origin as well as other countries. Transnationalism is more about the quality of the contact and how it affects everyday life. These interacting processes emerge as the salient aspect for diasporics rather than their aforementioned structural categories (Singla, 2015).

The broader context of the majority of society gains salience in comprehending these processes. Scandinavian countries often see themselves as "innocent" and outsiders when it comes to colonialism and racism, and there is a resistance to talk about these exclusions (Poddar, 2014; Benign Colonialaim, 2015).[8] Mulinari et al. (2009: 2) note the absence of critical discussion in relation to these racial processes in these countries: "[Nordic countries] never went through a clear period of critique of colonialism and its presence in everyday environments and encounters, as did the colonial centers in the aftermath of the dismantling of the empires".

Danish society is characterized by an illusion of homogeneity, a collective amnesia and official silence regarding mixedness through the past centuries (Singla, 2015). The shadows of the past combined with 21st-century anxieties have influenced present immigration policy, which is reflected in the negative experiences of some of the Indian diaspora participants, especially the Danish partners' critique of exclusionary and discriminatory practices. Thus, the belonging and marginality of the young Indian diasporics should be perceived in this context as argued by Kalra et al. (2005), that diaspora shifts attention away from viewing migration as a one-way process. They appeal for an understanding of the complex transnational identities and conceptualize diaspora as both a *positive embracing* of transnational affiliation in the context of South Asian postcolonial history and a defensive posture by communities in the face of a hostile host telling them they *do not belong*.

The current sociopolitical situation in Denmark thus contributes to a feeling both of belonging educationally and workwise and of being marginal socially—while empirical studies of the Indian diaspora in the United States, focusing on a relatively younger age group, indicate both similarities and differences.

A Comparative Perspective: The Young Indian Diaspora in the United States

As the third-largest ethnic minority group, Indian Americans currently number approximately three million. Only the Chinese and the Filipinos (Bhatia, 2007; Kurien, 2005) outnumber them. It is in the increasingly multicultural environment in the USA that the Indian American diaspora, both adolescents and their families, have to develop an identity, with differing issues for the first and the second generations. The pejorative term *American-Born Confused Desi* (ABCD) has often been used to describe the exigencies faced by this second generation who are neither Indian nor American or may be both at the same time. They have been described as confused, with a lack of understanding about their cultural identity and having a host of individual problems (Poulsen, 2009). The development of identity is crucial for adolescents and may be additionally difficult for adolescents from ethnic groups. Developing a bicultural identity was a primary concern for adolescents, between the demands of their families, on one hand, and the demands posed by their peer group and the wider society that they met in school and other social settings, on the other. The process of developing a hyphenated Indian–American identity, which incorporated elements of being Indian and American, occurred in *a third space*, distinct and different from the family and the peer group (Bhabha, 2004). They used a process of selective acculturation (Portes and Rumbaud, 2001) in deliberately choosing what they want to incorporate from the host society, along with retaining some of the family ideals and beliefs, while being embedded in family and community networks. The values and ideals espoused by the family may often be in direct contradiction with what is expected by the host nation (Sriram, 2014; Moinian, 2009; Sodhi, 2008).

Added to the *burden* of defining identity is the need to accommodate being a part of a *model minority*. The dilemmas associated with model minorities have to be resolved by the second generation (Bhatia, 2007; Dhingra, 2007; Kibria, 2002), a process made more complex because the host country continues to see them through old lenses and expects similar standards of behavior to that shown by the first generation. It is important to consider the inheritance of a particular human and social capital from the parents and its effects on shaping the identity of the second generation (Sriram, 2014).

Many of the young people spoke of two distinct selves: an American self contrasted with an Indian self. Both these self-structures were seen as distinct entities emerging in different contexts. The Indian self was seen at home and in interactions with siblings, family and the wider Indian community. The American part of the self came into prominence in school, where there were few Indian children, and the Indian self faded into the background, in order to blend in and not stand out. Fifteen-year-old Divya said, "The American part comes out in school, while the Indian part comes out over the weekend." In the words of 20-year-old Razia,

I think every Indian kid goes through this ABCD idea, because his or her culture clashes with American culture. Their parents have this one idea of them, they bring their ideas from India, and then they have to reconcile those ideas they have with the ideas of American culture. In addition, that is the hardest thing. I think ABCD is a good description of sometimes the way you feel. Confusion—I am American, I am definitely American, and I am Indian . . . It is this weird, in-between middle ground that you have.

While many of the families celebrated Indian festivals, it was rare for the children to invite friends from other races and religions for the celebrations. As 15-year-old Divya said,

American/white friends are not called for Diwali[9] and Kollu,[10] they may feel left out. Not because I would feel embarrassed, but just because do not want them to feel left out. I have never tried it, maybe I should. I generally feel that's the time for Indian friends.

It was during these Indian festivals that the youth wore Indian clothes. Girls tended to wear traditional Indian clothes more often than the boys did. However, many of the youth expressed reservations about wearing Indian clothes to school or in situations where there were few Indians. As 17-year-old Swati says,

Indian clothes for Indian festivals, when I get to see other Indian people, at the Diwali mela.[11] I won't wear Indian clothes to school— it's awkward, too bright, they stand out, not the kind of thing that people wear to school in America. I wear *kurtis*[12] to school. I would not wear *churidar*[13] and *kurta* to school. It's out of the norm, and not something that I would like to wear. . . . School is not related to Indian clothes, people would think it weird. Wearing jeans and a top or shorts makes me fit in better.

School was often the first place where Indian American children *encountered prejudice* in the form of name-calling, teasing and taunting. Some Indian American children and their parents spoke of bullying in middle school, when they were taunted about smell. The notion of curry and of smelling of curry was mentioned by many children. This was accompanied by the reluctance to take Indian food to school as part of their bag lunches. As 16-year-old Maya said, "I don't think any Indian kids bring Indian food to school. We eat it at home, but to school, we bring American-type food. Indian food is kind of messy". Many Indian parents also spoke of how their children refused to eat Indian food.

Prejudice and bullying were felt more often in middle school than in elementary and high school. In elementary school, teachers acted as a buffer between the second-generation Indian American children and the majority white community children. In middle school, this buffer was less evident, and many children spoke of being teased. Many of the children had Indian names, which were made fun of. Arushi, at age 18, spoke about how her younger brother called Manu had been called *Manure* through middle school. The Indian accent was made fun of as well, and many children said they spoke differently at home and at school. By the time the adolescents entered high school, many spoke of being better able to deal with the teasing and taunting.

While a majority of the adolescents and youth who took part in the study considered the Indian self to be an important part of who they were, a few young people could be considered whitewashed. The term *whitewashed* was used by Indian-origin youth as a derogatory reference to someone who had forgotten, or who refused to accept, the Indian part of the self. As 22-year-old Sparsh says, "You saw Indian kids in school who were completely whitewashed. They didn't want to associate with a single thing about being Indian." A case in point was that of 21-year-old Deven. Deven introduces himself to new acquaintances as Devon; he would respond only when addressed as Devon, rather than Deven. In his own words,

> I see myself as an American; I identify more with my American side than I do with my Indian side. I've grown up here; I've never spent any time in India, for more than a month. Most of my interactions have been with American society. My friends have been American. I don't agree with everything that is American, but at the end, I say that I am American.

Most of the second-generation Indian American youth *had limited access and fluency* in an Indian language. Many of the youth said that they could understand what was being said, if it was said slowly and clearly. While many of the youth watched Bollywood movies, they used the English subtitles to understand the dialogue and the drama. There were gender differences, with more girls than boys saying they were fluent in an Indian language. The familiarity with an Indian language was directly associated with the connection with India. Young people who had extended families in India and who visited India regularly were more likely to have access to an Indian language. When the parental generation did not communicate in an Indian language, there was limited opportunity to use the language. While there were classes in languages such as Hindi and Gujarati being offered along with religious training, few young people availed themselves of these opportunities. In Razia's words,

> Indian kids my age, we don't talk to each other in Hindi or Tamil . . . We talk to each other in English. Unlike Chinese kids who talk to each other in Chinese, even though they're born and brought up here. We just talk to each other in English. In India as well, everyone talks in English. India uses English so much, there's no need to use another language.

Similarly, in her 2010 study of young immigrants of Indian origin in Pittsburg and New Jersey in the United States, Rayaprol argues that some young Indians resist cultural pressures from the previous generations and form their own *unique identity* that is different from that of the parental generations. However, some of them may find themselves to be more traditionally Indian than their counterparts in India and thereby experience marginality in that context. She sums up:

> The essence of being Indian undergoes a natural dynamic social change and takes on new meanings in the diasporic context. . . . Race, ethnicity, class, religion, language, gender and sexuality are some of the components of their identity that shape their perceptions of who they are and how they like to be perceived by others.
>
> (Rayaprol, 2010: 146–147)

Moreover, there are differential levels of belonging to both *here* and *there*, depending on aspects such as life-course positioning, gender, socioeconomic position and the number of years living in the country of residence.

These narratives highlight some of the processes, including paradoxes and dilemmas, of the Indian diaspora in different age groups, ranging from related to belonging, inclusion and exclusion from various groups in the country of origin as well as the country of residence, along with their transnational engagement. These processes reflect both a changing pattern of emigration from India—as illustrated through diaspora-related policies in India, such as PIO and OCI discussed earlier—and immigration-related policies in Denmark and the United States, such as the "green card schemes", as well as changing connectivity related to technological changes—Internet, Skype and so on. Thus, there is an intertwining of the micro and macro levels in comprehending the similarities such as a sense of belonging in the country of residence along with connection with the country of origin for the Indian diaspora in the Danish and the American contexts.

The de-territorialized Indianness plays an important part in self-understandings of diasporics in both contexts. While the contradiction of *here* versus *there* exists, the dual connectedness through sociocultural ties via filial connections on one side and daily interactions and identification with the host society on the other are negotiated by the nuances of hyphenated beings such as Danish Indian or Indian American. Furthermore, the filial connectedness is at times enhanced by changes in Indian policies facilitating easier connections and thereby strengthening the sense of belonging. In addition to this, collective religious organizing as an illustration of social innovation—a process of addressing unmet needs as well as a strategy of dealing with religious belonging—is outlined in the next section.

Religious Organizing: Addressing Unmet Social Needs

With the increase in the Indian diaspora in Denmark and the United States, it is relevant to consider the role played by religion in the dynamics of immigrant belonging in host societies. Warner (2007) refers to the importance of considering religion in the assimilation and integration of immigrants into the host society. The earlier paradigms of considering assimilation through Judeo-Christian frameworks no longer holds true for the United States, with migrants coming from varied religious backgrounds. For many of the Indian diaspora in California, there was continued allegiance to religion and religious organizations. Most immigrant groups experience a degree of religious freedom not found in many countries (including where the state religion is Islam), which allows them to express their religiosity with fervor. In both countries of residence and India, the state allows freedom of religious expression and practice, although Denmark is a Protestant, Lutheran country.

In Denmark, there is Bhartiya Mandir, a Hindu temple representing different forms of Hindu gods, established in 1997, and Sri Vinayar Mandir, established in Næstved in 2012. In addition, there are temples in smaller towns such as Brande, Herning and Slagelse, a Hare Krishna temple and a couple of Sikh temples in Greater Copenhagen. The temple's role in Sri Lanka and India is of a more social nature than is usual in Denmark (Opinionen, 2014). Nonetheless, both religious and social needs are met through these institutions.

In California, most of the Hindu diasporics had small shrines dedicated to various Hindu gods in their homes. The city had larger temples, which served both religious and secular functions. The Shri Mandir in San Diego, established in 1994 in an area referred to as Little India, was conceptualized as a commonplace of worship for Hindus from all regions of India. The three priests in the temple were trained in India and carried out religious rituals and worship observances according to the Hindu calendar.

The other Hindu temples in the city were the Hare Krishna temple and the Shiva Vishnu temple. Though the Hare Krishna temple in San Diego is the oldest Hindu temple, most Indians did not visit it except during Janmashtami. The temple was perceived as too secular and did not seem to be truly Indian. The Shri Mandir and the Shiva Vishnu temple held classes on Indian cultural traditions for young children on Sundays and combined social as well as religious functions.

The presence of these temples in both contexts reflects the attempt to re-create socio- religious structures from the country of origin, albeit in a transformed form. The feelings and practices associated with belonging to a particular faith are related in a complex manner to the marginalization process in the country of residence and are beyond the scope of this chapter. However, these temples reflect that they function as a community center serving social, cultural and religious needs of the diaspora, in line with Vertovec's 2000 analysis of Hindu temples in London. Both in the United States and in Denmark, Hindu and Sikh groups outnumber other migrant religious groups; it is important to recognize the presence of Muslim and Christian Indians. In the United States, they have their own religious spaces and practice. There is a mosque meant only for *desis*. There is a collective of Christians from India, called the Indian Christian Fellowship. As the number of Indians from these religious groups has increased, there is a desire to establish distinct spaces for the practice of religion. In Denmark, on the other hand, they make use of existing mosques and churches used by members of the same faith from other countries. Re-creation of the social space through collective religious practices is facilitated by the presence of such places of worship in both the Danish and the American contexts. The presence of these institutions, without any state assistance, reflecting continued religious social practices, implies both awareness, resource mobilization, and participation of the diasporics in their own development in this context, along with self-reliance and long-term sustainability, documenting the people-centered framework's five critical foundations (Cox, 1998).

Reigniting Belonging and People-Centered Social Innovation

To conclude, we have some suggestions for promoting interconnections and links between the country of origin—India—and the country of residence based on people-centered social innovation.

While analyzing varied aspects of belonging among the Indian diasporic community in Denmark and the United States, we interpret that parallel processes of articulation of needs of belonging by the diaspora, on one side, and policy and process interventions by national governments for the "better", on the other, may be leading to worse connectedness. As Cox (1998) argues, the misplaced priorities and inequalities in the distribution of power in the dominant development paradigm make it necessary to put people at the center of development discourse. Applying such a paradigm for establishing strong connectedness of a diasporic community with the country of origin, the authors feel that the articulations of belonging as narrated in the previous sections need closer analysis, and integration of the same is crucial for building better connectedness. This necessitates the adoption of innovative approaches in integrating such articulations of belonging as intrinsic human needs way beyond the material benefits of entry relaxations and economic engagements. Thus, uniting the fulfillment of human needs to active engagement and changes in (social) relations (Hulgård and Shajahan, 2013) essentially integrates the people-centered approach and theories of social innovation in engaging with the diasporic community.

Some diasporics feel a positive affiliation, a pull toward the country of origin, which can be enhanced and sustained by diaspora-related policy changes such as entry relaxations. These could be perceived as procedural ease for overseas Indians, leading to the creation of an invigorated sense of belonging, which earlier used to be nonfacilitative and ambiguous in nature. Furthermore, a series of welfare and supportive provisions have made it easy for the Indian diaspora to relate to and even engage in economic activities like any Indian citizen can do. However, there are still bureaucratic barriers to carrying out economic activities, and there are useful lessons to learn from countries like China and Mexico, which encourage dual belonging of their diasporas through diverse policies and strategies (Portes and Rumbaut, 2014).

Among young people in the empirical studies, in spite of some experiences leading to feelings of not belonging, especially due to the restrictive policies for foreigners in the past few years in Scandinavian countries, paradoxically most young adults feel at home mostly *here* but also *there*, as they had hardly addressed *the myth of return* characterizing the diaspora processes in their self-definition and life trajectories now.

Analysis of return-migration programs in recent decades indicated limited success in India and some return of skilled migrants to countries such as China and the Republic of Korea, along with transnational involvement with both country of origin and destination, moving away from the simple brain-drain/brain-gain model of the 1960s (Tejada and Bhattachatya, 2014). This study of highly skilled returnees to India emphasizes their suggestions related to better infrastructural function, better remuneration packages, adaptation of anticorruption measures and increased governmental support (Tejada et al., 2014). These suggestions contribute to an understanding of limited return to India by the diasporics studied in Denmark and the United States. This limited return-migration coexists with the concept of *emotional citizenship* and *flexible citizenship* (Lum, 2012) entailing the process of affective transnationalism. However, we cannot predict the future pattern of transnationalism or return, and thus the long-term, generational sustainability of transnational institutions (Cox, 1998), illustrated here as meeting the religious-social needs of Indian people, is difficult to predict.

Acceptance of dual cultural affiliations and belonging of diasporics to the country of residence are significant. The lesson for the parental diasporic generation is illustrated by the historical suggestion in 1905 to the Indian diaspora in Mauritius by Mahatma Gandhi: "Educate your children and participate in the public life of your country of adoption" (Gayan, 2003: 43).

An important aspect to consider relates to the changes in perception of minority groups in the host country. The idea of *integration with real involvement of the diaspora*, rather than assimilation on its terms set by the state, allows a minority culture to retain aspects of the culture of origin. The metaphor of a mixed salad rather than a melting pot has been used in the United States. In the Danish context, however, the state provides a rather rigid, emotionally violent frame for dealing with the issues of difference and belonging in relation to migrants under the name of state-managed "integration", where the concept of migrants' belonging to the diaspora is almost nonexistent.

Our case studies, especially with regard to the organization of temples for meeting unmet needs, documents that working alongside formal state integration, efforts are much richer, nuanced processes where the local diaspora can reach out to newcomers, provide networks of information and resources both to facilitate awareness-raising, respect and, eventually, various forms of belonging. A people-centered social innovation perspective would involve harnessing the potential in these nongovernmental organizations and coupling them to the formal state system of provision, hopefully contributing to solving the problem for Denmark, the United States and Europe that is integration of new arrivals solely on terms set by the state, both in the short and in the long term.

One of the suggestions concerns the positive flow of media images and messages through global technologies, for example, the Internet and Indian films, to enhance online transnationalism, considering that these global media processes are also about feelings of longing, re-creating representation and a sense of belonging (Guzder and Krishna, 2005).

In recent decades, the international migration of semiskilled and highly skilled Indians has seen an upsurge due to demand in certain sectors such as the software industry thus directing attention to the Indian diaspora far more visibly, among others through a people-centered social innovation approach to enhance interconnections between the country of residence and the country of origin and to address the issues of marginality.

According to Nayyar (2012), there is a need for both inclusion and rights for diasporics in both contexts. Development must also enhance the well-being of people in terms of expanding freedoms. These must be extended beyond freedom from hunger, disease and illiteracy so that development has an impact on capabilities, creates economic opportunities and social inclusion and ensures political liberties for people.

Notes

1. Scandinavian countries consist of Denmark, Norway and Sweden, while Nordic countries also include Iceland and Finland.
2. The first author is part of the Indian diaspora in Denmark, the second and third authors live in India with experience of working internationally, and the third author has researched the Indian diaspora in the United States.
3. Transnational: composed of prefix *trans* meaning "through" and *national*, phenomena that takes place through nations.
4. Denmark scrapped the green card scheme in June 2016, but the current holders were spared.

5. Indians are concentrated in Asia, Western Europe, North America and the Caribbean. Taking 1,500 as the minimum figure, there are Indians in 53 countries.
6. They have established a firm in the field of pharmacy, as her husband had master's degrees in pharmacy and biotechnology.
7. Breaking down of artificial barriers to the flow of goods, services, capital, knowledge and (to a lesser extent) people across the border (Stiglitz, 2002: 9).
8. *Benign colonialism* is a controversial concept that refers to an alleged form of colonialism in which benefits outweighed risks for indigenous populations whose lands, resources, rights and freedoms were preempted by a colonizing nation-state. Literature challenging this has not been as widely publicized.
9. Diwali refers to the Hindu Festival of Lights, which is celebrated by most Indian diasporics who follow Hinduism.
10. Kollu is the traditional women's festival from South India celebrated during Navratri (Nine Nights) during fall.
11. Mela is a fair.
12. Short tunics, worn with leggings.
13. Tight leggings, traditional Indian clothing.

References

Aspinall, P. and Song, M. (2013). *Mixed Race Identities*. Basingstoke: Palgrave Macmillan.

Baumann, Z. (1998). *Globalization: The Human Consequences*. New York: Columbia University Press.

Benign Colonialism. https://oceanflynn.wordpress.com/speechless-glossary-of-terms/benign-colonialism/ (Accessed on 14 June 2015).

Bhabha, H. (2004). *Location of Culture*. London: Routledge.

Bhachu, P. (1999). "Multiple Migrants and Multiple Diasporas: Cultural Reproduction and Transformations Among British Punjabi Women in 1990s Britain," in Singh Thandi (ed.), *Punjabi Identity in a Global Context*. New Delhi: Oxford University Press.

Bhat, C. and Bhaskar, T. (2007). "Contextualising Diasporic Identity: Implications of Time and Space on Telugu Migrants," in G. Oonk (ed.), *Global Indian Diasporas: Exploring Trajectories of Migration and Theory*. Amsterdam: Amsterdam Unversity Press, pp. 89–118.

Bhatia, S. (2007). *American Karma: Race, Culture and Identity in the Indian Diaspora*. New York: New York University Press.

Bhatia, S. (2018). *Decolonizing Psychology: Globalization, Social Justice, and Indian Youth Identities*. New York: Oxford University Press.

Bryceson, D. and Vuorela, U. (2002). *The Transnational Family: New European Frontiers and Global Networks*. Oxford: Berg.

Bucieck, K. and Juul, K. (2007). " 'We are here, yet we are not here'—The Heritage of Excluded Groups," in Brian Graham and Peter Howard (eds.), *Heritage and Identity*. Ashgate: Aldershot.

Charsley, K. (ed.). (2012). *Transnational Marriage: New Perspectives from Europe and Beyond Research in Transnationalism*. London: Routledge.

Convert PIO Cards. (2017). http://indianexpress.com/article/india/convert-pio-cards-to-oci-by-june-end-pm-modi-tells-indian-diaspora-4464845/ (Accessed on 23 January 2017).

Cox, D. (1998). "Towards People-Centred Development: The Social Development Agenda and Social Work Education," *The Indian Journal of Social Work Education*, 59(1), pp. 513–530.

CPH, India. (2016, August). *India- Denmark Relations Special Supplement*.

Dencik, L. (2014). "The Dialectics of Diaspora in Contemporary Modernity," in E. Ben, J. B. Liwerant and Y. Gorny (eds.), *Reconsidering Israel-Diaspora Relations*. Brill, pp. 405–428.

Dhingra, P. (2007). *Managing Multicultural Lives: Asian American Professionals and the Challenge of Multiple Identities*. Stanford: Stanford University Press.

Drèze, J. and Sen, A. (1989). *Hunger and Public Action*. Oxford: Oxford University Press.

Dufoix, S. (2008). *Diasporas*. Berkeley, CA: University of California Press.

Faist, T. and Kivisto, P. (2010). *Beyond a Border: The Causes and Consequences of Contemporary Immigration*. New Delhi: Sage.

Gayan, S. (2003, January). "Mauritius Beholden to India," *India Perspectives*.

Guribye, E. and Overland, G. (2014). "Introduction," in O. Gwynyth, E. Guribye and B. Lie (eds.), *Nordic Work With Traumatised Refugee Do We Really Care* (pp. 1–13). Newcastle upon Tyne: Cambridge Scholars Publishing.

Guzder, J. and Krishna, M. I. (2005). "Mind the Gap: Diaspora Issues of Indian Origin Women in Psychotherapy," *Psychology and Developing Society*, 17(2), pp. 121–138.

Hickey, G. M. (2006). "Asian Indians in Indiana," *Indiana Magazine of History*, 102(2), pp. 117–140. www.jstor.org/stable/27792707.

Hulgard, L. and Shajahan, P. K. (2013). "Social Innovation and People Centred Development," in F. Mouleart, D. MacCallum, A. Mehmood and A. Ham (eds.), *The International Handbook on Social Innovation: Collective Action, Social Learning and Transdisciplinary Research*. Cheltenham: Edward Elgar.

Indian Embassy. (2017). www.indian-embassy.dk/indiadenmark.html (Accessed on 8 February 2017).

Jayaram, N. and Atal, Y. (2005). *The Indian Diaspora: Dynamics of Migration*. New Delhi: Sage.

Kalra, V., Kaur, R. and Hutnyk, J. (2005). *Diaspora & Hybridity*. New Delhi: Sage Publications.

Kapur, D. (2003). "Indian Diaspora as a Strategic Asset," *Economic and Political Weekly*, 38(5), pp. 445–448. www.jstor.org/stable/4413159.

Kibria, N. (2002). *Becoming Asian American: Second-Generation Chinese and Korean American Identities*. Baltimore: Johns Hopkins University Press.

Kurien, P. (2001). "Religion, ethnicity and politics: Hindu and Muslim Indian immigrants in the United States," *Ethnic and Racial Studies*, 24(2), pp. 263–293. doi:10.1080/01419870020023445

Kurien, P. A. (2005). "Being Young, Brown and Hindu: The Identity Struggles of Second Generation Indian Americans," *Journal of Contemporary Ethnography*, 34(4), pp. 434–469.

Lum, K. (2012). *India's Engagement with Its Dispora in Comparative Perspective with China CARIM India Robet Schuman Center for Advanced Studies*. European University Institute.

Mahalingam, M. (2017). *Indian Diaspora Policy & Foreign Policy: An Overview*. www.grfdt.com/PublicationDetails.aspx?Type=Articles&TabId=30 (Accessed on 23 January 2017).

Merger of PIO & OCI (2017). www.balglobal.com/bal-news/merger-of-pio-and-oci-cards-benefits-indian-diaspora-and-family-members/ (Accessed on 23 January 2017).

Mirdal, G. M. (2006). "Stress and Distress in Migration: Twenty Years After," *International Migration Review*, 40, pp. 375–389.

Moinian, F. (2009). " 'I'm Just Me': Children Talking Beyond Ethnic and Religious Identities," *Childhood*, 16(1), pp. 31–48. doi:10.1177/0907568208101689.

Mulinari, D., Keskinen, S., Tuori, S. and Irni, S. (2009). "Introduction: Postcolonialism and the Nordic Models of Welfare and Gender," in S. Keskinen, S. Tuori, S. Irni and D. Mulinari (eds.), *Complying with Colonialism: Gender, Race and Ethnicity in the Nordic Region*. Farnham: Ashgate, pp. 1–16.

Naidoo, Josephine. (2005). "Editorial: The Asian Indian Diaspora," *Psychology and Developing Society*, 17(2), pp. v–vii.

Nayyar, D. (2012). "Foreward," in A. D'Costa (ed.), *A New India? Critical Reflections in the Long Twentieth*. New Delhi: Anthem Press.

Noujoks, D. (2009). *Emigration, Immigration, and Diaspora Relations in India*. www.migrationpolicy.org/article/emigration-immigration-and-diaspora-relations-india (Accessed on 17 July 2015).

Opinionen. (2014). http://opinionen.dk/tema/naestveds-hinduer-byder-til-pooja (Accessed on 8 February 2017).

Poddar, P. (2013). Professor Inaugural Lecture. *Cultural Encounters Post Colonialism*, 15, pp. 11. Roskilde University.

Portes, A. and Rumbaut, R. (2001). *Legacies: The Story of the Immigrant Second Generation*. Berkeley: University of California Press.

Poulsen, S. S. (2009). "East Indian Families Raising ABCD Adolescents: Cultural and Generational Changes," *The Family Journal: Counselling and Therapy for Couples and Families*, 17(2), pp. 168–174.

Raghuram, P. and Sahoo, A. K. (2008). "Thinking 'Indian Diaspora' for Our Times," in P. Raghuram, A. K. Sahoo, B. Maharaj and D. Sangha (eds.), *Tracing an Indian Diaspora: Contexts, Memories, and Representations*. New Delhi: Sage Publications, pp. 1–28.

Raghuram, P. et al. (eds.). (2008). *Tracing Indian Diasporas: Contexts, Memories, and Representations*. New Delhi: Sage Publications.

Rayaprol, A. (2010). "Being American, Learning to Be Indian. Gender and Generation in the Context of Transnational Migration," in M. Thapan (ed.), *Transnational Migration and the Politics of Identity*. New Delhi: Sage Publications, pp. 130–149.

Root, M. (2001). *Love's Revolution: Interracial Marriage*. Philadelphia: Temple University Press.

Sahoo, A. and Kruijf, J. (2014). *Indian Transnationalism Online: New Perspectives on Diaspora*. Surrey: Ashgate.

Sheth, P. (2001). *Indians in America: One Stream, Two Waves, Three Generations*. Jaipur: Rawat Publications.

Singla, R. (2004). *Youth Relationships, Ethnicity & Psychosocial Intervention*. New Delhi: Books Plus.

Singla, R. (2005). "South Asian Youth in Scandinavia: Inter-Ethnic and Intergenerational Relationships," *Psychology and Developing Society*, 17(2), pp. 215–235.

Singla, R. (2008). *Now And Then – Life Trajectories, Family Relationships and Diasporic Identities: A Follow-Up Study of Young Adults*, Vol. 46. Copenhagen: Copenhagen Studies in Bilingualism, University of Copenhagen, Denmark.

Singla, R. (2011). "Plugged in Youth: Technology and Transnationalism among South Asian Diaspora in Scandinavia," in A. F. M. German and P. Banerjee (eds.), *Migration, Technology and Transculturation: A Global Perspective*. St. Charles, MO: CIGS Lindenwood University Press.

Singla, R. (2015). *Intermarriage and Mixed Parenting: Promoting Mental Health & Wellbeing*. Basingstoke: Palgrave Macmillan.

Singla, R. and Holm, D. (2012). "Intermarried Couples, Mental Health and Psychosocial Well-Being: Negotiating Mixedness in the Danish Context of 'Homogeneity'," *Counseling Psychology Quarterly*, 25(2), pp. 151–165.

Singla, R. and Varma, A. (2019). "Changing Demographics and Intimate Relation Patterns Among Indian Diaspora in Denmark," in I. Rajan (ed.), *India Migration Report—Diaspora in Europe*. Oxford: Routledge, pp. 279–243.

Sodhi, P. (2008). "Bicultural Identity Formation of Second Generation Indo-Canadians," *Candian Ethnic Studies*, 40(2), pp. 187–199.

Sriram, S. (2014). "Negotiating Identities in Immigrant Families: Indian Muslim Youth in the United States of America," in S. Salvatore, A. Gennaro and J. Valsiner (eds.), *Multicentric Identities in a Globalizing World*. Information Age Publishing, Idiographic Science, vol. 5.

Statistics Denmark. (2017). *Indvandrere 2017*. www.dst.dk (Accessed on 22 December 2017).

Stiglitz, J. (2002). *Globalization and Its Discontents*. New York: W.W. Norton.

Suurpää, L. (ed.). (1998). *Black Light, White Shadows: Young People in the Nordic Countries Write About Racism*. Nordic Council of Ministers, TemaNord: 538.

Tejada, Bhattacharya and Khadria, Kuptsch. (eds.). (2014). *Indian Skilled Migration and Development: To Europe and Back*. New Delhi: Springer.

Tejada, G. and Bhattachaya, U. (2014). "Indian Skilled Migration Migration and Development: An Introduction," in Bhattacharya Tejada and Kuptsch Khadria (eds.), *Indian Skilled Migration and Development: To Europe and Back*. New Delhi: Springer, pp. 3–27.

Times of India. (2018). https://timesofindia.indiatimes.com/india/india-retains-long-held-position-of-top-remittance-destination-of-migrants/articleshow/63903300.cms (Accessed on 30 July 2018).

Vertovec, Stephen. (2000). *The Hindu Diaspora: Comparative Patterns*. London: Routeledge.

Warner, R. (2007). "The Role of Religion in the Process of Segmented Assimilation," *The Annals of the American Academy of Political and Social Science*, 612, pp. 100–115. doi:10.1177/0002716207301189.

Williams, L. (2010). *Global Marriage: Cross-Border Marriage Migration in Global Context* Basingstoke: Palgrave Macmillan.

9 Innovations in Multistakeholder Partnerships for Sustainable Development
Fostering State–University–Community Nexus

Abdul Shaban and Prashant B. Narnaware

Introduction

How can we look at development alternatives or alternatives to development in an increasingly neoliberal world with its deepening marginalities? Such contemporary challenges highlight the need for newer strategies for development. Can social innovation provide an answer? *Innovation*— social and technological—is a current buzzword. High hopes are harbored for both types of innovation as an engine of economic growth (Minna Säävälä and Sirpa Tenhunen, 2014). However, considering that poor and marginalized people around the world face multiple challenges, single-sector innovations often increase rather than decrease or address such challenges. Innovations in multistakeholder partnerships could be a way forward. Using a case study of state–university–community partnership, this chapter delineates the importance of convergence across various sectors to reduce poverty, inequality and exclusion by increasing livelihood security and quality of services through people-centric innovation as a newer sustainable development pathway. *Development* and *sustainable development* have been variously defined and have remained contested expressions, although the key focus of sustainable development remains the reinforcing of the economic, social and environmental agenda. Millard et al. (2016) found that such positive socioeconomic-environmental improvements are typically undertaken by collaboration, new alliances and the cross-fertilization of ideas and practices among actors' ecosystems.

This chapter attempts to establish that there is a possibility of fostering an enabling and innovative multistakeholder partnership for creating sustainable impact and transformative change with local communities. It further delineates that the collaborative efforts among district administration (government), educational institutions and civil society groups in supporting innovation and entrepreneurship can play an extremely important role in livelihood security and empowerment of marginalized sections. The district administration of Osmanabad District, Maharashtra

State, India, has been able to realize this ambition by working together with Tata Institute of Social Sciences (TISS), Tuljapur Campus, and encouraging farmer-producer companies to take up the advantages offered by global and local markets.

Osmanabad district is economically and educationally one of the most underdeveloped districts of India (Government of Maharashtra, 2014). It is located in a semi-arid and drought-prone area with a population of about 1.7 million. It includes about 324,000 farmers, 70% of whom have land holdings of less than 4 hectares of mostly nonirrigated land. The district is also known for its high rate of farmer suicides due to economic distress and livelihood insecurity. The joint engagement of government (district administration), TISS (university) and civil society groups is able to turn around the narrative of development in the district from despair to hope and marginality to prosperity, growth and livelihood security. With much effort and engagement, approximately 14,600 farmer producer groups and 75 farmer-producer companies have been launched in the district. Innovations in production and the use of technology have been encouraged and the collectivization of smallholdings by farmers themselves has been recognized to take advantage of scale with a new approach, moving from individual to collective risk management. This has resulted in a rapid rise in the district's per capita income in the last few years—for example, it increased from INR 78,793 in 2015–2016 to INR 94,188 in 2016–2017, a growth of about 19.5% (Government of Maharashtra, 2018). The efforts are leading to rapid changes and redirection of the economy from subsistence and government dependence to self-reliance and entrepreneurialism.

This chapter outlines the transformation of a marginalized and underdeveloped district of India. The next section presents a background of the district with a focus on farmers' distress and is followed by a discussion of the mode of organization of elites and marginalized peoples under welfare and neoliberal regimes. After elaborating on the university–state–people's partnership for sustainability in development, we outline the impact that state–university engagement has had on the communities before presenting our conclusions.

Marginality Context and Sustainable Development Challenges

Development in Maharashtra, one of the economically developed states of India, is highly polarized by districts and cities. There is a vast territory of Marathwada and Vidarbha that suffers from underdevelopment. The development status of the districts in these regions is on a par with districts in the most underdeveloped states like Jharkhand, Orissa and Bihar (Government of Maharashtra, 2014). Osmanabad district comprises eight *tehsils*,[1] eight towns (Municipal councils), 622 *gram panchayats*,[2] and 728 villages (Census of India, 2011). The district is located in Marathwada region, which has remained relatively underdeveloped over the years: in comparison to four districts (Jalna, Nanded, Hingoli and Parbhani) in 2001, five districts of the region (Hingoli, Osmanabad, Nanded, Jalna and Latur) in 2011 fell into the category of low Human Development Index (HDI) districts of the state (Government of Maharashtra, 2014). The district of Osmanabad also registered the second-lowest improvement in the HDI during the 2001–2011 period. The per capita income in Osmanabad District is almost half (57%) that of the state average. For instance, in comparison to per capita income of INR 165,491 in 2016–2017 for the state, Osmanabad had a per capita income of only INR 94,188.

Although the growth of the population in Osmanabad District has been relatively low at 11.50% during the last census decade (the district's population increased from 1.487 million to 1.658 million during 2001–2011), this population increase adds to the problems of scarce cultivable land and water resources. The literacy rate in the district is 78.4%, compared to 82.3% in Maharashtra as a whole. The population in the district is largely dependent on agriculture and related activities. According to Census of India 2011, 38.4% of workers are cultivators, while 38.7% are agricultural laborers. This shows that there exists a very high economic and livelihood vulnerability in the district for a large section of the population. The declining ground- and surface water resources and increasing variability in the rainfall are further enhancing the livelihood vulnerability in the district. The district is largely dependent on rainfall for agriculture. Annual rainfall data from 1900 to 1999 for the district analyzed by the Central Ground Water Board shows severe drought conditions prevailing in the district during most of the years. In major parts of the district, during both pre-monsoon and post-monsoon, declining groundwater levels have been observed (Lamsoge, 2009). Drought conditions and loss of crops have led many farmers to commit suicide and pushed many into debt. Added to this water scarcity is the high nitrate content in the groundwater, which makes groundwater unsuitable for drinking without prior treatment. The extent and depth of poverty in the district are also high, and that forces people to migrate to cities in search of livelihoods or queue in front of centers/organizations where they can find daily employment. In 2004–2005, the poverty in the district was 58.8% (it was 31.2% in Maharashtra in the same year) and 50.8% in 1993–1994 (28.9% in Maharashtra; Government of Maharashtra, 2014). The infant mortality rate (IMR) in the district is also quite high. In 2006–2007, the IMR in the district was 50 in comparison to 44 in the state. The child sex ratio in the district is also very adverse: it was 867 females per 1000 males in 2011 as against 894 females per thousand males in 2001. This indicates a massive decline in the number of female children being born in comparison with males.

Farmers' Distress

According to district administration data, a total of 597 farmers committed suicide in Osmanabad district during the period between January 2011 and December 2017. Table 9.1 shows the distribution of suicides between 2011 and 2017 by *tehsils*. *Tehsils* in Osmanabad, Kallamb and Tuljapur are showing rising trends in farmer suicides and together they accounted for 384 suicides (64.3%) during the period. Farmer suicides are inversely related to the amount of rainfall in the district. The shortage of rainfall increased drought severity between 2014 and 2016, and that resulted in a rise in farmer suicides across all *tehsils*.

It is important to note that from March to May each year, when the water deficit remains high in the district, more farmers commit suicide. The main crops are produced between June and September and a majority of farmers cannot grow crops in the remaining months due to lack of water for irrigation. The income from agriculture dries out between March and June; this increases the severity of distress among farmers during these months.

The causes of suicide are mostly related to livelihood (Table 9.2). Debt, crop failure, and the effect of drought leading to multiple vulnerabilities are the major causes of suicides. Of the multiple causes that drove farmers to commit suicide, 74.3% were attributed to debt, and about 60% and 39% to crop failure and drought, respectively. Families of farmers who committed suicide have also outlined a number of other causes. Clearly, there is a need for radical changes to livelihoods and related strategies. Social innovations and entrepreneurship through the effective engagement of state and universities may be one strategy to help avoid the quagmire of hopelessness, debt and vulnerability.

Table 9.1 Reported number of farmer suicides in Osmanabad district by year, 2011–2017

Sr. no.	Tehsil	2011	2012	2013	2014	2015	2016	2017	Total
1	Bhoom	3	2	5	12	11	7	14	54
2	Kallamb	9	11	6	17	35	29	15	122
3	Lohara	0	1	0	4	3	9	5	22
4	Osmanabad	4	5	2	20	41	53	42	167
5	Paranda	0	0	8	3	13	10	10	44
6	Tuljapur	7	2	6	11	30	23	16	95
7	Omerga	1	1	0	2	11	15	14	44
8	Washi	1	0	1	2	20	15	10	49
	Total	**25**	**22**	**28**	**71**	**164**	**161**	**126**	**597**

Source: Office of the District Collector, Osmanabad.

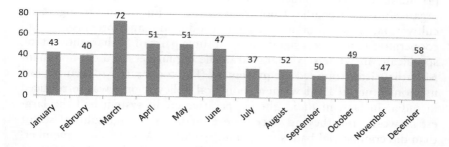

Figure 9.1 Number of farmer suicides in Osmanabad district by month, 2011–
2017

Source: Office of the district collector, Osmanabad.

Table 9.2 Causes of farmer suicides (multiresponse) in Osmanabad District

Sr. no.	Cause	Number of families	Percentage of total
1	Debt	284	74.3
2	Crop failure	230	59.9
3	Drought affected	151	39.3
4	Pressure of girls' (daughters'/sisters') marriage	77	20.1
5	Bore-well/well failure	69	18.0
6	Burden of educational expenses	49	12.8
7	Family dispute	47	12.2
8	Illness of own or family member(s)	46	12.0
9	Alcohol addiction	33	8.6
10	Financial issues	10	2.6
11	Business loss	7	1.8
12	Depressed due to death of other family members	5	1.3
13	Lack of fodder for livestock	5	1.3
14	Unemployment	5	1.3
15	Regular argument with spouse	3	0.8
16	Pending electricity bill	3	0.8
17	Scared of court cases	3	0.8

Source: TISS survey, October 2016–February 2017.

Organization of Elites and Marginals Under Welfare and Neoliberal Regimes

After India's Independence in 1947, the role of cooperatives was considered extremely important for the reconstruction of the rural economy. Cooperatives provided a philosophy and actionable agenda through which India could experiment with the Gandhian model of people- and community-based development. In Indian development planning, cooperatives are seen as part of the third sector (Ghosh, 2007), between private and public production and distribution systems and with local organizational strengths. Cooperative movements based on sugarcane cultivation, sugar production, milk production and processing, and cooperative banks grew significantly in some parts of Maharashtra State, specifically in Western Maharashtra. The big farmers and the dominant Maratha caste group led the movement. The cooperative movement lost its momentum in 1991 when a neoliberal policy regime was introduced in India. In fact, in India, the cooperative credit system had the largest network, and they advanced more credit to the agricultural sector than did commercial banks (Das et al., 2006). In Maharashtra, membership of cooperative societies had grown from 4 million in 1960–1961 to 26.9 million in 1990–1991 and further to 46.5 million in 2005–2006. However, real credit per capita by cooperative banks has not only stagnated but also declined in recent years. Many cooperative societies in the state suffer adverse financial health; that is, large numbers of repayments are late (Shaban, 2010). Although, given the number of members, cooperative societies present vast opportunities and potential for outreach, they suffer from "deep impairment of governance" (Government of India, 2005: 18). In fact, they have become a borrower-driven system, beset with losses, deposit erosion and poor portfolio quality (Government of India, 2005).

The failure of cooperative movements, combined with changes in agricultural policies under which agricultural inputs and outputs were thrown open to the market, led to the rise in input cost but a decline in output prices of farm produce, leaving farmers with little in the way of surplus margins. Even in drought-prone areas, farmers started shifting to cash crops such as sugarcane, which were easily absorbed by sugarcane factories linked to the cooperatives. Sugarcane cultivation in Marathwada region exploited surface and groundwater resources. The rising credit cost has led to a situation where most farmers are now in debt to moneylenders or to commercial/cooperative banks. This has led to a consistent rise in farmer suicides in the Marathwada region, with the Osmanabad District, in particular, one of those most affected.

The neoliberal regime made the elite-based cooperatives ineffective, as they came under mismanagement and overexploitation by those in power. Furthermore, the penetration of neoliberal ideologies and the reduction of caste-based domination also created a situation where erstwhile subordinated communities are moving away from domination by the upper castes. This has created communal disorganization in Indian villages where communities are caught in struggles for domination, competition with others, or avoiding domination by other communities. The villages in Marathwada and, specifically, in Osmanabad also show similar traits. Individual farmers who used to make decisions based on village community consensus now make their own decisions with regard to the type of crop they want to produce and the labor they want to engage. However, the adverse impact of this has been that individual farmers are now facing the vagaries of the neoliberal market themselves. Added to this are the vagaries of the weather/climate, which is now more erratic, and declining rainfall. The individual farmers have now become exposed to more risk from credit agencies, weather and market fluctuations. The overall impact of this has been a rise in farmers' distress.

To overcome the vagaries of the market, weather and individual exposure to credit risk, the farmers have started recollectivizing themselves by pooling their resources (e.g., land, machinery, financial capital, etc.) and collectively negotiating in the agricultural markets. This initiative is at a very early stage and is supported by the district administration and universities such as TISS. This new collectivization process is qualitatively and quantitatively different from the earlier cooperative movement, which was elite-based and located in only a few places. The neo-cooperative movement is marginalized-based, or non-elite-based, and almost every village has two or three such groups. These collectives are entrepreneurial in nature, as they envisage turning agriculture into business and engage in further processing of agricultural produce, adding value to farm produce. Many such collectives have also been engaged in off-farm activities and animal rearing to create alternative sources of reliable income in the wake of failing farming and crop production.

University–State–Community Links and Partnership for Innovative Entrepreneurial Initiatives

Neoliberal reform introduced a new vulnerability among Indian farmers, especially in certain states, such as Maharashtra. Marathwada (where Osmanabad District is located) and Vidarbha regions have seen thousands of farmer suicides over the last 25 years or so. Farm-sector policies, therefore, have come under severe criticism by scholars, civil society groups and left-wing political parties. The response from the state has not been in terms of providing more subsidies or regulating the market prices of agricultural inputs and outputs, and financial credit but, rather, to make farmers more self-reliant by infusing in them a sense of entrepreneurship. In these conditions, universities such as TISS, with the support of state administrators, have attempted to mobilize farmers to participate in social innovations and entrepreneurship with a philosophy of creating wealth for the broader society through a social business model. The TISS philosophy of community engagement for the social and economic development of India has been valuable here. In the following, we mention the major state initiatives and tenets on which TISS Tuljapur Campus has stood to accomplish change, which we describe in the next section.

State Initiatives and Links With Community and University

To counter extreme farmer hardship and bring a meaningful development into the area, the district administration has evolved a number of initiatives such as creating farmers' groups, encouraging group farming, providing incentives and information to farmers for effective marketing, etc. The district administration has also adopted a cluster development scheme based on agro-climatic suitability and Baliraja Chetana Abhiyan (BCA), a multipronged strategy to counter farmer distress through subsidies to encourage entrepreneurship. TISS, Tuljapur Campus, has been a partner in expanding community outreach for both these programs for the state and in motivating and educating farmers. The community leaders in the villages, called *sarpanchs*, were specifically contacted by both TISS and the state for the identification of beneficiaries. TISS also carried out the midterm evaluation of the program, which showed the massive success of this community development approach in a state–university–community partnership. This success has been achieved because of the involvement of the elected village panchayat (local governance) representatives, who have been motivated and counseled by both the university and district administration representatives. The presence of TISS or a university as a knowledge partner in the entire process further convinced the farmers to participate actively in implementing the scheme and selecting beneficiaries. It is important to note here that most government schemes fail because of the mistrust which has developed between beneficiaries/village representatives and the state because of the extremely top-down approach often adopted in the implementation and design of the schemes. In this scheme, the district administration independently designed and implemented the scheme with the help of TISS wherever it was required and was therefore able to understand the grassroots reality as TISS shared research and its experience and community expectations. This led to the rapid changes and redirection of the agricultural economy from subsistence and government dependence to entrepreneurialism, where the farmers are increasingly taking agriculture as a business and engaging in profit maximization rather than depending on it as a source of survival and subsistence. Farmers are thus being educated about climatic and market risks.

To counter distress among farmers, BCA was introduced as a pilot project in 2015 and was implemented shortly thereafter. The program aims to uplift the motivation and morale of distressed farmers in villages to enable them to lead a responsible, purposeful and meaningful life. It also attempts to raise awareness among journalists and to motivate them to publish news articles, stories and cases of success in order to mobilize local farmers and other key stakeholders to improve the farmers' situation. BCA also organizes awareness programs for farming communities in the villages through public lectures, *kirtan mandals* (a group of people devoted to singing religious songs), street plays, campaigns, dramas, *prabodhan* (motivational speeches) and so on. Finally, it aims to mobilize and organize farmers to take control of their decisions through appropriate positive feelings and to change their attitudes to fight against the conditions that cause their distress.

Apart from boosting morale and motivation, the program aims to provide assistance to farmers through the following two processes/steps: first, by identifying distressed families in villages and encouraging farmers to form groups (wherein at least one member is from distressed families) for business ventures. Second, it invites proposals from the farmers' groups for financial assistance to start a venture. The vision is to facilitate the movement of farmers to a corporate platform and at the same time to put the concerns of the marginalized and excluded groups center stage. Farmers are supposed to form their own groups—especially small and marginal farmers or distressed farmers. Furthermore, the scheme uses farmers' collective negotiation abilities to protect themselves from price shocks in the market. The constitution of farmers' groups is also meant to promote nonagricultural entrepreneurial activities and to divert them from sole dependence on agriculture. It has multiple implications such as buffeting farmers from drought, imparting them with skills and negotiating abilities, eliminating middlemen from agricultural produce and providing farmers with direct access to the market. The program has also encouraged the mechanization of agriculture. To encourage such farmers' groups, interest-free loans are provided to selected groups who are willing and eligible to take on business ventures.

The formation of farmers' groups (as shown in Figure 9.2) rose sharply after 2012, and the peak years for collectivization of farmers in the district have been 2012 to 2015. Almost all the farmers' groups studied by the authors had shown definite levels of progress in their ventures, except one group which was yet to start its activity. Dairy, goat and poultry farming are the three main business areas of the groups, with nearly 80% of the groups studied engaged in these activities (Table 9.3). The farmers

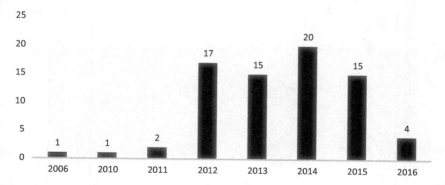

Figure 9.2 Establishment of farmers groups receiving financial assistance under BCA by year.

Source: Based on field survey by the first author.

Note: By July 2017, a total of 78 farmers' companies/groups were assisted by District Administration of Osmanabad under BCA. Of these, 75 were studied by the authors.

Table 9.3 Characteristics of farmers' groups in Osmanabad (as at November 2017)

Activities of the group	Number of farmers' group	% of total farmers' companies	Average monthly cash contribution by members (INR)	Total average investment by the group (INR)	Average worth of the companies (INR)	Average number of total members in the group	Mean age of the members	Average number of distressed families	Average number of Male members'	Average number of female members'	Average number of General Category members
Agro service center	1	1.3	0	20,000	200,000	15	46	2.0	13	2	11
Dairy	33	44.0	270	132,236	523,091	14	44	1.2	13	1	11
Goat farming	17	22.7	212	77,500	404,706	15	41	1.1	13	2	12
Goat & dairy farming	2	2.7	100	125,000	675,000	19	38	1.5	15	5	15
Goat & poultry farming	2	2.7	50	325,000	475,000	14	41	1.0	10	4	7
Grain/seed processing	3	4.0	208	116,667	533,333	13	44	1.0	6	7	11
Krishi Seva Kendra	3	4.0	233	116,667	700,000	13	43	2.0	8	5	11
Masala production	1	1.3	500	200,000	500,000	11	38	2.0	11	2	13
Milk collection	1	1.3	0	600,000	250,000	10	30	0.0	7	3	6
Onion dehydration	1	1.3	0	500,000	4,000,000	250	33	1.0	6	0	6
Poultry	9	12.0	178	315,144	425,111	12	41	1.0	9	3	7
Sericulture	1	1.3	50	50,000	400,000	20	50	1.0	18	2	19
Not yet started	1	1.3	500	60,000	300,000	11	44	1.0	7	5	11
Total	75	100.0	224	153,515	528,240	17	42	1.2	12	2	11

Source: Data collected by the authors.

Note: The 78 farmers' companies have received financial help (but total 75 companies were studies as mentioned in the table) from the district administration, and even if they have not contributed from their own side, the financial help under BCA is provided to them. The financial help under BCA generally has been of INR 200,000 per farmers' group.

have formed these groups and contributed a small sum of money on a monthly basis. The average sums contributed by them in all types of ventures have been below INR 500, but the average total worth of the groups has been INR 0.53 million. The largest sum of INR 0.40 million was raised by an onion dehydration group. These groups have been based on a large number of farmers, with an average of 17 farmers per group. However, the number of distressed families and female members in these groups has not been very high. The groups remain dominated by males, upper and middle castes and large farmers due to existing structural inequities.

However, it should also be noted that this is the beginning of a new movement and these are slightly advantaged farmers (with access to information and better landholding along with social capital) able to organize themselves. Nevertheless, there are signs that a grassroots movement for entrepreneurship and a new cooperative movement has begun in Osmanabad. This may have a very positive impact on sustainable and inclusive development in the district.

TISS Tuljapur Campus and Its Philosophy

TISS Tuljapur Campus was established in 1987 with the mission of promoting initiatives for sustainable, eco-friendly and equitable socio-economic development of rural communities. TISS Tuljapur seeks to contribute to the transformation and strengthening of the rural economy, society and polity and to promote alternatives in development. In order to achieve this, TISS Tuljapur has adopted a four-pronged strategy: teaching, research, training and field action. Over the years, it has built a strong team of academics and professionals drawn from economics, social work, sociology, history, agronomy, geography, political science, demography, engineering, mathematics and other related disciplines.

TISS Tuljapur has evolved as a campus with graduate, postgraduate and training programs with approaches based on equity, justice and sustainable development. Being located at Tuljapur Tehsil headquarters, and because of its proximity to rural communities and its close working relationship with central, state and district development administrations, it has started playing a significant role beyond the campus (see Figure 9.3). It is not only influencing local self-governance but also contributing to strengthening overall capacities, especially of marginalized and vulnerable communities and their access to state programs and decision-making processes. Based on its involvement with government agencies and programs, business organizations, civil society groups and communities, the campus has framed its larger role as a catalytic and transforming center for influencing socioeconomic development. In this regard, it has started developing responsible cadres of sensitive and sensible change agents who can help steer developmental processes in favor of the most deserving and

Figure 9.3 Conception of state, society and university links for sustainable development
Source: Authors.

marginalized sections of society. Major initiatives that the campus has taken up for community development relate to enhancing outreach and ensuring delivery of government programs in the villages of Osmanabad District, spreading awareness about the right to education, health and human rights, legal support services for women, dalit and tribal communities, watershed development as part of drought mitigation, capacity-building among communities through training and exposure visits for government officials and community leaders.

TISS Tuljapur Campus is a community-engaged campus. It works for sustainable development through its field action projects by interweaving equity, economy and environment. It emphasizes equity-based and ecosystem-based development and cultivation of use value of capital. At the center of its philosophy of sustainable development is neo-localism under which local communities, their contexts and products gain increased attention (Figure 9.4).

New Aspirations and Ideas

The state initiative, by exemplary leadership in district administration and willing cooperation from the university, led to the active engagement of the communities, which were looking for an opportunity to make a

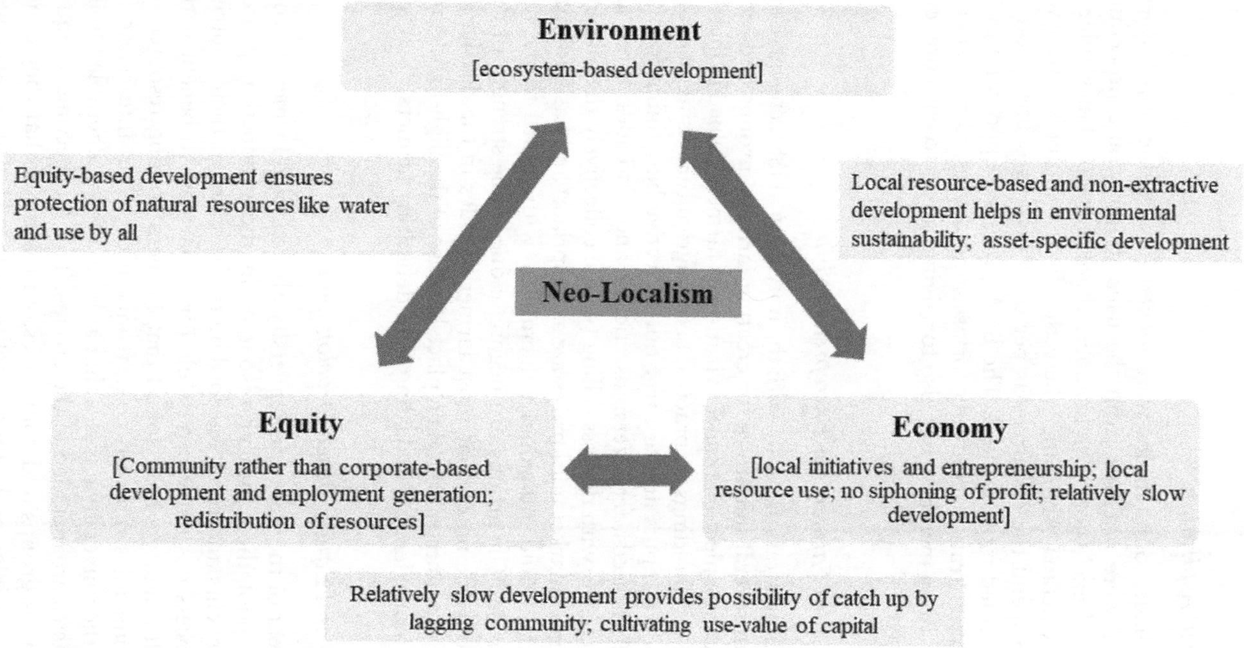

Local resource-based and non-extractive development helps in environmental sustainability; asset-specific development

Environment

[ecosystem-based development]

Economy

[local initiatives and entrepreneurship; local resource use; no siphoning of profit; relatively slow development]

Neo-Localism

Equity-based development ensures protection of natural resources like water and use by all

Equity

[Community rather than corporate-based development and employment generation; redistribution of resources]

Relatively slow development provides possibility of catch up by lagging community; cultivating use-value of capital

Figure 9.4 Sustainable development through neo-localism

Source: Authors.

difference to their situation. The morale of the communities has changed, and this has resulted in the following visible changes.

From Despair to Aspiration

Until 2013, village communities were locked into visible hopelessness. State initiatives were not free from the usual bureaucratic procedures and processes of exclusion. For instance, there was no plan similar to the Bali Raja Chetana Abhiyan, where the district administration was empowered to spend the resources as per their own assessments on the sectors they deemed most in need. The BCA provided opportunities for the district administration, not only for assisting distressed farmers and the families of ailing members but also for giving grants to entrepreneurs for new initiatives.

Collectivization of Farmers for Entrepreneurship

The district administration, along with the university (TISS), engaged with communities in several initiatives for creating farmers' groups and farmers' producer companies. The collectivization of farmers helped in increasing the size of landholdings to practice better agriculture using machines and other modern inputs and to carry out collective bargaining for market inputs such as seeds, fertilizers, insecticides and pesticides. It has also helped them to cope with distress selling (where collectively the output is withheld from the market until prices are appropriate) and has minimized the risk of default and individual vulnerability with regard to the market or bank credit. The groups can negotiate due to the strength of their number. It should be noted that most farmer suicides in the district and elsewhere in the country have taken place because of the high-handedness of banks and moneylenders in dealing with defaulting farmers.

Participatory and Equity-Based Development

The engagement of the state and university also enabled farmers to come together and pool their meager resources in the production process, sharing the benefits and profits according to the share of their contribution. This process has made it possible for all farmers to benefit within the group. Although we have found that farmers pooling resources for groups and companies generally come from one caste, the intervention by the state and the university ensures that at least a few vulnerable families from other castes are included in the groups. This has become a requirement for farmers groups and companies, and without that they cannot receive state subsidies and other benefits. This has ensured an equity-based development where wealth is produced and shared by a large number of farmers rather than by individuals.

Creating a Sense of Neo-Localism and
Context-Based Development

The state initiative and the effective engagement of universities such as TISS, the Indian Institute of Technology, Bombay, and Parbhani Agricultural University have also created a sense of geographic or local belonging among the communities where they are cultivating a sense of the place where they belong and of the environment they live in. The sense that they belong to Osmanabad and the Marathwada region of the state has been enhanced. One sign of this is that they now want to brand their products based on local geographic names and local deities. They have also started cultivating a sense of the environmental context in which they live, where the use of available resources in a sustainable manner is emphasized. For instance, limiting the cultivation of sugarcane in the drought-prone area for saving scarce surface- and groundwater is now practiced. The renewed sense of geographic belonging also provides communities with further possibilities of cultivating a sense of the local in a quickly globalizing world where geographies and a sense of space are collapsing.

Conclusion

Osmanabad district has been one of the least developed districts of the country since independence. For almost seven decades, economic development has proceeded in ways that have created enormous vulnerability among farmers while only marginally raising their standard of living. Such development resulted in farmers being in debt, erosion of local environmental resources, the emergence of small elite groups from dominant castes and the marginalization of larger sections of society and the farming community. New programs have emerged with discernible active engagement of the state and universities with the communities, creating the possibility of long-term sustainable development. This development—the Osmanabad model of development—is context-based, market-based, people-based, and equity-based. Farmers are looking forward to engaging as collectives with new possibilities and aspirations. However, as mentioned earlier, collective processes still remain dominated by elites in the community including men, middle-class and privileged caste groups. Although there have been efforts at inclusion through processes of community mobilization, structural inequities remain formidable impediments. However, in this initiative the effort has been to be conscious of such societal inequities. Conscious efforts have been made to overcome barriers through compulsory inclusion of at least one distressed family in a farmer group and to create separate venture platforms for women.

In spite of some of the abovementioned challenges, this form of collectivization alongside universities, the state and communities is not visible elsewhere in the country. This new emerging model has created enormous hopes and possibilities in a globalizing neoliberal era.

Notes

1. *Tehsils* are the intermediate administrative units in Maharashtra state between block and district.
2. *Gram panchayats* are the lowest development administrative units in India and are governed by elected representatives from a single or a group of villages. Gram panchayats mainly use development funds provided to theme from district level but also are empowered to impose some minor taxes for land use change and so on.

References

Census of India. (2011). *Primary Census Abstract*. Data on CD.

Das, Banishree, Palai, Nirod Kumar and Das, Kumar. (2006). *Problems and Prospects of the Cooperative Movement in India Under the Globalization Regime*. Paper presented at XIV International Economic History Congress, Helsinki.

Ghosh, Arun Kumar. (2007). "Cooperative Movement and Rural Development in India," *Social Change*, 37(3), pp. 14–32.

Government of India. (2005). *Repost of Task Force on Revival of Cooperative Credit Institutions*. New Delhi: Ministry of Finance.

Government of Maharashtra. (2014). *Maharashtra Human Development Report 2012*. New Delhi: Sage Publications.

Government of Maharashtra. (2018). *Economic Survey of Maharashtra 2017–18*. Mumbai: Directorate of Economics and Statistics, Planning Department.

Lamsoge, Bhushan R. (2009). *Ground Water Resources and Development Potential of Osmanabad District, Maharashtra*. New Delhi: Central Ground Water Board.

Millard, J., Weerakkody, V., Missi, F., Kapoor, K. and Fernando, G. (2016). *Social Innovation for Poverty Reduction and Sustainable Development: Some Governance, Policy Perspectives*. Published in the Proceedings of the 9th (ICEGOV2015–16). Montevideo, Uruguay: The ACM Press.

Säävälä, Minna and Tenhunen, Sirpa. (2014). "Innovation: Transforming Hierarchies in South Asia," *Contemporary South Asia*, 22(2), pp. 121–129.

Shaban, A. (2010). "Institutional Credit and Economic Entitlement: Emerging Regional and Sectoral Divides in Maharashtra," in C. Sen and S. Corbridge (eds.), *Democracy, Development and Decentralisation in India: Continuing Debates*. New Delhi and London: Routledge, pp. 111–146.

10 Social Innovation in Africa

An Empirical and Conceptual Analysis

Jeremy Millard, Mohamed Wageih and Bev Meldrum

Introduction and Methodological Approach

This chapter describes and analyses the development and prospects of social innovation in Africa. It draws to a great extent on insights from the large-scale empirical research, mapping and analysis of social innovations around the world undertaken between 2014 and 2017 by the SI-DRIVE project (Schröder et al., 2014). It also examines other relevant evidence related to social innovation and sustainable development, as well as drawing on development and social theory to assist placing the analysis in context and drawing conclusions about social innovation and social enterprise in Africa. In order to reflect a people-centered social innovation and solidarity economy approach, three scales are tackled: (a) examining Africa as a whole (Millard, 2017b), justified by the many common themes shared across the continent, which together show clear contrasts with the generality of social innovations implemented elsewhere (Millard, 2018); (b) the important cultural, historical, political and social distinctions between Northern Africa[1] and sub-Saharan Africa; and (c) a more detailed focus on the experiences of individual countries, particularly Egypt, South Africa and Ghana, in order to provide a deeper sense of context (see Figure 10.1).

The empirical evidence is taken from data collected using a comprehensive analytical definition of social innovation, describing it as a new combination or figuration of social practices. Using this analytical lens, the project's 25 partners from around the world, including two from Africa,[2] mapped and analyzed more than 1,000 initiatives of social innovation from all inhabited continents, as well as undertaking more than 80 in-depth case studies (SI-DRIVE Project, 2014–17). Because of large differences in how social innovation is defined and practiced in different parts of the world, as well as the highly variable access possible for mapping and analyzing social innovation initiatives on the ground, these samples cannot be described as statistically representative. However, SI-DRIVE partners were selected as key observers of, and researchers in, social innovation in their respective regions, and were thus most likely

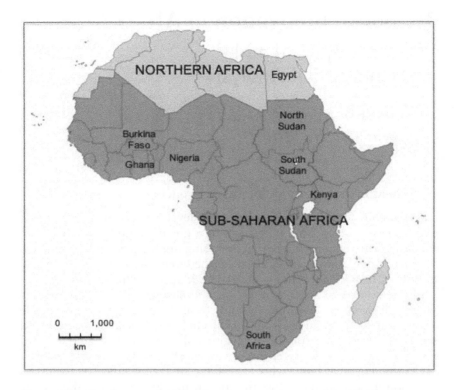

Figure 10.1 Sketch map of Africa showing countries mentioned in the text

to have detailed knowledge of the range and types of social innovations taking place. Their decisions concerning which social innovations to map and analyze were, of course, constrained by the access they could obtain, but their final samples were, in all cases, judged by them and their peers to be the most representative samples that could, in practice, be obtained.

Apart from the empirical material, extant surveys and studies of social innovation in Africa at a continental level are limited and largely restricted to Nwuneli (2016) and Awuah (2012). However, there are numerous country, regional and sectoral studies, some of which have been consulted, especially Hart et al. (2012, 2014), Junge (2015), Romisher (2015) and CSESS (2011) in Francophone countries. These are drawn on and referenced as appropriate in the text that follows. As a tentative exercise in understanding the nature of social innovation in Africa, this chapter must only be seen as a first attempt to fill some important gaps, although it can only partially achieve this from a largely empirical perspective.

Analysis of the empirical case studies showed a clear tendency for social innovations and social enterprise supporting poverty reduction and sustainable development to adopt a strong *human condition* and *human dignity* approach. This takes the real human condition of poor/vulnerable people directly into account by addressing their needs, aspirations and behaviors holistically. The evidence shows how the most successful social innovations and social enterprises tend to be undertaken in a manner that treats the individual with dignity, recognizing their full value as a human being in their efforts to increase both their welfare and their prosperity. This approach thus also involves a strong focus on gender, basic human attributes and idiosyncrasies, as well as human rights (Millard, 2017a). These findings echo Hart's human economy approach from an economic anthropology perspective; that is, that by "calling the economy human we put people first, making their thoughts, actions and lives their main concern" (Hart, 2008). Moulaert et al. (2013) make similar observations concerning human-centered social innovation when they recognize the past failures of conventional service delivery to tackle poverty and social exclusion and seek to promote new ways of doing things, grounded in the social relations and experiences of those in need. These attributes and approaches are strongly reflected in the evidence, analysis and discussion presented in this chapter.

In order to set the scene and provide an initial generalized overview of social innovation in Africa compared to social innovations elsewhere, Figure 10.2 compares the data samples of both African and non-African social innovation initiatives in terms of their focus on the three pillars of sustainable development as defined by the United Nations.[3] The

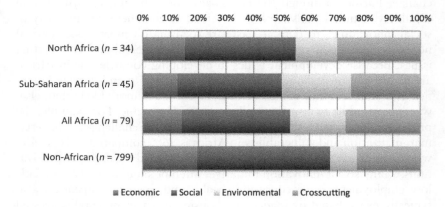

Figure 10.2 Sustainable development pillars of African and non-African social innovations

Source: SI-DRIVE data.

figure shows that 878 of the 1,000 initiatives collected contained sufficient data across all relevant indicators used in this chapter to compare the 79 African cases with 799 cases from other parts of the world. The African sample is further subdivided into Northern Africa and sub-Saharan Africa in order to illustrate both their similarities and their differences.

It can be seen from Figure 10.2 that there are clear contrasts between African and non-African social innovations. Just under 50% of non-African initiatives focus on the social pillar tackling issues like quality of life, health, education, culture, awareness raising and knowledge and skills development, as well as social exclusion and inequity. Almost 20% are concerned with economic issues such as financial security, financial safety nets, income, wages, savings, jobs and vocational training. In contrast, environmental concerns with a focus on the human-constructed environment (habitation, infrastructures, food, utilities, facilities and amenities) and the natural environment (land and water reclamation, pollution, climate change and biodiversity) compose only 10% of all initiatives. Just under a quarter of initiatives focus on two or three pillars simultaneously, so are as described as *crosscutting*. Although African initiatives are also characterized by a focus on the social pillar, this is less dominant than non-African cases at 39%, though still the most important pillar overall. Economic initiatives are much less important at only 14% of the total, while crosscutting initiatives at 27% and environment initiatives at 20% take second and third place respectively.

The data seem to indicate some special concerns in Africa generally compared with other global regions, as also indicated by Nwuneli (2016). These include the greater everyday environmental stresses confronting African societies, due both to massive population growth and to climate change. Further, although the challenges posed by unemployment and suitable vocational skills are high in Africa as elsewhere, the majority of social innovations, to date at least, are focusing on more basic survival needs (such as hunger) related to social, environmental and crosscutting issues. Because development issues in developing countries, as in Africa, are highly interrelated and often need to be tackled in an integrated manner, individual African social innovations are much more likely than elsewhere to straddle two or three pillars at the same time. For example, the proportion of initiatives focusing on combatting the challenges of poverty, marginalization and vulnerability in Africa is 36% compared to 16% elsewhere, and such challenges tend to be underpinned by multiple deprivations. Many social innovation initiatives attempt simultaneously to tackle low employment, poor education, health and financial insecurity, also typically exacerbated by inadequate housing in environmentally stressed areas. Such social innovations thereby attempt to be fully people-centered by designing initiatives which integrate, coordinate and cut across two or more pillars at the same time, often deploying a bottom-up approach. Their purpose is to ensure initiatives are fully focused on the all-round needs of the individual or group, rather than treating distinct needs separately in a silo fashion. It is also noticed that many such social innovations intend to relieve the symptoms of the people suffering, rather than challenging the real causes of these problems, an issue addressed more fully in the section Applying the Agency–Structure Framework later in the chapter.

Figure 10.2 also indicates that, as far as the overall sustainable development focus is concerned, the differences between Northern Africa and sub-Saharan Africa are much less than the differences Africa has with the rest of the world. The only apparent noteworthy distinction is the even greater focus on the environment in sub-Saharan Africa compared to Northern Africa, coupled with a further reduction of concerns for economic development. These differences might be at least partially explained by the fact that Northern Africa is mainly an Arab and Muslim region, while sub-Saharan Africa is a mainly Negroid and largely non-Muslim region. This also coincides, in very general terms, with different cultural and socioeconomic mores and norms, also derived from their very different historical experiences. The former region has been closely associated with broader Middle East, European and Asian historical development for at least 4,000 years, so tend to be relatively more economically aware and integrated internationally. The latter region, however, only experienced extensive contact with other parts of the world over the last 200 years, geographically bestride the equator and encompass a much greater range of disturbed and fragile environments. Social innovators in these two regions, together with their government and other sponsors and donors, are therefore likely to be more focused on these specific regional challenges. Being the most affected regions in the world with the impact of climate change (water scarcity and the raising of temperatures and sea levels), there is a real need to empower social innovations that consider the environmental challenges across Africa (Van Hofwegen and Svendsen, 2000; NASA Big DataSet, 2015).

Concepts and Understanding of Social Innovation in Africa

Rapid population growth and environmental stress across the continent pose the major challenges for social innovation in Africa, so the focus is often on problems such as the provision of food, housing, education, health care, energy, transportation, water and sanitation. The purpose is to ensure that the value created accrues primarily to society as a whole, but despite many successes, with most interventions reaching hundreds and even thousands, they struggle to achieve impact on the necessary scale by reaching millions of people across the continent (Nwuneli, 2016; Awuah, 2012). (See also the Social Innovation Capacities and Actions section later in this chapter.)

In South Africa, according to Hart et al. (2014), the country's post-1994 innovation policies aim to support strategies that yield social outcomes and include rural development as an important theme in this context. The policy challenge is how to promote innovations that yield direct positive outcomes that benefit the poor and marginalized members of society. Many policy statements refer to social innovation, but what this means in practice is unclear. South Africa is struggling to implement a pro-poor innovation focus but is finding it difficult to translate this effectively into action, also because of a lack of clear understanding about the multifaceted dynamics of innovation. Although the South African 1996 white paper on science and technology recognized that an exclusive focus on technical innovation was insufficient and that social innovation should be included, little subsequent progress has been made. Thus, in 2012, a Ministerial Review of Science, Technology and Innovation examined what social innovation could encompass by equating it with innovation for development, stating that it should address priorities arising from unemployment and poverty. In other words, social innovation must have social purposes and involve the full range of societal actors, including the public sector, private sector, civil society and the poor themselves with a strong people-centered approach. It was also stated that pro-poor development needs to recognize the huge potential for creative and active agency within poor communities while also noting that existing structural conditions limit the ability of such communities and individuals to exploit this potential. Thus, there is a need to make appropriate support available to these actors in order to ensure the desired outcomes (Hart et al., 2014).

According to an earlier Hart paper (Hart et al., 2012: 2–3) three definitions of social innovation in a South African and broader African context are important. First, social innovations are products (goods and services) with immediate human welfare or social benefits, such as better education, health, improved water access, cost-efficient energy devices and products that improve communication and transportation. Second, social innovation also considers the organization or arrangement of people and things within enterprises or social settings (informal or formal organizations and arrangements). Examples range from trade unions and worker forums to savings groups, neighborhood committees, rural neighborhood work parties and even various marketing practices. Key here is the social collaboration of people themselves in ways that add value for their own livelihoods and their relationships with other actors. Third, social innovation can also be seen as a combination of the first two, that is, as both those new products, services, models and practices that meet social requirements and those that involve new social collaborations (Hart et al., 2012). This approach to social innovation resonates with the European approach as articulated by BEPA (2010): that social innovations aim to achieve social ends by using social means.

Junge (2015) supplements Hart by outlining ten trends of social innovation in South Africa that demonstrate all aspects of especially poor and vulnerable people's lives. On one hand, these range from shifting the way people view and undertake farming as a sustainable and vital part of society rather than something done simply to subsist. On the other hand, they include improving access to information and knowledge through simple mobile phones that allow them to communicate and receive basic information, for example, about work, market prices or the weather. Also noted as important are innovating public service provision at the basic level, improving literacy and evoking people's everyday stories at the community level, social entrepreneurship creating new livelihood opportunities, products and services, as well as learning from elsewhere, for example, in housing and education.

African Social Innovation in Practice

Social Needs, Challenges and Opportunities
Driving Social Innovation

In contrast to South Africa and many other sub-Saharan countries, social innovation is not a well-known concept in much of Northern Africa, possibly because there are fewer development aid and donor interventions supported by developed countries. Even so, it can be argued that the main challenge in Northern Africa is to achieve a paradigm shift in the field of development in general. Society and economy are characterized by a very strong, top-down, government-led development model that has been focused mainly on economic output factors. The private sector has been dominated to a large extent by military and economic elites, while small-scale entrepreneurs and civil society have not traditionally played a significant role in solving development challenges until very recently. However, the Arab region, in contrast to much of Europe and North America, has seen decreases in poverty levels over the last 20 years, although this is still a significant challenge and other challenges remain. The Arab Spring of 2011 and its aftermath have seen these other challenges become much more acute, such as the absence of peace and security; high levels of unemployment, illiteracy and hunger; remaining high poverty in some countries, such as in both North and South Sudan; and high population growth rates, as well as drought, desertification and the overconsumption of natural resources like water and agricultural land. However, these conflicts and stresses have had the effect of motivating civil society to begin to take many more initiatives themselves by deploying social innovation practices throughout the region.

The basic development challenge lies in the educational and other capacities of the whole of society, and the general attitude toward taking active responsibility for solving existing challenges, but neither institutions nor behaviors are changing fast enough. A true shift to social innovation in any field can therefore only be expected to come about with the coming of the next generation and must go hand in hand with an increasing focus on education. Many of the countries in the Arab region have embarked on major reforms of their education and training systems in order to make them more relevant to their needs. Recent educational developments have seen the progressive closing of the gender gap in formal education in many countries, although significant gaps continue to exist in adult literacy. There are numerous social innovation initiatives in the field of education in the Arab world, the majority of which attempt to reduce educational disadvantages and to expand basic education to marginalized groups. Most of these initiatives are government-led in collaboration with international organizations, like UNESCO and UNICEF.

Other social innovations, like those in the energy sector in Arab countries, include the transition toward renewable energy. The top-down regulatory framework makes this slow going, so local initiatives and organizations are usually supported by international development organizations that are also keen to disseminate and replicate successful initiatives. For example, Egypt has a very large population with high population growth, but only about 6% of the total land surface is inhabited. The rising urbanization problems in Cairo and the challenges of food security mean that large numbers of people will have to move into the desert to live and produce food. Social innovations around the water–energy–food nexus are becoming established, for example in the SEKEM Development Foundation agricultural and light industry community based on biodynamic farming.[4] There are also initiatives in the desert based on new technologies such as hydroponics that grow plants without soil, using mineral nutrient solutions in a water solvent under controlled temperature and light conditions. However, technology alone cannot be seen as the solution. Community development, including the necessary social institutions, is crucial in order to attract people to new areas and form the basis for sustainable development.

Looking at sub-Saharan Africa, generally, and South Africa, specifically, the national government has enacted a number of policies that promote social innovation and entrepreneurship, but without any specific policy for the sector. For example, there is a long history of initiatives promoting cooperatives in South Africa, particularly in the agricultural and craft sectors. Government funding is available for establishing cooperatives through the Cooperatives Incentive Scheme, and support organizations provide training for cooperatives that are starting out. However, many cooperatives have either remained small organizations or have failed, due to little ongoing support. The list of South African cooperatives includes numerous small, localized cooperatives producing beadwork or leather goods or selling vegetables to local communities. Kaap Agri is one of the few cooperatives that has scaled, starting as a cooperative of a small group of farmers who joined together to purchase fertilizer in 1912. Since that time, they have amalgamated with other small, local cooperatives initially and then large provincial organizations. In 1995 they made the decision to convert from a cooperative to a company, although they continue to pride themselves in an approach that focuses on the empowerment of the people that work there.

As social innovation and entrepreneurship began to be discussed in South Africa, resistance was seen from some academics to widening the definition to include anything other than cooperatives. Current formal policies are instead centered on purely commercial enterprises and economic development, such as the Competitiveness Fund, administered by the Department of Trade and Industry, that provides assistance to entrepreneurs, and the Junior Achievement South Africa program that runs a number of initiatives to encourage youth entrepreneurship. In the last 20 years, the country has made the transition from apartheid to democracy but remains beset by persistent social inequality and poverty. In this context, taking health and social care as an example, although there have been substantial improvements, a heavy burden of disease remains alongside an inequitable quality of healthcare service provision. In conjunction with major health reform investments, the South African government has embarked on steps to establish a National Health Insurance (NHI) system. The goal of the NHI is to foster health care reform that will improve service provision and health care delivery among socioeconomic groups while also partnering with providers and organizations within the private sector in the delivery of health care. The main challenges within the social care environment in South Africa include poverty, unemployment and access to the basic requirements of life such as clean water, nutrition, sanitation and education. These factors ensure that the demand for social assistance remains high and constant.

Along with the work of the International Labour Organization in South Africa, and the now-closed African Social Entrepreneurs Network, universities in South Africa have been one of the driving forces behind the growth of social innovation and entrepreneurship in the country. The University of Johannesburg launched the first social enterprise project, with support from the Department of Trade and Industry. It focused on supporting and marketing the work of cooperatives in South Africa. The Gordon Institute of Business Science at the University of Pretoria has run a successful social entrepreneurship program for a number of years. The Graduate School of Business launched the Bertha Centre for Social Entrepreneurship and Innovation in 2013 and it is now recognized as one of the top five university-based social impact centers in the world. Its work has seen social innovation and entrepreneurship become part of the mainstream MBA and MPhil curriculum within the business school. It provides scholarships to African students to study social innovation at the school, has prepared numerous resources and guides for those in the sector and has piloted projects such as the first social impact bond in South Africa.

The Western Cape provincial government in South Africa commissioned the Bertha Centre for Social Entrepreneurship to develop a formal social innovation and social entrepreneurship strategy for coordinating government efforts in this area. This province is one of nine in the country, and, although it is one of the more prosperous provinces, it is still confronted with high levels of unemployment and a range of social problems. The Western Cape Government also realized that, lacking the resources to tackle these problems head-on, it could collaborate with the Bertha Centre to harness the power of social entrepreneurship, social innovation and social enterprise. It was also recognized that this was best done through creating an enabling environment where these phenomena can thrive. Hence, the strategy was intended to act as an overarching framework that government departments could use to guide their activities in this area and to synchronize much of the successful work that was already being done. There were four distinct steps involved in developing this government strategy:

1. Examination of the experiences of other governments in this area. This was matched with local research to create a conceptual framework.
2. Gathering the insights of various stakeholders. In-depth interviews were conducted with government officials and experts. Sixty-nine people participated in eight focus groups, and 144 people expressed their views through an online survey.
3. Development of a draft strategy and obtaining feedback from experts and government using an interactive process.
4. The fourth step subjected the draft strategy to a prescribed consultation process within the Western Cape government.

The strategy identified five distinctive areas where activities should be focused, which were

- to increase market access,
- to improve access to finance,
- to ensure access to business support,
- to demonstrate the impact of social entrepreneurship and
- to build the brand of social entrepreneurship.

Each of these five pillars was then matched with four priority projects that would help to lay the foundation for the enabling ecosystem it seeks to create. Some interesting insights from this emerged about how the strategy should be implemented, the foremost being the importance of the government working with trusted organizations in the field, and not duplicating infrastructure. However, the strategy was never formally adopted, so little happened in practice.

South Africa's health innovation policy currently resides within the Department of Science and Technology. Government across all departments is a key provider of basic services, with MomConnect, the biggest government innovation to date, firmly driven by the minister for health. However, social innovations are primarily developed at the frontlines of health care delivery by individuals and communities in response to a pressing need, often not met by government services. These social innovations take various forms, from technological products to processes, novel organizational models or market mechanisms. Social innovation is most often implemented and tested at a local, grassroots level before being pushed out to the district, provincial, and national levels and adopted in an ad hoc fashion. No formalized channels exist for grassroots innovators to interact with government officials. Several individual examples exist of social innovations that have been developed by grassroots innovators in response to a pressing need and only later adopted by the government or contracted by the government to support service delivery. This has also been the development trajectory of a grassroots education initiative in Ghana, as described later.

In Africa as a whole, according to Ginies (2013) focusing on social entrepreneurship, there is increased concern over the tragic waste of human potential, given that 20,000 highly qualified Africans leave the continent annually. If they remain in Africa, most of them are either unemployed or underemployed. In order to help create employment opportunities for young Africans, Ginies has set up 2iE, the International Institute for Water and Environmental Engineering, in Burkina Faso as a nonprofit association of public utility. This supports engineers from 27 countries and actively works for social innovation through entrepreneurship in Africa by a combination of training and entrepreneurship programs, joint research centers, start-up support and incubators. Awuah (2012: 17–18) notes that a pattern can be discerned underlying every challenge Africa faces, that is, barriers consisting of "people in positions of responsibility who were neither fixing problems nor creating solutions. Very few seemed to care, and even those who did were resigned to the status quo". Both sources point to the need for "a revolution in African education," especially at postschool and higher levels, away from traditional narrow subject matter, where students are tested on recall, toward thinking outside the box, ethical leadership, civic engagement and innovative thinking on "a leveraged path to a new Africa" (Awuah, 2012).

Another major challenge for Africa is infrastructure and public utilities. For example, in an article in the *Stanford Social Innovation Review*, Romisher (2015) pointed to the lack of electricity as one of the prime causes of poverty and inadequate economic growth and social development. Worldwide, 1.3 billion people live without access to electricity, while another 1 billion experience significant rolling blackouts. Nearly

97% of them live in sub-Saharan Africa and developing Asia, and the lack of reliable electricity creates a massive drain on education, manufacturing, and retail. More than 50% of businesses in sub-Saharan Africa identify electricity as a major constraint to their operation, compared with just 27% citing transportation.

In early 2018, a Danish information and communication technology (ICT) company,[5] in collaboration with the Ministry of Communications in Ghana, launched another affordable and sustainable *connecting the unconnected* project in four rural communities in the Western region of Ghana, prior to it being rolled out all over the country. The core of the solution is a base station powered 100% by solar energy that establishes a Wi-Fi hotspot with a range of up to 1 kilometer in diameter. The hotspot is connected to the internet by existing infrastructure, such as microwave link and fiber, or by satellite, balloons or drones, bringing connectivity to even the most secluded areas of the world. As the solution is based on Wi-Fi, people can browse the web, stay in touch or participate in educational programs using any smartphone, tablet or laptop. A local cloud is established at the base station providing fast and easy access to e-learning, e-health, and e-government services and allows citizens to share information, for example, about health care, education and agriculture, as well as communicate online with government authorities. Farmers can watch training videos to help them make the most of their land and to sell their crops at a fair price. Local doctors gain access to lifesaving information and much more. The hotspots are also being used in public establishments such as schools, hospitals, banks, police stations and market places.

Social Innovation Strategies and Themes

The challenge described by Romisher (2015) of lack of access to reliable electricity to tackle poverty and inadequate economic growth and social development, and the role that social and other innovations can play, consists of seeing the solution as requiring a multipronged approach. This illustrates some general issues about social innovation strategies and processes in Africa (Romisher, 2015) that require structural (i.e., macro and institutional) changes:

- The need, on one hand, for Africa to focus on technological innovation and technology leapfrogging, for example by taking advantage of the rapidly declining price of solar energy, increased battery capacity per dollar and the proliferation of mobile phone commerce. On the other hand, however, there is also a need to understand that solutions are not only, or indeed largely, technological but are, for example, also related to state capacity and the local political economy, especially how local elites share the spoils of the political game, such as the control of energy infrastructure.

- Given that the poor at the bottom of the pyramid do not have money and are not rendered bankable nor creditworthy even now they have mobile phones, it is important to focus not just on technological innovations but also on financial leapfrogging and empowerment at the lowest economic rung of a country. This also implies that the regulatory and political climate must simultaneously constitute an ecosystem of empowerment of opportunity, income and wealth, for example, through innovative consumer finance techniques and creative for-profit business models.

It is also important to recognize that many rural families in Africa have family members or *representatives* in towns who generate income and send it home as remittances, often in the form of goods that are unaffordable for the rural poor. Migrants in urban areas and abroad are a major source of economic leveling and provide many rural poor people with their material goods, as well as services like school fees. A disadvantage is that such migrants may thereby also be burdened with the needs of their extended family, which can both reduce their own personal prosperity as well as spreading the benefits of prosperity too thinly (Romisher, 2015).

Figure 10.3 maps the different types of underlying strategies and themes used to design and implement social innovations in African and non-African countries. It shows that empowerment of, for example, disadvantaged or marginalized groups is the most important strategy adopted and that this is closely followed by the related strategies of knowledge and human resource development, social enterprise, a focus on gender and other inequality issues and the use of ICT. Apart from greater emphasis on empowerment in Africa, there are only minor differences between African and non-African initiatives, which arguably points to

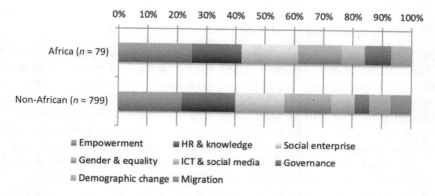

Figure 10.3 Main strategies addressed by African and non-African social innovations
Source: SI-DRIVE data.
Note: HR = human resource; ICT = information and communication technology.

a set of global core strategies characteristic of social innovation. There is, however, a greater focus on the goal of achieving better governance of related initiatives in Africa, which is likely to be related to the larger number of initiatives integrating and coordinating across two or more development pillars at the same time, as illustrated in Figure 10.2. It is also noticeable in Figure 10.3 that there are no migration-related initiatives in Africa compared to 7% outside Africa, despite the fact that both regions otherwise focus equally on demographic change issues, such as fertility, family size and age-related challenges, at 7%. Social innovations with migration strategies perhaps require significant political will and reach at regional or national levels to be viable, a situation not yet generally seen in Africa.

Other SI-DRIVE data also show some small differences between Northern Africa and sub-Saharan Africa, with the former more likely to adopt strategies focused on social enterprise, while the latter tends to focus more on gender, equality, diversity and empowerment. As generalizations, these differences can readily be seen to reflect the overall concerns and the current situation in the two regions, despite their very large internal differences, and also tend to be reflected in Figure 10.3. The Northern African focus on social entrepreneurship appears to be more closely aligned with conventional private market measures and strategies, while the South African use of social enterprise tends to adopt a more holistic approach. As noted earlier, the Bertha Centre for Social Entrepreneurship and Innovation in South Africa promotes social enterprise as a support and market conduit for the work of cooperatives in the country. This also reflects the argument in Moulaert et al. (2013) that there is a break between old social change analysis focusing more on broad approaches to social innovation and more recent social innovation analysis, where the conventional economy is prioritized.

Governance, Networks and Actors in Social Innovation

In Northern Africa as well as the wider Arab Region, pan-national bodies like the League of Arab States (LAS), the Economic and Social Commission for Western Asia (ESCWA), and the Mediterranean Commission on Sustainable Development (MCSD) are the chief governance structures designed to help achieve the United Nations' Sustainable Development Goals, 2016–2030.[6] The LAS has different specialized councils and sectors to design and manage the regional sustainable development and poverty reduction framework in all Arab states. Agenda 21 is the Arab countries' master plan for sustainable development and fighting poverty. At the national level, central governments and different ministries are the main, and in some countries the single, governance structures for social innovation practices. The main social innovation actors in Northern Africa and the Arab region are both regional and national government ministries, although the involvement of both the private sector and, especially, civil society has increased significantly over the last two decades.

In a sub-Saharan context, as perhaps exemplified by South Africa, Hart et al. (2014) point to the South African 1996 white paper on science and technology. This recognized the importance of, on one hand, formal government, higher education, research institutions and the private sector and, on the other hand, both formal civil organizations and informal households and individuals as part of the National System of Innovation. As described earlier, this is in some contrast to Northern Africa, as also evidenced by other SI-DRIVE data. The overall African picture is depicted in Figure 10.4 and largely reflects the sub-Saharan Africa situation. The figure shows, in fact, that although there is an almost equal balance of public, private and civil actors in non-African cases, indicating that the aim of involving all types has largely been achieved, in Africa civil actors by far outweigh public and private actors. This perhaps points to the relatively underdeveloped, still relatively small-scale and possibly informal nature of social innovations, particularly in sub-Saharan Africa.

Figure 10.4 can also be better understood by Hart et al.'s (2014) explanation that, although more than half of the non-profit-sector initiatives (designated as civil actors in Figure 10.4) innovate for social improvement, a large minority innovate as social entrepreneurs for commercial purposes but with the aim of meeting otherwise unmet social needs. This might be because of the high level of competition for resources to provide services in this sector and the resultant need to supplement grant income in creative ways, for example, innovations that increase income. It might also result from the fact that some nonprofit enterprises, especially those linked to government projects and community groups, aim to generate an income for members as part of poverty reduction strategies. In contrast,

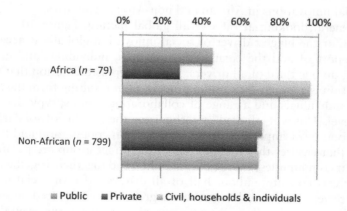

Figure 10.4 Combinations of actors in African and non-African social innovations
Source: SI-DRIVE data.[7]

private-sector innovators who cite social improvement purposes are often thinking about more indirect poverty alleviation outcomes through, for example, job creation resulting from greater profits, increased food security as a result of the use of new seeds or greater credit for poor people through profitable microfinance schemes. Overall, therefore, Hart et al. (2014) conclude that the perceptions of innovators across the sectors about the purpose and beneficiaries of social innovation are blurred, and clear boundaries do not exist, although there is an indication that the poor or less fortunate should benefit most directly.

Much social innovation in Africa is mainly focused on tackling poverty and promoting sustainable development, compared to many more economically advanced countries. Sub-Saharan Africa and Northern Africa tend to tackle these challenges using different governance systems and a different disposition of actors. In the former, the approach has typically been largely from the bottom up; informal; promoted by civil society, including social entrepreneurs; and unrelated to the traditional types of innovation practiced in the private sector, in research institutions and even in the public sector. In Northern Africa, on the other hand, social innovation is more likely to be characterized by a top-down government, institutional and private-sector approach. Although social innovation in more economically advanced countries is also characterized by all these approaches, many other types of social innovation are also found, such as much greater interlinking with the traditional approaches to research, innovation and cooperation found in the public sector and in research and private institutions.

Drivers and Barriers

Figure 10.5 summarizes the main types of drivers, or enablers, of successful social innovations in African and non-African countries.

In general, looking at the overall global picture, Figure 10.5 shows that by far the biggest driver of social innovation globally is access to, the support of and the creation of networks, individuals and groups, making up one third of all drivers. This underpins the notion that social innovation is a largely bottom-up process often resulting from the action of key individuals and a range of collaborating groups, typically at the local level. This is reinforced by recognizing the benefits of solidarity, as the second most important driver, arising from cooperation and mutual action that ensures that the interests of the target group are paramount and that communities and societies should stand together. Together, these two drivers constitute about half of all drivers. African social innovations are very similar, although there is greater weight placed on solidarity with consequentially less importance given to networks, even though these two drivers are often two sides of the same coin. It is clear that notions of solidarity are even stronger in Africa, given that the challenges

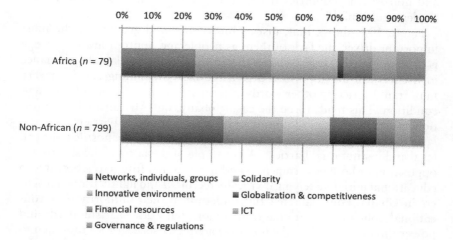

Figure 10.5 Main drivers of African and non-African social innovations
Source: SI-DRIVE data.
Note: ICT = information and communication technology.

of poverty, marginalization and exclusion tend to be even more acute than elsewhere.

Globally, the presence of a local and contextually appropriate innovative environment that enables and promotes innovation and the more macro pressures and opportunities of globalization and competitiveness are both important drivers. However, the latter has little relevance in Africa where socioeconomic conditions in situations where social innovation takes place are rarely linked to more than local and regional structures. Financial resources do not seem to be decisive drivers, although they are somewhat more important in Africa, probably given the fact that much social innovation is more likely to be driven by resources in kind and, as noted earlier, the cooperative efforts and mutual actions characterizing notions of solidarity. Similarly, the opportunities afforded by ICT are of only minor importance to date, although there is clearly much potential for this in Africa (World Bank, 2012), as illustrated earlier by the Wi-Fi hotspot example in Ghana. Clearly, the potentially large impacts of ICT appear to date not to have been adequately explored by social innovators. Finally, governance and regulations are likewise only occasionally important drivers, which again shows social innovation to be a largely bottom-up local process often working away from the limelight, regardless of prevailing structural frameworks and more formal programs.

Turning to the barriers to social innovation, Figure 10.6 summarizes the main types which typically hinder social innovations in African and non-African countries from starting up or being successful during implementation.

Figure 10.6 shows that, just as individuals and groups are the most important driver, the lack of them as people and appropriate knowledge is the main barrier. It also shows that, although the availability of finance in itself is not an important driver, the lack of funding can be a very important barrier; in other words, it is often a necessary but not sufficient condition. This tends to be the case globally, but African social innovations differ in relation to a number of other important barriers, particularly the inhibiting effects of nonconducive or even more hostile political, legal and institutional barriers. An example of the latter is the short-term opposition of both governmental and institutional forces to a bottom-up educational initiative relying on locally recruited and lightly trained teachers in Ghana. Politicians felt this undermined their authority over educational policies and national trade unions felt both their standards and power threatened. When the initiative adapted aspects of its approach to ensure that politicians could take some credit for its success, as well as by encouraging their teachers to go on to formal training colleges, thereby also helping to ease the acute teacher shortage in Ghana, the initiative went on to be highly successful (see also the following discussion for more details of this example). In non-African countries, political barriers tend to be much less important, although legal and institutional barriers are often mentioned. Finally, the problems resulting from competition are sometimes important outside Africa but rarely within, reflecting the roles both play in international globalization and competition. Also, a lack of access to media communication and the promotion of an initiative are

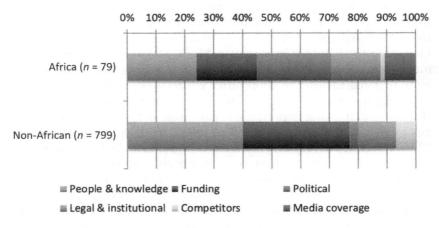

Figure 10.6 Main barriers to African and non-African social innovations
Source: SI-DRIVE data.

not a problem in non-African countries, although can be in Africa given the much less developed media environment.

According to Nwuneli (2016), efforts at implementing and scaling social innovations in Africa generally reflect the preceding observations. She notes that social innovation is limited by a number of factors, including unsuitable business models, access to creative capital, a poor enabling environment and weak infrastructure, shortage of human capacity with the requisite skills to drive growth without sacrificing quality and impact and institutional barriers to cross-sector collaborations.

Social Innovation Capacities and Outcomes

An Economist Intelligence Unit study from 2016 devised and calculated an index measuring the capacity for social innovation, using both quantitative and qualitative indicators. Of the 45 countries surveyed, 4 are from Africa: South Africa, Kenya, Ghana and Nigeria, with the results generally reflecting the earlier conclusions across the four pillars examined:

1. Policy and institutional framework: all African countries are in the bottom third of the rankings: South Africa (rank 31), Kenya (34), Ghana (41) and Nigeria (42)
2. Financing: similar to pillar 1: South Africa (rank 31), Kenya (35), Ghana (38) and Nigeria (39)
3. Social entrepreneurship: all African countries are in the top third of the rankings: Kenya (4), South Africa (rank 6), Ghana (12) and Nigeria (14)
4. Civil society: all African countries are in the middle third of the rankings: Kenya (15), South Africa (rank 16), Ghana (34) and Nigeria (35).

These data clearly show the existing capacity for policy, institutions and financing to be relatively low when compared with non-African countries. This aligns with the findings noted above that political, legal and institutional barriers figure higher in African compared to non-African countries. Also, the existence of financial resources is an important driver in African countries when it is available but is typically not a barrier simply because many social innovation initiatives are not dependent on external funding due to their in-kind nature, often driven by notions of solidarity, pointing to a generally low financial capacity.

African countries, however, rank relatively high globally in terms of social entrepreneurship. As stated in the Economist Intelligence Unit's report,

> [s]ome African countries are well positioned to benefit from social enterprise. That social entrepreneurialism is seen as a sustainable solution in Africa is the result of what some experts call the continent's

"crisis of development" and the failure of either the state or the market to deliver results. The way is open for dynamic, socially minded enterprises—or what some have termed "Africapitalism"—to solve social problems, in many cases using new technology that can "leap-frog" into wider use in developing economies.

(Economist Intelligence Unit, 2016: 6)

The fact that civil society capacity is about average in global terms arguably reflects the fact that, on one hand, CSOs are much more important for social innovation in Africa, with the state and the market correspondingly less important as noted by the Economist Intelligence Unit, compared to elsewhere. On the other hand, this shows that civil society is not particularly well developed, being mainly local and often not strongly institutionalized.

In contrast to measuring capacity, there is little readily available systematic evidence of the real achievements of social innovation in Africa, apart from the anecdotal effects produced by individual initiatives. Thus, the data provided by the SI-DRIVE project is timely, even though it only partially fills this gap. A simple initial analysis of the SI-DRIVE cases in relation to the type of evidence on outcomes provided showed that

- Northern African cases: 47% of the 34 cases provided quantitative data on outcomes,
- sub-Saharan African cases: 67% of the 45 cases provided quantitative data on outcomes,
- total African cases: 58% of the 79 cases provided quantitative data on outcomes and
- non-African cases: 79% of the 799 cases provided quantitative data on outcomes.

These data clearly show that sub-Saharan African cases are more likely to be using quantitative data measures in evaluating their results, compared to Northern African cases, but also that the proportion of non-African cases that do so is much higher than both African regions. It is also the case that, in Africa, much of this is self-measurement by initiatives taking place on a local and often case-by-case basis, so perhaps the fact that measurement is more common in sub-Saharan Africa reflects the more bottom-up local- and civil-led nature of initiatives here. This evidence might also, however, reflect the fact that international funding for sub-Saharan African initiatives also brings a requirement for measurement that the initiatives might not otherwise prioritize.

Overall, however, more than half of all African cases are at least at the stage of collecting data as opposed to only relying on qualitative, and perhaps sometimes anecdotal, evidence, although this latter type of evidence can also be highly important, especially in understanding how and why given outcomes are achieved. There is increasing pressure on initiatives of all types to demonstrate real impact and value for the efforts and inputs put in, especially in a context of increasingly scarce resources and competition between initiatives. Meaningful measurement requires both awareness of its importance and that processes are in place to undertake it. In non-African countries, many initiatives have better access to staff with the necessary skills, as well as being part of structured programs which require measurement.

According to BEPA (2010), there are three societal levels at which the outcomes of social innovations may arise. In this perspective, social innovations

1. respond to *social demands* that are traditionally not addressed by the market or existing institutions and are directed toward vulnerable groups in society. These are typically seen at the micro level. Examples might include community-focused initiatives that give beneficiaries the confidence and skills to start their own small enterprises, thereby providing jobs and contributing to the local economy.
2. tackle *societal challenges* through new forms of relations between social actors, respond to those societal challenges in which the boundary between social and economic blurs and are directed toward society as a whole. These are at the meso level. Examples might include primary educational initiatives that aim to change the relationships between pupils, parents and teachers, on one hand, and the educational authorities, on the other, by giving the former more resources and decision-making powers to make contextually relevant educational decisions.
3. contribute to the *systemic change* or reform of society in the direction of a more participative arena where empowerment and learning are both sources and outcomes of well-being. These are at the macro level. Examples might include national policy and regulatory changes that enable locally based and initiated renewable-energy projects to start up and be successful, such as when legal restrictions against local energy production are removed.

As deployed by SI-DRIVE (Howaldt et al., 2016) and as analyzed by Millard et al. (2017), this BEPA methodology represents an approach that is both conceptually and operationally sound when ascertaining social innovation outcomes. It links directly to ideas of social change, as well as focusing on those changes that are favorable to participants and beneficiaries, that is, people-centered social innovations. Figure 10.7 shows the relative importance of the three BEPA outcome levels in African and non-African initiatives.

In general terms, Figure 10.7 shows, not unexpectedly, that most innovations achieve outcomes at the more micro level of social demand, somewhat fewer outcomes at the meso level of societal challenge, with the more ambitious systemic change level achieving the fewest outcomes.

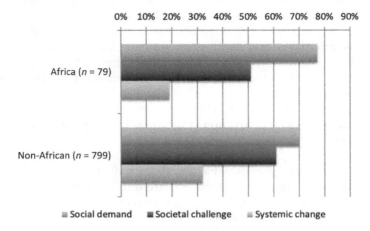

Figure 10.7 Combinations of outcome levels in African and non-African social innovations

Source: SI-DRIVE data.[8]

However, it is also clear that all levels are achieving important outcomes, whether measured quantitatively or qualitatively. Again, it is the case that African social innovations tend to achieve outcomes more weighted toward the micro level than those outside Africa, as well as achieving fewer outcomes overall. This is in line with the earlier observations that, in Africa generally, social innovations are more likely to be highly local- and civil-society-initiated and -led, aiming in the first place to fulfill the urgent demands of the local community, and less likely to be part of larger scale policy and innovation programs. The latter tend, in contrast, to be more common in the more developed global regions.

Some Conceptual Lessons and Considerations

The detailed mapping and analysis of social innovation in Africa, presented earlier, can also be tentatively placed in the context of a more conceptual and theoretical framework. First, relevant issues derived from development theory are examined, followed by the social theory of agency structure. Second, related conclusions are drawn regarding social innovation in Africa.

The Relevance of Development Theory to African Social Innovation

Development theory is a collection of theories about how desirable change in society is best achieved with a specific focus on so-called *developing* countries and *emerging* economies. However, it also relates directly to any context that requires socioeconomic development or improvement, normally through planned or coordinated actions. It therefore draws on a wide range of social science disciplines and approaches (Allen and Thomas, 2000; Sachs, 1992). *Development* can thus be seen as a multifactor and cross-sectoral issue, potentially cutting across all areas of social, economic, environmental, political, cultural and technological change, and attempts to link these areas together to account for their combined effect at different scales and levels. Traditional development theory tends to address mainly macro and typically global societal change, as what is experienced in one country or region is perceived as being intrinsically part of larger scale and often pervasive trends (Millard, 2014). The evidence presented above from African social innovations indicates that they are indeed highly cross-sectoral, contextually embedded and address the full range of social, economic, environmental and related concerns. However, especially in Africa, social innovations have not been much focused on larger scales and often find it difficult to scale and have an impact beyond the local and specific context in which they take place.

More recently, postdevelopment and human development theories reveal the fundamental cultural and mental constructivism that underlines much theorizing and practice of social innovation, and this also helps to strengthen understanding of the behavioral and psychological processes and contexts in which innovations take place. As seen with many social innovations, this, in turn, emphasizes the importance of local cultures and local knowledge in addressing social need challenges, sometimes up to the level of systemic social change (Santos, 2008). Embedded within these new development approaches and reflected in African social innovations are issues such as gender, vulnerability, exclusion and welfare economics, as well as developments of the sustainability concept that employ theories of ecology and ecosystems that are not simply biological or physical, but also social and cultural.

Also relevant is the recent focus in developmental concepts on dimensions of morality, ethics, fairness and justice in innovation and societal change, including the move away from a needs-based and toward a rights-based approach. These help to underline the need to see economic and development processes as being just as much cultural, social, economic and institutional as they are technological, financial and market-based, as emphasized in bottom-of-the-pyramid (Prahald, 2004) and similar theories. Moreover, this shift involves greater emphasis on the capabilities and aspirations of people and communities rather than only their needs, on people-centric approaches and on inclusive and frugal innovation which underlie the appreciative inquiry approach. Here the focus is mainly on resource-poor people and communities and how they can be mobilized both to help meet their own objectives and needs and to become important actors in their own right. This includes becoming potential partners and innovators in creating new business models that mutually benefit both companies and communities. In turn, the theory-of-change approach focuses attention on the sequence of changes and processes necessary to reach a longer-term goal using participatory and bottom-up processes to meeting social needs. Social change processes are no longer seen as linear but as having many feedback loops that need to be understood in a process that can be seen as experimental and socially innovative (Millard, 2014).

Applying the Agency–Structure Framework

As noted earlier, social innovations, especially in Africa, readily use the first two social change mechanisms but are less successful with the third. In turn, this helps illustrate and analyze the agency–structure distinction (Archer, 1982; Emirbayer and Mische, 1998; Giddens, 1984), viz.

- structure: the recurrent patterned arrangements of rules and resources, habits, conventions, institutions and cognitive frameworks that influence or limit the choices and opportunities available to societal actors and
- agency: the capacity of individuals and collectives to make sense of structures, to act on them, reason and make choices.

Structure and agency in this view are complementary forces. Structure both constrains and enables human behavior, and humans are capable of reiterating or changing the social structures they inhabit, although this typically requires collective action on a relatively large scale and time-frame, so can be difficult to do. Many of the preceding examples have illustrated the importance of linking achievements, especially in relation to the agency of target beneficiaries, to the structural context in which they find themselves. Often this is not done, or not done successfully, leading to fewer real outcomes than might otherwise be achieved.

As we have seen, there is a major role in social innovation for CSOs[9] in Africa compared to elsewhere and a greater focus on crosscutting social innovations that simultaneously tackle two or three of the sustainable development pillars as part of one development process. CSOs in Africa tend to find it difficult to work with other actors (although not with the target beneficiaries) and especially with the public sector, which is often seen as remote and occasionally hostile. Thus, although much success at the agency level is being achieved, this is not seen so clearly at the structural level, which would otherwise increase rollout, scaling and impact. However, structural links do tend to be stronger in social innovation in Northern Africa—although there are many questions around what the most appropriate structures are—where they are correspondingly less strong in developing the agency of target beneficiaries and intermediaries on the ground, although this is now starting to change. The reverse is typically the case in sub-Saharan Africa, while again, there are many signs that structural frameworks are being strengthened and becoming more appropriate.

For example, close collaboration with international development donors, including philanthropies (which, by and large, practice people-centered social innovation but do not call it this) is often good in Africa. Thus, social innovation in Africa is often characterized by dissemination and scaling being relatively low in a given context and country (e.g., within a given governmental jurisdiction) but relatively high internationally. There are, however, an increasing number of valuable exceptions to this generalization. For example, an education and poverty-reduction social innovation in northern Ghana that significantly enhances the agency of beneficiaries spent about 10 years battling against both central and local government and prevailing structures but finally got their approach mainstreamed across the country when it became part of official government policy. This resulted in close to half a million children, who otherwise would have had none, being provided with a basic education, as well as providing a pathway to more advanced education (Millard, 2017a).

Examining social innovation development paths and trajectories is thus illuminating. For example, the Ghanaian case mentioned well illustrates some of these often complex interrelationships in a social innovation run by a CSO in the north of the country. The CSO started not by attempting to find a solution to a given problem but, instead, by recognizing an opportunity to use the latent talents and capacities of local inhabitants possessing some basic education by training them as so-called *barefoot* teachers. They then noticed the many children in nearby villages who had no possibility of any education and so married the two together by deploying these barefoot teachers to provide basic literacy and numeracy skills to children. However, instead of focusing purely on facilitating children's education, the CSO soon realized that the actual key to success was to work on simultaneously changing local power structures through wide and painstaking consensus and capacity building, particularly by empowering women in village life, to ensure broad acceptance and consensus that such education was good for all. Significant success in all aspects ensued, and from this, in turn, other complementary innovations were simultaneously both required and enabled. These included involving women in local entrepreneurship schemes and supporting local radio stations and media productions as job opportunities for some of the locally educated youth. This example also illustrates the need to address, as far as possible, some of the structural root causes—in this case, local power structures and the role of women as well as government intransigence—in order to meet a number of immediate social needs, like child education and female employment.

Other Important Considerations

Basic questions need to be asked about how the social needs and issues addressed by social innovation are articulated. For example, on one hand, people in poverty typically find themselves in a condition of over-all relative powerlessness, while, on the other hand, the poor—and especially the communities in which they live—possess huge potential, resilience and latent ability to be a big part of their own solution, as seen in the Ghanaian example. As this example also shows, this will often mean there should be less focus just on problem solving and much more on the opportunities open to the poor in their specific context so that awareness raising, advocacy and mobilization of the poor people and their communities, especially in Africa, as much as possible through their own efforts, is critical. The SI-DRIVE results revealed that many more than expected of the social innovation cases examined are aban-doning the traditional focus purely on trying to solve an immediate problem of social need, such as low income. This can, of course, be important, but many instead start from the possibilities, opportunities, capacities and aspirations already existing rather than what might be missing (Millard, 2017a). Indeed, other recent research has led to related conclusions, such as the WILCO project,[10] which found that investing in capabilities rather than deficits is an important trend in service inno-vation. Similarly, a conclusion from innovation studies more generally noted that most innovations do not, in fact, arise from attempting to solve a particular problem, whether this is a pressing social need as is typically the case in social innovation but, instead, arise from dreams, visions and possibilities (Dijkgraaf, 2017).

From the perspective of governments, funders and civil organizations, this implies that a coordinated approach which cuts across administra-tive silos and links together a range of complementary actors is needed, depending on the specific requirements of each initiative. Given that pov-erty, deprivation and social needs more generally, as the main foci of social innovation in Africa, all result from—as well as themselves cause—multiple deprivations across a range of issues, this is a fundamental issue. In this context, CSOs often play a special role as trusted third parties which can link other actors across silos and sectors. This typically seems to work well in Africa, as elsewhere, given they are seen as not having their own commercial or political interests and are thus better able to be neutral mediators. For example, in the Ghanaian case cited, a local non-governmental organization partially supported by Danish development funding has successfully managed to mediate and coordinate appropri-ate all-around solutions by combining the efforts and resources from a range of actors. These include both central and local governments, trades unions, local microenterprises, radio and TV outlets, village chiefs and councils, as well as international donors and experts.

Summary and Conclusion

Social Innovation Today in Africa

The main social innovation focus in Africa at present is on alleviating poverty, marginalization and exclusion from the social and economic benefits of development, while also ensuring that progress is sustainable in both environmental and socioeconomic terms. All aspects of development are being tackled, given the acute needs recognized, and all actor types are involved, although the majority of initiatives are started and led by civil organizations and, sometimes, informal groups. These are close to the beneficiary target groups they are assisting, which themselves normally play a vital role in determining the objectives and implementing initiatives so that people-centric, and indeed people-driven, strategies are important characteristics.

On this basis, most social innovations in Africa are bottom-up and focus on empowering the target group, especially women and disadvantaged groups, developing human resources and knowledge, as well as social enterprise. As noted earlier, African countries appear to have relatively high social entrepreneurship capacity in global terms, given the continent's so-called crisis of development and the failure of either the state or the market to deliver results. Networks, relationships to individuals and groups and notions of solidarity are, by far, the most important drivers of social innovation, counterpoising the often unaware, weak and/or unsympathetic and even occasionally road-blocking public sector, as cited in the Ghana example, although there are very large variations.

Social innovations in Africa often start informally and some remain so, but there is also an increasing tendency for closer cooperation between civil society and the public and private sectors through more formalized arrangements, and this is also reflected by international donors and investors who increasingly look to civil society to undertake development work through social innovation, but also typically insist that such partnerships are active and take outcome measurement seriously. Indeed, an increasing number of externally funded social innovations are channeled through and led by the public sector and/or commercial companies, although in such cases, civil society, whether formal or informal, is typically also involved. As in many global regions, but even more so in Africa, a lack of appropriate personnel and knowledge is often the most important barrier to social innovation, but a lack of funding and of political support and understanding can also be critical.

The Future of Social Innovation in Africa

The backdrop to the future of social innovation in Africa is rapid population growth which, although it is starting to reduce quite significantly, will remain a challenge over the next 10 to 20 years, and perhaps longer, as the present youthful population cohort rises through the age pyramid. Linked to this, but likely to continue unabated in at least the foreseeable future, is rapid urbanization as Africans move increasing from rural villages to towns and cities, where the population is rising even faster due to better medical and other facilities in these areas. Another significant ongoing trend that social innovation needs to address is increasing inequality in all African countries, despite the overall significant reduction in absolute poverty that has been experienced over the past 20 years. This is, in fact, a global phenomenon but is particularly acute in Africa, as well as other developing countries in Asia and South America. This might threaten the quite shaky—although real and significant—development gains there have been so that continuing sustainable development is not yet assured and might easily be reversed or set back.

It is clear that the African continent can benefit from the purpose, sense of direction and targets specified in the United Nation's Sustainable Development Goals (SDGs) for the 2016 to 2030 time frame, agreed in New York in September 2015.[11] The 17 SDGs cover the whole spectrum of development required across the three development dimensions of economic, social and environmental, to which poverty eradication has been added as an informal fourth dimension. The SDGs are, of course, guidelines but have the huge advantage of building directly on the relatively successful Millennium Development Goals that preceded them. The SDGs are also attracting significant financial support from various international and private donors, as well as valuable mutual support and learning between countries, South–South, North–South and North–North, given that the SDGs are universal and apply to all countries. They have the additional advantage of including, for the first time, a focus on institutional capacity and development as a key enabler of delivering the targets. The SDGs also recognize that all actors, especially civil society and the private sector, alongside governments and public administrations, have a very important and increasing role to play. Social and inclusive innovation is a critical part of this recognition.

Notes

1. Northern Africa (UN classification): Algeria, Egypt, Libyan Arab Jamahiriya, Morocco, Tunisia, Western Sahara.
2. UCT (South Africa) and Heliopolis University (Egypt).
3. www.un.org/en/ga/president/65/issues/sustdev.shtml (Accessed on 16 November 2014).
4. www.sekem.com/en/index/.
5. https://bluetown.com/solution/.
6. https://sustainabledevelopment.un.org/content/documents/21252030%20 Agenda%20for%20Sustainable%20Development%20web.pdf.

7. Numbers add up to more than 100%, as almost all initiatives have more than one actor.
8. Numbers add up to more than 100%, as almost all initiatives report outcomes at more than one level.
9. CSOs are termed Community Service/Support Organizations in Northern Africa.
10. www.siresearch.eu/blog/wilco-final-conference.
11. https://sustainabledevelopment.un.org/content/documents/21252030%20 Agenda%20for%20Sustainable%20Development%20web.pdf   (Accessed on 25 January 2018).

References

Allen, T. and Thomas, A. (2000). *Poverty and Development into the 21st Century*. Oxford University Press.

Archer, M. S. (1982). "Morphogenesis Versus Structuration: On Combining Structure and Action," *British Journal of Sociology*, 33(4), pp. 455–483.

Awuah, P. (2012, Summer). "Path to a New Africa," *Stanford Social Innovation Review*, pp. 17–18.

BEPA (Bureau of European Policy Advisers). (2010). *Empowering People, Driving Change. Social Innovation in the European Union*. Luxembourg: Publications Office of the European Union.

CSESS (Le Conseil supérieur de l'économie sociale et solidaire). (2011, décembre). *Rapport de synthèse du groupe de travail innovation sociale*.

Dijkgraaf, R. (2017, July 3). *Director and Leon Levy Professor, Institute for Advanced Study*. Princeton University Press. Reported at the European Commission Conference Research and Innovation—Shaping Our Future. Brussels.

Economist Intelligence Unit. (2016). *Old Problems, New Solutions: Measuring the Capacity for Social Innovation Across the World*. London: Economist Intelligence Unit.

Emirbayer, M. and Mische, A. (1998). "What Is Agency?" *American Journal of Sociology*, 103(4), pp. 962–1023.

Giddens, A. (1984). *The Constitution of Society*. Cambridge: Polity Press.

Ginies, P. (2013). *Social Innovation Through Entrepreneurship in Africa*. Published by the Philadelphia Social Innovations Journal. http://philasocialinnovations.org/site/index.php?option=com_content&view=article&id=552:social-innovation-in-africa-qthe-footprintq-of-2ie&catid=19:disruptive-innovations&Itemid=30.

Hart, T., Jacobs, P. and Mangqalaza, H. (2012). *Key Concepts in Innovation Studies: Towards Working Definition*. RIAT Concept Paper Series—Concept Paper 2. Pretoria: HSBC.

Hart, T., Jacobs, P., Ramoroka, K., Mangqalaza, H., Mhula, A., Ngwenya, M. and Letty, B. (2014, March). *Social Innovation in South Africa's Rural Municipalities: Policy Implications*. Policy Brief of the Human Sciences Research Council. Department of Science and Technology, Republic of South Africa.

Howaldt, J., Schröder, A., Kaletka, C., Rehfeld, D. and Terstriep, J. (2016). *Comparative Analysis (Mapping 1): Mapping the World of Social Innovation: A Global Comparative Analysis Across Sectors and World Regions*. Deliverable D1.4 of the SI-DRIVE Project, June 2017. www.si-drive.eu.

Junge, J. (2015, April 20). *Ten Trends of Social Innovation in South Africa*. Published by Social Innovation Exchange. www.socialinnovationexchange.org/categories/read/top-10-trends-of-social-innovation-in-south-africa.

Millard, J. (2014, September). *Development Theory*. Chapter 3 in Deliverable D1.1 (Theoretical Approaches to Social Innovation: A Critical Literature Review) of the SI-DRIVE Project. www.si-drive.eu.

Millard, J. (2017a, January). *Social Innovation in Poverty Reduction and Sustainable Development: Case Study Results*. Deliverable D10.3 of the SI-DRIVE Project. www.si-drive.eu.

Millard, J. (2017b, June). *Summary Report on Social Innovation for Poverty Reduction and Sustainable Development*. Deliverable D10.4 of the SI-DRIVE Project. www.si-drive.eu.

Millard, J. (2018, February). "Social Innovation in Africa: Huge Diversity but Common Themes," *Atlas of Social Innovation*. Prepared by the SI-DRIVE Project. www.si-drive.eu.

Millard, J., Holtgrewe, U. and Hochgerner, J. (2017, December). *Objectives: Social Demands, Societal Challenges and Systemic Change Addressed*. Chapter 3 in Deliverable D1.6 (Towards a General Theory and Typology of Social Innovation) of the SI-DRIVE Project. www.si-drive.eu.

Moulaert, F., MacCallum, D., Mehmood, A. and Hamdouch, A. (2013). *The International Handbook on Social Innovation*. London: Edward Elgar.

NASA Big DataSet. (2015). *Temperature Patterns Around the World by 2100*. Release 15–115. www.nasa.gov/press-release/nasa-releases-detailed-global-climate-change-projections (Accessed on September 2018).

Nwuneli, N. O. (2016). *Social Innovation in Africa—A Practical Guide for Scaling Impact*. Series. Routledge Studies in African Development, Routledge.

Romisher, J. (2015, April 24). "Five Innovations That Will Electrify Africa," *Stanford Social Innovation Review*. http://ssir.org/articles/entry/five_innovations_that_will_electrify_africa.

Sachs, W. (ed.). (1992). *The Development Dictionary: A Guide to Knowledge as Power*. Zed Books.

Santos, B. S. (ed.). (2008). *Another Knowledge Is Possible: Beyond Northern Epistemology*. London: Verso.

Schröder, A., Weerakkody, W., El-Haddadeh, R., Kapoor, K., Butzin, A., Boelma, V. Scoppetta, A., Weber, M., Schaper-Rinkel, P., Dhondt, S. and Oeij, P. (2014, December). *Methodology Review: Research Propositions, Data Collection and Analysis Framework*. Deliverable D2.1 of the SI-DRIVE project. www.si-drive.eu.

SI-DRIVE Project. (2014–17). *Social Innovation: Driving Force of Social Change*. Funded by the European Union's Seventh Framework Programme for Research, Technological Development and Demonstration Under Grant Agreement no 612870. www.si-drive.eu.

Van Hofwegen, P. and Svendsen, M. (2000). *A Vision of Water for Food and Rural Development*. World Water Vision Sector Report. hubrural.org/IMG/pdf/waterfor_foodvision.pdf (Accessed on September 2018).

World Bank. (2012). *eTransform Africa—the Transformational Use of Information and Communications Technologies in Africa*. Washington, DC: The World Bank and the African Development Bank with the Support of the African Union.

11 Social Innovations as Heretical Practices

Silla Marie Mørch Sievers

Introduction

Social innovation is in fashion. It is praised as the solution to state as well as market failures and politicians dream of social innovation as a vehicle to create more efficient social services—to do more for less. This chapter is a theoretical investigation of social innovation that seeks to challenge the simplistic notion of social innovation as an improvement machine. The word *innovation* is derived from the Latin *innovare*, which comes from *in-* (into) and *novus* (new). Bringing something new into the world has historically been seen as threatening. As Godin (2015b) points out, the positive perception of innovation is a relatively recent phenomenon. From the Reformation to the 19th century, innovation was regarded as unwelcome, and innovators were often perceived as heretics who disturbed an order (Godin, 2014, 2015b). In this chapter, it is argued that the disturbance of order can be viewed as a key feature of social innovations. This aspect is also central to, for example, Schumpeter's idea of innovation as "creative destruction". In the social innovation literature, however, there seems to have been an imbalance favoring *creativity* and other positive or productive aspects of innovation, whereas the *destruction* aspect has been more overlooked. Drawing on Spinosa, Flores and Dreyfus's (1997) notion of disclosive spaces, this chapter argues that innovations are essentially disharmonic and challenge a given order, a given standard, and force us to reconfigure new disclosive spaces and, with them, new standards or infrastructures. In this way, social innovation is not primarily about doing things *better* but more about doing things *differently*.[1] Here, social innovation can be viewed as a marginal practice that does not simply subject itself to existing standards and orders but (sometimes radically) challenges and changes them. It is therefore essential not to view social innovations as isolated phenomena but to analyze them against the backdrop of the historical and societal developments and contexts in which they emerge. As suggested earlier, social innovations can be regarded as *heretical* (Godin, 2015b). This may help us explain why it seems to be difficult to succeed in creating lasting social innovations despite political attention and desire. In this way, this chapter can be understood as an attempt to challenge what is commonly referred to as the pro-innovation bias (see Rogers, 1976). This bias is the tendency to focus only on the positive aspects of innovation, forgetting its limitations or weaknesses.

The chapter concludes by outlining some of the methodological implications of understanding social innovation as a heretical endeavor.

Social Innovation: A Beloved and Contested Concept

The popularity of the concept of social innovation seems to be ever growing. Former US president Obama launched an Office of Social Innovation and Civic Participation, and the European Commission has launched a social innovation community called Social Innovation Europe, which seeks to connect people and projects across Europe (European Commission, n.d.; White House, n.d.). Several local, regional and national initiatives tap into the same discourse, and in Denmark we now have a Ministry of Public Innovation that, among other things, wishes to involve civil society more in public welfare.

The past 10 to 15 years have seen a growing interest in social innovation in politics as well as academia. Social innovation is called on to challenge some of society's wicked problems and manages to unite politicians across the political spectrum in one common vision. It is often linked to either civil society or to cross-sector collaborations and hopes are that new innovative solutions can be the remedy that ensures the survival of a challenged public sector. "Burning platform" stories that demand innovations in order to maintain the current service level for citizens are often told. We hear of market failures and state failures (Gerometta et al., 2005; Swyngedouw, 2005; Teasdale, 2011), which refer to a situation where the state is incapable of providing services or social insurance for all its citizens or is powerless to balance out the inequities created by market forces (Teasdale, 2011: 103). We see people who are not capable of participating under market conditions. At the same time, the state is criticized for being too ineffective, bureaucratic and sluggish (Dees, 2007). Failure of the state is also often explained by the wickedness of the problems or the pressure on the public sector because of changing demographics and a strained economy. A radically changed and continually changing reality means that social innovation is often linked to a conservative wish to maintain the status quo and keep services as they are. In this perspective, social innovations are mainly seen as a reactive endeavor—social innovation is called for when market or state fails.

Despite the popularity of social innovation, its precise meaning remains challenged (see, e.g., Moulaert et al., 2013; Pol and Ville, 2009; Roy et al., 2014). It could be argued that social innovation to some extent functions as a floating signifier or a quasi-concept with multiple definitions and

meanings (Jenson, 2016: 90), and as Pol and Ville put it, " '[s]ocial innovation' is a term that almost everyone likes, but nobody is quite sure of
what it means" (Pol and Ville, 2009: 881).

Notwithstanding the diversity of perspectives, definitional work continues. Some view social innovation as a means to fight social exclusion
(Roy et al., 2014); as the solution to unmet social problems or needs (see,
e.g., Mulgan et al., 2007); as a way to create social change and social
value in a more effective, efficient and sustainable way than existing
solutions (Phills et al., 2008: 36); as a guide for collective action (Klein,
2013); as a means to improve social relations (Moulaert et al., 2013);
as a way to create enhanced life quality and life quantity (Pol and Ville,
2009); or as "a novel way to reconfigure market relations in support of
social policy initiatives" (Jenson, 2016: 89).

The influential Young Foundation understands social innovations as

> new solutions (products, services, models, markets, processes etc.)
> that simultaneously meet a social need (more effectively than existing
> solutions) and lead to new or improved capabilities and relationships
> and better use of assets and resources. In other words, social innova-
> tions are both good for society and enhance society's capacity to act.
> (The Young Foundation, 2012: 18)

And Geoff Mulgan from Nesta favors a simple version: "innovations
that are social in their ends and their means" (Nesta, 2017).

The common denominator of most of these definitions and approaches
is that they tend to focus on the positive effects of social innovation.
Social innovations are innovative ways to solve social problems, and this
leads to an understanding of social innovation as an advanced problem-
solving approach. The limitation of this approach is that, often, *social
value* is only vaguely defined, if at all. Social value is approached as if
it were a concept that could be understood unambiguously. However,
as experience will tell us, social value is not uniform or universal across
time, perspectives, people or situations.

Consider, for instance, any municipality, and see how the values and
aims for the citizens vary across departments. A citizen may enter several different municipal departments and be met with many different
understandings of social value. In the employment service, getting a job
is the primary task; in the family center, the citizen may be met with
the objective of creating a stable life for her children; in the municipal
health center, the aim is to tackle the person's chronic disease or lifestyle
issues. These different aims and the interventions initiated to tackle them
may not be compatible, and sometimes they may even undermine each
other. Add to this the citizen's own perspective on what is valuable in
his or her life, and the picture gets even more complex. Not only do the
understandings of value vary across the pillars of the public sector or

across sectors; they also vary across time. Alexander (2010), for instance, describes how the traditional focus in third-sector organizations used to be on social welfare, health, social justice and so forth. In the past two decades, this focus has shifted in the Anglo-Saxon context (and similar trends can be seen across many European countries) to support for the unemployed and developing work integration programs. According to Alexander, this tendency "accords with the Anglophone political mantra in the last decade that welfare should not be an end in itself but should channel people back to work" (Alexander, 2010: 220). This development is perhaps best reflected in the increased interest in the social economy, especially in work integration social enterprises.

A glance at practice shows that the question of social value is far from simple. Social value is packed with ambiguity and dilemmas, and the notion of social innovation as a problem-solving strategy seems to reinforce what has been named the *pro-innovation bias* (Rogers, 1976). The pro-innovation bias is a bias that "assumes that the innovations studied are 'good' and should be adopted by everyone" (Rogers, 1976: 295). This causes a methodological blind spot that ignores or externalizes negative or problematic aspects or effects of the innovations and ignores the fact that social value may be contested.

Social value is dependent on the situation, context, period in history and perspective. Social innovations should therefore not be studied as isolated phenomena but be analyzed in their context, in relation to norms (of, e.g., which values are deemed most important), standards and obstacles that challenge and shape them. Hence, we need to view them against the backdrop of historical and societal developments (Moulaert et al., 2010).

Illegality and Heresy

The previous section presented different perspectives on social innovations but also some of the challenges of the concept that arise as a consequence of viewing social innovation as merely creating social value or solving social problems. In the following section, I challenge the blind spot that emerges when we focus exclusively on the positive aspects of social innovations. A starting point for this investigation will be to interrogate the concept of *innovation*.

A very simple definition is that innovations are new ideas that work (Albury, 2005: 51). This is a broad and quite general definition yet it might point to some of the inherent tensions innovation seems to contain. Derrida argues that inventions qua "something new" contain a degree of illegality (Derrida, 1992: 312),[2] or a critique of the existing: "An invention always presupposes some illegality, the breaking of an implicit contract; it inserts a disorder into the peaceful ordering of things, it disregards proprieties" (Derrida, 1992: 312). At the same time, however, innovations and inventions demand recognition (Derrida, 1992: 315).

They must be recognized as something that "works". Innovation exists stretched out between breaking conventions and longing for recognition.

In much literature on innovation, the emphasis seems to be on the "works" aspect. Innovation is often equated with streamlining, optimization and improvement, just as it was shown earlier that social innovation is about *improving* quality or quantity of life (Pol and Ville, 2009) or meeting social needs *more effectively* (The Young Foundation, 2012). Yet if social innovation is to be a concept in its own right, we have to be able to distinguish it from other types of changes—and from mere improvement. As Hartley says, "innovation should not be conflated with improvement, or better performance, or success. Some very interesting innovations are not successful" (Hartley, 2014: 227). Despite this, social innovations are often talked about as precisely that. Here, exploring the *newness* of social innovation might provide a way forward. Schumpeter has described the innovation process as one of *creative destruction* (Schumpeter, 2003). Yet the focus in social innovation literature seems to be primarily on creativity and the productive elements of social innovation and less on the destructive forces. This favoring of the problem-solving properties is what has enabled (social) innovators and (social) entrepreneurs to be celebrated as heroes.

That, however, is not the whole story. If we turn to Spinosa, Flores and Dreyfus and their view on the entrepreneur, we meet a figure that opens new spaces for human action and engagement in a history-making process (Spinosa et al., 1997). Entrepreneurship is history-making in the sense that it "changes the way in which we understand and deal with ourselves and with things" (Spinosa et al., 1997: 2). In this perspective, entrepreneurship and innovation is not a frictionless endeavor. Rather, concepts such as anomaly and disharmony begin to appear (Berglund and Schwartz, 2013; Spinosa et al., 1997). The entrepreneur manages to identify disharmonies in her life and then hold on to these (Spinosa et al., 1997). Initially, the anomalies or disharmonies do not prompt the entrepreneur to try to avoid, solve or dismantle them. He or she might instead try to relate to or even embrace them (Berglund and Schwartz, 2013: 243) and, through this relating, identify a new marginal practice (Spinosa et al., 1997). This is a remarkable difference from the innovators-as-problem-solvers approach. Instead, the entrepreneur reconfigures *disclosive spaces* based on anomalies (Spinosa et al., 1997: 164). Spinosa, Flores and Dreyfus define a disclosive space as "any organized set of practices for dealing with oneself, other people, and things that produce a relatively self-contained web of meanings" (Spinosa et al., 1997: 17). Engaging in a marginal practice is seldom celebrated or praised. Often the practice of the entrepreneur will be considered absurd or outrageous (Spinosa et al., 1997: 167). What Spinosa, Flores and Dreyfus are proposing is that the entrepreneur (or innovator), in Lavoie's words, "shifts interpretive frameworks" (Lavoie in Spinosa et al., 1997: 58). Not only are new products or services produced; entrepreneurship is also about enacting new practices and new understandings. Entrepreneurs and innovators do not simply solve problems but create new ways to approach and understand the problems, and perhaps most important, they change or, to use Peter Drucker's word, *transmute, values* (Spinosa et al., 1997: 35). In this sense, entrepreneurship or innovation is a second-order practice that produces metachanges (Spinosa et al., 1997: 44).

Social innovations are, then, not 1:1 solutions to social problems or needs. They become solutions to problems that had not been identified or formulated prior to the innovation: solutions to problems we did not know existed in advance.

Hence, social innovation results in new understandings of a situation and a problem and becomes something more than simply a new, more effective solution. This transformative aspect of social innovation also means that social innovation processes are not linear. Social innovations must be conceived as complex processes with unknown and unanticipated outcomes; they have a certain open-endedness to them. Spinosa, Flores and Dreyfus add that the innovative entrepreneur is not someone who predicts the needs of people and satisfies these needs: "Once the needs are determinate, an average businessperson can catch on and try to catch up; the entrepreneur is the person who determines which needs will seem important" (Spinosa et al., 1997: 36). Social innovation introduces qualitative changes to practices, and it becomes not so much about the quantitative change often called for, such as doing more of the same for less, but, rather, about qualitative change. These qualitative changes introduce new ways of being and new ways of relating to one's environment, which differ from the canonical ways of doing things. Introducing a new, marginal practice functions as a criticism of the existing order. It is the duality of the creative destruction of Schumpeter, namely, production and destruction at the same moment. Hillier's Deleuze-inspired methodology describes how social innovations often emerge from conflict "as challenges to institutionalized or normalized legitimacy" (Hillier, 2013: 170).

The destructive aspect of innovation has historically led people to turn away from innovation, sometimes even to despise it. Benoit Godin traces the origins of the word, concept and term *innovation*, describing how it has gone from being derogatory to being praised, and adds that *innovation* was used as the secular term for heresy (Godin, 2015b: 6). He argues that innovation is "full of ambivalence and tensions" (Godin, 2015b: 7) because innovations are about individuals (or groups) who "take the initiative or liberty of introducing something of their own and foreign to the custom" (Godin, 2015b: 6). Historically, this has been seen as threatening a given order:

> From the Reformation onward, innovation is strictly pejorative. Whether one looks at religion, politics, philosophy, science or social

reform, innovation is negative. As 'introducing change into the established order', innovation is a polemical weapon used against those who attempt to change things.

(Godin, 2014: 8)

In this view, innovation is closely related to *liberty* or *choice*, which the Scottish philosopher Thomas Reid was also aware of when he described innovation as a "'liberty which, even when necessary, creates prejudice and misconstructions, and which must wait the sanction of time to authorize it' (Reid, 1796)" (Reid, as cited in Godin, 2015a: 18). Godin also notes how the innovator is introducing something that is different from the established order and tradition (Godin, 2015a: 18). Innovations act as the centrifugal forces of society (Bakhtin, 1981) in that they stratify and challenge the official and monologic order. This resonates with the aim of people-centered social innovation (PCSI) to move beyond Western models of monologic understanding toward one which is more dialogical (Hulgård and Shajahan, 2013: 95).

Given the great interest in innovation and social innovation, the overriding questions become: Have we simply just learned to accept and even celebrate such heretics? Have we accepted the ones who try to overthrow our world order? Or, do we actually mean something different and less radical when we call for *more* innovation?

Social Value Contested/Revisited

Heretics disturb and undermine the given social order. They also catalyze change and push society in new directions. They reconfigure disclosive spaces (Spinosa et al., 1997). If we acknowledge this, we must also acknowledge that social innovation is a situated practice—it does not emerge in a vacuum. If disharmony in a disclosive space triggers a social innovation, this social innovation will be shaped and given form by the context in which it emerges. Furthermore, social innovations do not emerge by themselves. They emerge as effects of action. Etymologically, the word *heresy* is derived from the Greek *haeresis*, which translates as "choice", because "each one chooses that which seems to him to be the best" (Etymologies, VIII, 3 as cited in Godin, 2015a: 18). The emphasis on choice raises questions because who has the right to choose and on whose behalf? This is the ethical question that resides at the heart of social innovation: "Who gives practitioners the authority to 'judge' which are 'good' and which are 'bad' actants, encounters and potentialities? Whose definition of 'good' and 'bad' is employed?" (Hillier, 2013: 175).

Since the value of social innovations may be contested; since only time can decide the value of them, as Reid suggests; and since innovations are about sailing unknown waters, then how is it determined which innovations we should chase? When Reid is suggesting that only time can sanction the innovations, what he is saying is that the standards used for judging the innovation will only be established after the innovation. That makes it extremely difficult to assess the value of the innovation in advance. Heresy presents a conceptual framework that captures some of the ambiguities inherent to innovation, whether social or not.

We now begin to approach a potential conflict with the political visions and hopes that permeate the field. As noted earlier, social innovation is often understood as a means to optimize and improve. Social innovation as a heretical practice questions existing truths and standards rather than improving them. In PCSI this is recognized as the need for a *"paradigm shift* in addressing issues of urban poverty, marginalization and vulnerability" (Hulgård and Shajahan, 2013: 98, my italics). This is perhaps also the key to understanding why social innovations seem rarer and harder to scale up and out than one would expect in view of the policies that seek to promote them. The infrastructures needed by social innovations to grow and spread are the exact same infrastructures that the innovations are criticizing. *Infrastructure* is here used as an umbrella term for institutionalized standards, regulations, financial channels and so on. With regard to social innovations, these may be certain legal and regulatory infrastructures, financial infrastructures where social projects often must adjust to certain aims, methods or definitions of target groups in order to receive funding or standards to evaluate whether a project or an approach creates social value or not. Infrastructures are not everlasting; they are created by people (in communities of practice) and may therefore also be changed. They are seamless and almost invisible until they meet cases that do not fit (Bowker and Star, 2000). Social innovations are precisely the cases that do not fit, and in order to gain traction, social innovations need new infrastructures. To change infrastructures or develop new ones, however, is extremely difficult—much more difficult than introducing a new marginal practice.

Social innovation as a heretical practice means that we must imagine that the innovation may be far more conflictual than the implication when social innovation is regarded as the solution to a problem. It is widely accepted that social innovations may arise from conflict (see, e.g., Moulaert et al., 2013) or, as noted earlier, from disharmonies (Spinosa et al., 1997). However, not only are conflicts the starting point for social innovation in this perspective, conflict is omnipresent in social innovation, at least until time has sanctioned it, allowing it to evolve from an innovation to an established and accepted practice. The innovation claims that something could be different, and it thereby represents a break from an incumbent order. Social innovations predate the standards by which they are to be judged. They will therefore always fall short when assessed against existing standards. A perspective on social innovations as heretical is not merely a theoretical exercise; it has methodological implications. Some of these will be introduced in the following section.

Methodological Perspectives

Focusing on the heretical elements of innovations has several methodological implications. First, it challenges us to move beyond the pro-innovation bias. Social innovations are by definition ambiguous because they challenge existing standards, norms, infrastructures or logics. By focusing exclusively on outcomes, we risk overlooking potential social innovations simply because they are not regarded as unequivocally positive in relation to existing standards or innovation attempts that may be hampered and made invisible by existing standards and norms. Social innovations, if they are genuine innovations, require new standards and they require time, as Reid argued, before they can be recognized. There is an element of uncertainty in innovation and this means that the effects of social innovations cannot be predicted completely in advance. This calls for an approach that is process-oriented rather than outcome-oriented. The process-oriented approach is central to PCSI, where key ingredients are community participation, changes in social relations (Hulgård and Shajahan, 2013) and the destabilization of existing power structures that, among other things, keep people trapped in poverty or marginalization.

A process-oriented approach allows us to research social innovations as they emerge and to analyze any obstacles they may meet. In doing so, we can become more aware of the situations that may inhibit the realization of potential social innovations. Taking inspiration from Deleuze, this would mean thinking of social innovations as "always-incomplete processes of becoming" (Hillier, 2013: 172). A process-oriented approach allows us to pay attention to both positive and negative aspects of social innovations and to potentially transformative aspects that push our values in new directions.

A second and related methodological implication is that a focus on social innovations as heretical requires us as researchers to pay closer attention to the question of social value. In line with much of the literature presented here, Hillier describes social innovation as performing: "an ethical re/making of social space" (Hillier, 2013: 169). Researching social innovations in this perspective therefore requires a strong focus on the issues of ethics and social value. In other words, what are the assumptions on which we build our understandings of what is good and what is bad? This means that research on social innovations should always include an analysis of what Spinosa, Flores and Dreyfus (1997) would call *disclosive spaces*. What are the characteristics of the disclosive spaces from which a social innovation emerges, and what new marginal practices and disclosive spaces are constructed or partly constructed during the innovation process? This calls for analyses that are historically and socially situated and where social value is researched as thoroughly as the newness.

A third methodological issue that emerges when we view social innovation as heretical is that we need to add an analysis of power relationships between strategic actors (Hillier, 2013: 169). As Moulaert, MacCallum and Hillier note, "SI [social innovation] is very strongly a matter of process innovation of changes and dynamics of social relations including power relations" (2013: 17).

Questions of power become relevant when one disclosive space is challenged or even replaced by another one. For example, Swyngedouw (2005) points out how new types of horizontal, networked and distributed forms of governance empower new actors while disempowering others. What he names *governance-beyond-the-state* leads to increased and new possibilities to participate (Swyngedouw, 2005). Simultaneously, this type of arrangement may lead to a democratic deficit, as governance through network-based modes is less transparent and questions of representation become more blurred than in traditional liberal democracy. In other words, networked modes of governance provide voice and increased access to participation for new groups of actors. At the same time, however, it also becomes less clear who is given voice and who becomes silenced. Which stakeholders are invited to express their voice and which actors are marginalized, ignored or unable to speak up in ways that give access to participation? Social innovation studies should, in other words, not only include analyses of the expansive forces that may empower and fight social exclusion but also pay attention to what new forms of exclusion are created, what new dilemmas emerge and what kinds of pain appear in the slipstream. This may also provide a way to move PCSI forward. PCSI calls for an *epistemological openness* that asks us to challenge existing knowledge and practices (Hulgård and Shajahan, 2013: 102). As such, PCSI must also look back at the new emerging practices, critically examine these new attempts to innovate and make this a central part of its own methodology.

The question of power also becomes relevant in relation to the creation of new infrastructures and standards. An analysis of the play between centrifugal forces (the challenging of existing infrastructures) and centripetal forces (the preservative forces; Bakhtin, 1981) and their reciprocal power relations may help us understand why some social innovations take off while others wither. This is important since it must be presumed that the centripetal forces are normally stronger than the centrifugal forces and may therefore overshadow and repress these innovation attempts.

Concluding Remarks

Godin states that users of the concept of innovation, including theorists, usually have an agenda (2015b: 7). This has also been the case in this chapter. Contrary to Godin, who descriptively traces the historical uses of the concept and explores the different meanings of innovation over time, my agenda has been to actively reintroduce the historical reticence to social innovation in order to understand some of the inherent tensions in the concept and the practice of social innovation. This has been achieved with two agendas in mind.

First, social innovation and innovation, in general, seem to be used interchangeably with a multitude of other kinds of change processes. If social innovation is to be a concept in its own right, it is crucial that theorists engage in theory development that moves beyond the pro-innovation tendency. Introducing heresy or illegality as an aspect of social innovation is a suggestion of how to do this—as a way of rendering the concept more dangerous. Sometimes, what we need might not be social innovation at all; in some cases, improvement and linear problem solving are exactly what we should pursue, and here a conflation of the concept is less helpful.

Second, social innovation seems difficult to develop in practice, despite political hopes and investments. Understanding social innovation as a practice that is inherently criticizing existing systems, standards and perhaps values, it becomes easier to understand why social innovations are difficult to develop, scale and disseminate. Social innovations are not simply good and effective ideas; they are new practices that require new standards and new infrastructures. This is a very demanding task that takes time and effort and raises questions of both power distribution and ethics.

This chapter has attempted to challenge the taken-for-grantedness of much social innovation thinking. In the previous section, it was suggested that innovation is distinct from improvement and optimization. It is not just about meeting social needs, but, more important, also about changing them. Similarly, it is not merely concerned with creating social value, but also with redefining what is considered to be valuable.

A view of social innovations as heretical calls for new areas of attention with regard to methodology. In this chapter, it was argued that a heresy perspective requires a process-oriented approach, a close analysis of the often-used concept of social value and, last, a careful analysis of the power relationships surrounding the social innovation. These types of analyses may provide a way to center actors, in other words, to move forward toward a people-centered approach to social innovation. A critical self-reflexivity toward PCSI was suggested in order to support epistemological openness but also to avoid the pro-innovation bias being repeated in PCSI.

I posed the question of whether the positive valorization of social innovation and innovation, in general, was an expression of a development where we had learned to accept changes and perhaps even heresy to a greater extent than in earlier times or whether the concept of innovation simply had changed meaning to something less radical and less dangerous. Concluding this chapter, I propose that both explanations may have some truth to them. There is no doubt that social innovation as a concept has been somewhat diluted in both research literature and in politics, where it is used as a synonym for less dangerous forms of change. At the same time, it could be argued that we have become more tolerant of change than, say, in medieval times. We are increasingly exposed to different ways of living, different cultures and thereby also different values. Changes happen at a rapid pace in technology, for example, and constantly force us to deal with ourselves and the world around us in ever new ways. In that way, we are continuously met with the awareness that things *could be different*.

Notes

1. As I have elaborated elsewhere (Sievers, 2016).
2. Derrida is referring to invention, but I believe his idea could equally well be applied to innovation.

References

Alexander, C. (2010). "The Third Sector," in K. Hart, J-L. Laville and A. D. Cattani (eds.), *The Human Economy*. Polity Press, pp. 213–224.
Albury, D. (2005). "Fostering Innovation in Public Services," *Public Money and Management*, 25(1), pp. 51–56.
Bakhtin, M. M. (1981). *The Dialogic Imagination: Four Essays*. Edited by M. Holquist. Austin: University of Texas Press.
Berglund, K. and Schwartz, B. (2013). "Holding on to the Anomaly of Social Entrepreneurship Dilemmas in Starting Up and Running a Fair-Trade Enterprise," *Journal of Social Entrepreneurship*, 4(3), pp. 237–255.
Bowker, G. C. and Star, S. L. (2000). *Sorting Things Out*. The MIT Press.
Dees, J. G. (2007). "Taking Social Entrepreneurship Seriously," *Society*, 44(3), pp. 24–31.
Derrida, J. (1992). "From Psyche—Invention of the Other," in D. Attridge (ed.), *Acts of Literature*. New York and London: Routledge, pp. 310–443.
European Commission. (n.d.). *Innovation Union*. http://ec.europa.eu/research/innovation-union/index_en.cfm (Accessed on 7 December 2015).
Gerometta, J., Häussermann, H. and Longo, G. (2005). "Social Innovation and Civil Society in Urban Governance: Strategies for an Inclusive City," *Urban Studies*, 42(11), pp. 2007–2021.
Godin, B. (2014, October 20). *The Vocabulary of Innovation: A Lexicon*. Project on the Intellectual History of Innovation, Paper no. 20. 2nd CASTI Workshop, Agder, Norway. Montreal: INRS.
Godin, B. (2015a). *Innovation: A Conceptual History of an Anonymous Concept*. Project on the Intellectual History of Innovation, Working Paper No. 21.
Godin, B. (2015b). *Innovation Contested: The Idea of Innovation Over the Centuries*. New York and Abingdon: Routledge.
Hartley, J. (2014). "New Development: Eight and a Half Propositions to Stimulate Frugal Innovation," *Public Money & Management*, 34(3), pp. 227–232.

Hillier, J. (2013). "Towards a Deleuzean-Inspired Methodology for Social Innovation Research and Practice," in F. Moulaert, D. MacCallum, A. Mehmood and A. Hamdouch (eds.), *The International Handbook on Social Innovation*. Cheltenham and Northhampton, MA: Edward Elgar, pp. 169–180.

Hulgård, L. and Shajahan, P. K. (2013). "Social Innovation for People-Centred Development," in F. Moulaert, D. MacCallum, A. Mehmood and A. Hamdouch (eds.), *The International Handbook on Social Innovation*, Cheltenham and Northhampton, MA: Edward Elgar, pp. 93–104.

Jenson, J. (2016). "Social Innovation: Redesigning the Welfare Diamond," in A. Nicholls, J. Simon and M. Gabriel (eds.), *New Frontiers in Social Innovation Research*. Houndsmills: Palgrave Macmillan, pp. 86–106.

Klein, J-L. (2013). "Introduction: Social Innovation at the Crossroads Between Science, Economy and Society," in F. Moulaert, D. MacCallum, A. Mehmood and A. Hamdouch (eds.), *The International Handbook on Social Innovation*, Cheltenham and Northhampton, MA: Edward Elgar, pp. 9–12.

Moulaert, F., MacCallum, D. and Hillier, J. (2010). "The Role of Theory in Social Innovation Analysis: History and Challenges," in F. Moulaert, D. MacCallum, A. Mehmood and A. Hamdouch (eds.), *Social Innovation: Collective Action, Social Learning and Transdisciplinary Research* (KATARSIS final report), pp. 13–22. https://cordis.europa.eu/docs/publications/1243/124376771-6_en.pdf (Accessed on 11 February 2019).

Moulaert, F., MacCallum, D. and Hillier, J. (2013). "Social Innovation: Intuition, Precept, Concept, Theory and Practice," in F. Moulaert, D. MacCallum, A. Mehmood and A. Hamdouch (eds.), *The International Handbook on Social Innovation*. Cheltenham and Northhampton, MA: Edward Elgar, pp. 13–24.

Mulgan, G., Tucker, S., Ali, R. and Sanders, B. (2007). *Social Innovation—What It Is, Why It Matters and How It Can Be Accelerated*. Oxford Saïd Business School, Skoll Centre for Social Entrepreneurship, The Young Foundation.

Nesta. (2017). *Social Innovation—the Last and Next Decade*. www.nesta.org.uk/blog/social-innovation-last-and-next-decade (Accessed on 8 April 2017).

Phills, J. A., Deiglmeier, K. and Miller, D. T. (2008). "Rediscovering Social Innovation," *Stanford Social Innovation Review*, 6(4), pp. 34–43.

Pol, E. and Ville, S. (2009). "Social Innovation: Buzz Word or Enduring Term?" *The Journal of Socio-Economics*, 38(6), pp. 878–885.

Rogers, E. M. (1976). "New Product Adoption and Diffusion," *Journal of Customer Research*, 2(4), pp. 290–301.

Roy, M. J., McHugh, N. and Hill O'Connor, C. (2014). "Social Innovation: Worklessness, Welfare and Well-Being," *Social Policy and Society*, 13, pp. 457–467.

Schumpeter, J. A. (2003). *Capitalism, Socialism & Democracy*. Taylor and Francis e-Library, Routledge.

Sievers, S. M. M. (2016). *Social innovation i civilsamfundet—kætteri og flertydigheder i arbejdet med socialt udsatte [Social Innovation in Civil Society: Heresy and Ambiguities in Work with Socially Vulnerable People]*. Roskilde University.

Spinosa, C., Flores, F. and Dreyfus, H. L. (1997). *Disclosing New Worlds*. Institute of Technology.

Swyngedouw, E. (2005). "Governance Innovation and the Citizen: The Janus Face of Governance-Beyond-the-State," *Urban Studies*, 42(11), pp. 1991–2006.

Teasdale, S. (2011). "What's in a Name? Making Sense of Social Enterprise Discourses," *Public Policy and Administration*, 27(2), pp. 99–119.

White House. (n.d.). www.whitehouse.gov/administration/eop/sicp/about (Accessed on 15 December 2015), www.whitehouse.gov/administration/eop/sicp/about.

The Young Foundation. (2012). *Social Innovation Overview: A Deliverable of the Project: "The theoretical, empirical and policy foundations for building social innovation in Europe"*. (TEPSIE), European Commission—7th Framework Programme. Brussels: European Commission, DG Research.

Notes on the Authors

1. Editors

Swati Banerjee, PhD, is Professor and Chairperson at the Centre for Livelihoods and Social Innovation, School of Social Work, Tata Institute of Social Sciences (TISS), Mumbai, India, and Coordinator of the Right Livelihood College–TISS. She has been a postdoctoral fellow at Lund University, Sweden, and has been a visiting faculty at many universities across the world including Roskilde University, Lund University and the University of British Columbia. She is also a recipient of several fellowships from national and international organizations including the German Academic Exchange Service, the Indian Council of Social Science Research (ICSSR), the Ford Foundation, Erasmus Mundus and Erasmus Plus. The key thematic focus of her research includes people-centered social innovation, human-centered and inclusive design thinking; collective entrepreneurship development and empowerment of women and marginalized communities; and livelihoods and postdevelopment concerns of marginalized communities (with a focus on particularly vulnerable tribal groups, nomadic tribes, etc.). She uses participatory methodologies with a focus on "ecologies of knowledges" and is involved in global discussions on social innovation, poverty reduction and achievement of sustainable development goals through the United Nations Economic and Social Commission for Asia and the Pacific and other Asia-Pacific regional forums.

Stephen Carney, PhD, is Associate Professor in Comparative Education Policy at Roskilde University in Denmark. His research focuses on global educational reform and the comparative method. He has studied community participation in education in Nepal, school development in China and social enterprise policy in Tanzania. He has led the master's program in Social Enterprise and Management at Roskilde University and currently leads its bachelor's program in Global Humanities, where the focus is on promoting awareness of ecologies of knowledge. He has been President of the Comparative Education Society in Europe (CESE) since 2016.

Lars Hulgård, PhD, is Professor of Social Entrepreneurship, Roskilde University, Denmark, and Visiting Professor at Tata Institute of Social Sciences, Mumbai, India. Between 2015 and 2017, he was also full Professor of Social Innovation and Social Entrepreneurship at the University of Southeast Norway to assist in establishing a research platform on social innovation. In 2018–2019, he was a visiting professor at Universidade de Coimbra in Portugal. His PhD in 1994 was on social innovation in social work. At Roskilde University he serves four main functions: (1) Co-founder of EMES European Research Network (President 2010–2016), (2) Professor at the MA in Social Science in Social Entrepreneurship and Management, (3) Co-director, Centre for Social Entrepreneurship and (4) research, teaching and consultancy in innovation, solidarity economy, social innovation, social policy, social economy, social entrepreneurship, public service, social enterprise, civil society and transformation of the welfare state. He is the co-editor of Routledge Studies in Social Enterprise and Social Innovation.

2. Contributors

Adriane Vieira Ferrarini, PhD, is Full Professor at the Post-Graduation Program in Social Sciences at the Universidade do Vale do Rio dos Sinos, São Leopoldo, Brazil. She holds a PhD in Sociology from the Universidade Federal do Rio Grande do Sul (Brazil 2007). She coordinates the research group on "Solidarity and Cooperative Economy". She has experience with research on, teaching and consultancy in social innovation, social policy, solidarity economy, epistemology of the South, social work and local development.

Luise Li Langergaard, PhD, is Associate Professor in Social Entrepreneurship at Department of People and Technology, Roskilde University. She works with empirical, critical and conceptual studies in social entrepreneurship, public-sector innovation and social sustainability and resident democracy in Danish nonprofit housing. The focus is on critical and normative perspectives on welfare organization, social change and forms of citizen engagement in particular.

Linda Lundgaard Andersen, PhD, is Professor in Learning, Evaluation and Social Innovation at Roskilde University; Co-director, Centre for Social Entrepreneurship; and Director, PhD School of People and Technology. Her research interests include learning and social innovation in welfare services, democracy and forms of governance in human services, psycho-societal theory and method, ethnographies of the public sector, social entrepreneurship, voluntary organizations and social enterprises. Recently, she has been researching neoliberal transformations and shifts of paradigms in the Danish and Scandinavian welfare services focusing on a renewed discourse and practice of co-creation, coproduction and partnership.

Bev Meldrum, BSc, MA, is a PhD student at the Graduate School of Business, University of Cape Town, South Africa. Her research focuses on social entrepreneurship and innovation, in particular, within the informal economy in sub-Saharan Africa. She is also a social entrepreneur, having established social enterprises both in the United Kingdom and, more recently, in South Africa. Her most recent venture is Grow Recruitment, a social enterprise recruitment agency focused on reducing unemployment among disadvantaged youth in South Africa.

Jeremy Millard, BSc, MSc, is Director of the consultancy Third Millennium Governance and holds senior research positions in Denmark and the United Kingdom. He has more than 40 years' global experience and publications in numerous transdisciplinary areas, including governance, information and communication technology and the fourth Industrial Revolution, open and social innovation, sustainable and socioeconomic development, tackling poverty and exclusion, entrepreneurship, the new economy, urbanization and nature-based solutions tackling societal challenges. He has published extensively in these and related areas.

Andres Morales, PhD in Social and Solidarity Economy, is Co-Founder and Chief Operating Officer of Minca Ventures Ltd and Living in Minca. He has international experience, working as both a researcher and a consultant in more than 40 countries. Beyond his empirical work, he has published many pieces of research that includes journals and books. He has also designed and delivered a social enterprise Massive Open Online Course (MOOC) that reached out to more than 50,000 beneficiaries in 190 countries.

Silla Marie Mørch Sievers, PhD, holds a master's degree in psychology and a PhD in social entrepreneurship. She is a knowledge worker in a social enterprise in Denmark and a part-time lecturer at Roskilde University. Her research interests include social innovation, social entrepreneurship, civil society and urban development.

Prashant B. Narnaware is an Indian Administrative Services officer and is currently the Collector and District Magistrate of Palghar, Maharashtra, India. He was also an adjunct faculty at Tata Institute of Social Sciences, Mumbai. He has a PhD in Health Policy. He was also Collector of Osmanabad District and has dealt with drought and farmer suicide issues, achieving great success. Presently as Collector of Palghar District, he is dealing with issues such as malnutrition, child deaths, infrastructure development and coastal security. He is also working toward empowerment of tribal communities in his district.

Michael Ngoasong, PhD, is a Senior Lecturer in Management and Director of Masters Programmes at The Open University Business School, UK. He holds a PhD in Science, Technology and Society from the University of Nottingham, UK. His research interests include the role of informal institutions on development-led entrepreneurship in developing countries. He has published in leading journals such as the *Journal of Small Business Management*, the *Annals of Tourism Research*, *Tourism Management* and the *Journal of Small Business and Enterprise Development*.

Silvia Sacchetti, PhD from the University of Birmingham, UK, is currently Associate Professor of Economic Policy at the University of Trento, Italy, and collaborates with Euricse (the European Research Center on Cooperative and Social Enterprise). Her research addresses in particular on the study of participatory governance structures and resource coordination mechanisms. She focuses on cooperative firms and social enterprises, recently studied in the context of welfare and cultural services. Silvia is Co-Chief Editor of the *Journal of Entrepreneurial and Organizational Diversity* and Associate Editor of *European Management Journal*.

Sunil D. Santha, PhD, is Associate Professor at the Centre for Livelihoods and Social Innovation, School of Social Work at the Tata Institute of Social Sciences, Mumbai. As an academic with keen interests in the field of environmental risks, climate justice and livelihood uncertainties, Dr. Santha strives toward understanding the role of social institutions and participatory action in reducing vulnerabilities and strengthening community resilience and just adaptation practices. He believes in action research toward innovating participatory methods of entrepreneurial action and emergent livelihoods.

Devisha Sasidevan is Assistant Professor at the Centre for Livelihoods and Social Innovation, School of Social Work at Tata Institute of Social Sciences, Mumbai. She has a keen interest in the field of changing ecosystems, knowledge systems, livelihoods vulnerabilities and resource management. She has also worked extensively in the field of risk and water scarcity.

Abdul Shaban, PhD, is Professor at the School of Development Studies, Tata Institute of Social Sciences, Mumbai. He has published several papers in various journal and authored a book on *Mumbai: Political Economy of Crime and Space* (Orient Blackswan, 2010). He has edited three books, namely, *Lives of Muslims in India: Politics, Exclusion and Violence* (Routledge, 2012), *Muslims in Urban India: Development and Exclusion* (Concept Publishing, 2013) and co-edited book on *Mega-urbanization in Global South: Fast Cities and New*

Urban Utopias of the Postcolonial State (Routledge, 2016). He has also produced several reports for the government of Maharashtra, the government of India, the World Bank and national and international corporate groups and has been Visiting Professor at various universities in different countries. He has engaged in extensive grassroots research and action in India, including the innovative and pioneering work in rural Maharashtra with drought-affected farmers.

P. K. Shajahan, PhD, is Professor of Social Work at the Tata Institute of Social Sciences (TISS), Mumbai. He was formerly Dean, Social Protection, Dean Students' Affairs and Chairperson, Centre for Community Organisation and Development Practice at TISS. He is currently Member of the Board of Directors, International Association of Schools of Social Work and Vice-President, International Council on Social Welfare. He, along with colleagues from Europe, the Americas and Africa, founded global academic alliances: Critical Edge Alliance and Solidarity Economy Reciprocity and Social Innovation. His research, publications and areas of expertise include participatory development, social innovation, social protection and social policies, international social work, diversity and social cohesion, community and civic engagement and youth development.

Rashmi Singla, PhD, is Associate Professor in psychology at Roskilde University, Denmark. She migrated from India to Denmark in 1980. Her research concerns movements across borders, family and "peer" relations, ethnicity and psychosocial interventions. One current interest concerns the interplay between Eastern and Western psychology in areas such as meditation, yoga, and organizational diversity management. Her latest major publication was *Intermarriage and Mixed Parenting: Promoting Mental Health and Wellbeing* (2015). She is currently part of the research project Living Apart Together, Transnational Couples: Mental Health and Wellbeing promotion.

Roger Spear, PhD, is Emeritus Professor of Social Entrepreneurship at Open University, Member of Ciriec Scientific Committee, and founder member of EMES research network. Currently he is Guest Professor in the Centre for Social Entrepreneurship at Roskilde University, contributing to International Masters in Social Entrepreneurship. His recent research includes mapping social enterprises and their eco-systems in Europe; social enterprise in the United Kingdom, models and trajectories; cities; the social economy; and inclusive growth.

Sujata Sriram, PhD, is Professor at the School of Human Ecology, Tata Institute of Social Sciences, Mumbai, and former Dean of the School of Human Ecology. In 2010 she was awarded a Fulbright Nehru Senior Research Fellowship to the University of California San Diego.

In 2017, she completed a study exploring stress among students in Kota, Rajasthan. She is currently working on a research project concerned with marital dissolution through the family court in Mumbai.

Mohamed Wageih, MSc, is Director of the Social Innovation & Business Incubation Center, SEKEM Development Foundation. In 2008, he joined the SEKEM Initiative and its Heliopolis University as Research and Innovation Advisor. He manages the Innovation and Research Observatory, responsible for developing its Response to Intervention strategy, as well as directing the Social Innovation Center. Since October 2018, he is Project Officer for the EU-PRIMA Programme in Barcelona. Mr. Wageih manages European Union projects in FP7, H2020, EuropeAid and ER+. He has published several international joint papers.

Index

abyssal thinking 7
acculturation 162
active citizenship 27, 78, 104
actorhood 8, 10
adaptive innovations: *asset conservation* 119–120; elements of 111; *informal entrepreneurship* 111–112, 121–124; *livelihood diversification* 116–119; market exchange strategies 120–121; *mobility* 113–116; *occupational shifts* 116–117; people centered development and 110–125; *reverse migration* 113–115; *risk pooling* 119; *rural–urban livelihood linkages* 118; *seasonal migration* 115, 118–119; *shifting worksites* 115–116; *storing perishable goods* 120; strategies 112–121
Africa: actors in social innovation 208–210; agency–structure framework 218–219; challenges driving social innovation 201–206; concepts and understanding of social innovation in 199–201; cooperative 202–203; drivers and barriers of social innovations 210–213; future of social innovation in 221–222; governance structures of social innovation 208–210; Indian diaspora 160; infrastructure and public utility challenges 205–206; networks in social innovation 208–210; opportunities driving social innovation 201–206; people-centered social innovation 198–199; relevance of development theory 216–218; social innovation capacities and outcomes 213–216; social innovation in 195–222; social innovation in practice 201–216; social innovation strategies and themes 206–208; social innovation today in 221; social needs driving social innovation 201–206
agency 8–9, 47–48, 61
agency–structure framework 218–219
alliances 54, 59–60
American-Born Confused Desi (ABCD) 167–168
anomaly 229
Arab countries 202
area development societies (ADSs) 73–74, 78, 85
asset conservation 119–120
association 136
association memberships 119
awareness 71, 79–80, 172

Baliraja Chetana Abhiyan (BCA) 186, 192
belonging 158, 161–163, 170, 174
benign colonialism 162
biodynamic farming 202
biofuels 3
Bolsa Família Program 101–103
bottom-up approach 84, 100, 198
Brazil: Bolsa Família Program 101–103; Citizen Constitution of 1988 101; overcoming poverty 100–105; social innovation in 89–90
BUDS schools 81
Buen Vivir (BV) development model: conceptualisation 130–133; criticisms of 133; interpretation 131–132; transformation of IOGs

into ICOs 133–152; values and pillars 130, 132–133
Bureau of European Policy Advisers (BEPA) 215

capacity building 149
choice 231
civil society: bottom-up initiatives spearheaded by 7, 103–104; hybridity of organizations 44; marketization in 6, 20, 106; organizations 50–63, 95–97, 214, 219; rankings 213; relationships between state institutions 84, 179–180, 185, 189, 221, 226; role in development 201; role of social participation 131; roots in public sphere 81–82; social entrepreneurship in 33
climate change 4, 118, 198–199
coercive isomorphism 135
collective action 53–54, 58–59, 61, 80, 82, 91, 218, 227
collective agency 45, 47–48, 61
collective amnesia 158
collective identity 78
collectiveness 142, 144
collective religious practices 172
collectivization 47–48, 80, 183–185
Colombia 128–152
colonialism 95, 129, 162
community 10
community development societies (CDSs) 74, 78, 80, 85
community values 130
community well-being pillar 130
complementarity values 145
conceptualisation 31–36
conscientization 80
constitutional amendments 76–77
contestation 129
context-based development 193
convergence 80
cooperative 135–136, 142, 184–185, 189, 202–203, 211
counterdiscourse 20, 23–30
country of origin 156, 172–173
country of residence 156
critical analysis 102
critical discourse analyses 23–26, 28–31
critical theory 26, 29, 95

critique: conceptualisation 20–21, 31–39; content of and arguments for 21–23; normatively informed 26–28; as research strategy in social entrepreneurship studies 19–31, 37–39
cultural affiliations 173–174
cultural identity 162

decolonization 89–90, 100–105
decolonization pillar 130
democracy: capitalist development under 103; constitutional 81–82; decentralization 76–77; deepening democracy 80; deliberative 22, 28, 98–99; *governance-beyond-the-state* and 234; hybrid organizations and 44; level in social innovation 98–100; normatively informed critiques 26–27, 29–31, 34; participatory 22, 28, 33, 75–78, 80, 97, 99, 104–106; "people's democracy" 38, 74; representative 98; role of active citizenship 27, 78, 104; transition from apartheid to 203
democratization pillar 130
Denmark: Indians in 158–160, 163–166, 170, 172, 174; Neighborhood Mothers 50–55, 61–63
desh 158
de-territorialized Indianness 170
development solidarity organizations (DSOs) 135
development theory 216–218
dialogical understanding 231
diaspora 157–158
diasporic communities: cultural affiliations 173–174; Indian diaspora 156–174; Indians in Denmark 158–160; Indians in United States 158–160; policies in India 160–161; post-1965 wave of migration 159; role of religion 171–172; use of Indian language 169; welfare and support provisions 161; young Indian diaspora in United States 162–163, 166–170
Dignity and Design (D&D): aim 58; alliances 59–60; challenges 60–61; drivers 56–57; implementation

strategies 59; institutional structures 57; overview 55–56; partnerships 59–60; potentials 60–61
disclosive spaces 225, 229, 231, 233–234
disharmony 25, 229, 231
dispositif 23–24
diversification 148

ecologist/developmentalist approach 131, 133
Economic and Social Commission for Western Asia (ESCWA) 208
economic pluralism pillar 130
Ecosol Group 100
emancipation 5, 89, 92–93, 95–97, 105
emotional citizenship 157, 173
empowerment: among women 17, 42–62, 69, 73, 86; level of democracy and 98, 106; of migrant informal workers 110, 119; people-centered development and 71–72; people-centered social innovation and 18, 38; political 69, 86; role in social change 38, 45; role of partnerships 179, 207–208; role of social innovation 215; social 86; social entrepreneurship and 23
energy sector 202
entrepreneurship 69, 229–230
epistemology 89
equity-based development 192
ethics 26, 157, 217, 233, 235
ethos 90, 92–100, 103, 105
exclusion processes 170, 211

farmers: collectivization for entrepreneurship 192; marginality context and sustainable development challenges 180–183; neo-localism and context-based development 193; organization of elites and marginalized peoples under welfare and neoliberal regimes. 183–190; participatory and equity-based development 192–193; state initiatives and links with community and university 185–189; suicide 180, 181
first-person voices 156
flatarchy organization 138

flexible citizenship 157, 173
foreign direct investment (FDI) 161
formal entrepreneurship 111

Ghana 206, 213, 220
governance-beyond-the-state 234
grant seeking 146–147
grassroots identity 25, 29
grassroots innovation 55–63, 124, 189, 205
grassroots mechanism 78
grassroots organizations 85
grassroots realities 10, 186

harmony and complementarity values 130
health innovation policy 205
hegemony 25, 128–129
heresy 231
human condition and *human dignity* approach 197
human economy approach 197
human rights 197
hybridity 44–45, 128–129, 134, 136, 143–146, 151

identity 78, 158, 161–163
inclusion: belonging 161–163, 170, 174; of bottom up entrepreneurship 100; ethnic-racial 104, 163; of excluded 72, 79–81; financial 43, 103; social 77, 90, 103–104; through processes of community mobilization 193; of women 78
indentured labor 158
India: diasporic communities 156–174; migrant workers 110–125; people-centered social innovation in Kudumbashree 69–86; transformation of marginalized and underdeveloped district 179–194
Indian language 169
indigenist approach 131, 133
indigenous community organizations (ICOs): capacity building 149; decision-making processes 143–146; development of 128–129; diversification 148; forms of governance 143–146; grant seeking 146–147; legal status 134–136; networking 150; organizational

strategies 146–150; organizational structure 137–138; ownership 134, 151; partnerships 150; production of goods and services 138–143
indigenous peoples' organized groups (IOGs): motivations in formalizing 135; production of goods and services 138; transformation into indigenous community organizations 128, 133–150
informal entrepreneurship 111–112
informal sector 110–111
informal workers 111; *see also* migrant workers
information and communication technology (ICT) 206, 207
infrastructures 225, 232–235
innovation 228–231
innovators-as-problem-solvers approach 229
institutional approach 84, 128
intersectionalities: Dignity and Design 55–61; of gender relations 47–48; intersectional learning 49, 61; Neighborhood Mothers 50–55
isomorphism 128–129, 134, 135, 149

Kenya 213
"Kerala Model of Development" 75–85
knowledge: ecologies of 6; exchange 164; indigenous 150; internal and external 149–150; modern 7; Southern knowledge 7
Kudumbashree (Kerala State Poverty Eradication Mission): components 69–70; development and participatory democracy context 75–77; overview 73–75; people-centeredness in 77–83; in perspective for institutionalization of PCSI 83–85; promotion of active citizenship 78; use of sluice model 81–82

League of Arab States (LAS) 208
L'EMergence de l'Entreprise Sociale en Europe (EMES) network 22, 33–34
liberty 231
lifeworld 81
livelihood: gendered 48–63; *livelihood diversification* 116–119; promotion 45

local self-governments (LSGs) 73–74, 77–78, 80, 85, 86

managerialism 20, 22, 27, 28, 30, 32, 37, 135
marginality 8, 42, 47–48, 82, 157, 161, 163, 166, 170, 174, 180
market exchange strategies 120–121
marketization 6, 20, 21, 22, 28, 30
Mediterranean Commission on Sustainable Development (MCSD) 208
microcredit 69
migrant workers: adaptive innovations among 110–112; *asset conservation* 119–120; *informal entrepreneurship* 121–124; livelihood adaptation strategies 113–125; *livelihood diversification* 116–119; market exchange strategies 120–121; *mobility* 113–116; *risk pooling* 119; *storing perishable goods* 120
migration 113–116, 118, 157, 159
mimicry 128–129, 134, 143, 151
mixedness 158
mobility 113–116
model minority 167
monologic understanding 231

neighborhood groups (NHGs) 73, 78, 85
Neighborhood Mothers (NM): alliances 54; challenges 55; drivers 51; implementation strategies 54–55; institutional structures 52–53; methods 53–54; overview 50–51, 61–63; partnerships 54; potentials 55
neoliberalism 28, 30, 184–185
neo-localism 193
networking 150
networks 208–210
Nigeria 213
normative isomorphism 149
normativity: critique as research strategy in social entrepreneurship studies 19; normatively informed 26–28, 38–39
North 95, 106
Northern Africa 195, 199, 201, 208, 214

occupational shifts 116–117
official silence 158
'old diaspora' 158
Osmanabad model of
    development 193
Overseas Citizen of India (OCI) 157,
    160–161, 170
Overseas Indians 157
ownership 134, 151

participation 71, 104–106, 145, 192
participatory video research approach
    140, 143
partnerships: Dignity and Design
    59–60; indigenous community
    organizations 150; Neighborhood
    Mothers 54; state–university–
    community 179–194
people-centered development (PCD):
    adaptive innovations and 110–125;
    foundations 71, 79–80; in
    international development 71–72;
    in Kudumbashree experiment
    77–83; origin of 70–72, 110
people centeredness 8–9, 71
people-centered social innovation
    (PCSI): in Africa 198–199;
    conceptualisation 69; conceptual
    issues 8–9; *epistemological
    openness* 234; gendered 43, 45–63;
    intrinsic pillars of 70, 86; overview
    4–8; politics of practice in 9–10
Persons of Indian Origin (PIO) 157,
    160, 170
plural economy 106, 148–149
plurinational state pillar 130
poverty: challenges in Africa 198,
    210; overcoming 100–105; use
    of Bolsa Família Program in
    overcoming 101–103
power 158, 212, 219, 233–234
power relations 29, 46, 62, 72,
    85–86, 106, 234–235
prejudice 168–169
process dimension 70, 72, 77, 86
process-oriented approach 233
product diversification 123
pro-innovation bias 226, 228, 235

qualitative empirical studies 157

religion 171–172
renewable energy 202

resistance 20, 23–30, 129
return-migration programs 173
reverse migration 113–115
rights of nature pillar 130
risk pooling 119
rural–urban livelihood linkages 118

seasonal migration 115, 118–119
self-governance 98–100
self-reliance 71, 79–80, 172, 180
shifting worksites 115–116
SI-DRIVE project 195, 214, 220
situated practice 231
skill enhancement 123–124
sluice model 81–82
social and solidarity economy (SSE) 7,
    71, 103, 128, 135–136
social capital 70, 81–85
social change: collective action and
    62–63; relationship to social
    entrepreneurship 8, 17–19, 30,
    34, 36, 45; relationship to social
    innovation 8, 90–91, 128, 156,
    208, 215, 217–218, 227; role of
    empowerment 38, 45; theories 9;
    use of critical analysis as driver for
    26, 28, 37
social entrepreneurship: in Africa 205;
    conceptual debates 17–18, 31–36;
    critical discourse analyses 23–26,
    28–31; critique as research strategy
    19–31; definition 17, 33–34;
    epistemological dimensions 35–36;
    normative dimensions 35–36;
    normatively informed critiques
    26–28; pragmatic dimensions
    35–36; relationship to social change
    8, 17–19, 30, 34, 36, 45; in South
    Africa 204
social innovation: in Africa 195–222;
    in Brazil 89–90; capacities and
    outcomes 213–216; conceptual
    issues 8; contested 231–232;
    controversies 90–92; definitions
    200, 226–227; ethical-political
    intentionality 96–98, 104; ethos
    of 92–100; gender and 45–47; as
    heretical practice 232, 234–236;
    implementation 4; inaccuracies
    90–92; institutional approach 84;
    level of democracy in 98–100;
    methodological perspectives
    233–234; in overcoming

poverty 100–105; overview 2–4; perspectives on 226–228; rationale underlying 93–96; relationship to social change 8, 90–91, 128, 156, 208, 215, 217–218, 227; societal levels of outcomes 215; transformative aspect of 228–231, 233; trends in South Africa 200–201

socialist/statist approach 131, 133
social justice 22, 42, 72, 79, 97–98, 106, 110, 228
social mobilization 71, 79–80, 172
social policy 84, 227
social psychological perspective 157
social value 32, 49, 70, 72, 90–91, 97–98, 227–228, 231–235
societal transformation 17–18
solidarity and reciprocity values 130
solidarity economy 7, 70–71, 83–84, 86, 99, 103, 104, 195
solidarity economy organizations (SEOs) 135
South 89–91, 94, 100–101, 103, 105–106
South Africa 199–200, 202–205, 209, 213
Southern knowledge 7
standards 225, 228, 232–235
state–university–community partnership: marginality context and sustainable development challenges 180–183; organization of elites and marginalized peoples

under welfare and neoliberal regimes. 183–190
storing perishable goods 120
strategic relationships 123
sub-Saharan Africa 195, 199, 202, 208–209, 214
suicide 181
sustainability 71, 79–80, 172, 210

third sector 7, 95
third space 129, 144, 167
TISS Tuljapur Campus 186, 189–190
top remittance 157, 165
transnational affiliation 158
transnationalism 156–158
twice-migrants 158

United Nations Sustainable Development Goals (SDGs) 71, 222
United States: Indians in 158–160, 172, 174; young Indian diaspora in 166–170
urban resilience 111

videsh 158
volunteerism 142

whitewashed 169
WILCO project 220
women's collectives: collective action and 53–54, 58–60, 62–63; conceptual framing 42–49; Dignity and Design 55–61; Neighborhood Mothers (NM) 50–55